Also by Sylvia Vaughn Thompson:
Economy Gastronomy

The Budget Gourmet

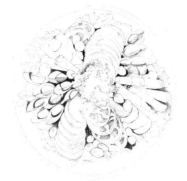

The Budget Gourmet

Sylvia Vaughn Thompson

Random House
New York

Library of Congress Cataloging in Publication Data

Thompson; Sylvia Vaughn Sheekman.
    The budget gourmet.

    1. Cookery.   I. Title.
TX652.T45   641.5'52   74–29608
ISBN 0–394–49915–8 (hardbound)
ISBN 0–394–73034–8 (paperbound)

Some of the recipes in this book are taken from the following previously published articles: "Cold Soups and Hot Salads," "Dinner Well in Hand," "Casseroles Your Whole Family Will Love," "Vegetables Absolutely No One Can Resist," "Stuffed Guests For Dinner," and "Share Your Thanksgiving" were originally published in *Woman's Day Magazine*, a Fawcett Publication; "Remembering La Bretagne," "Tina's Cucina," "A Taste of Paris Aux Fines Herbes," and "The Venerable Quince" first appeared in *Gourmet Magazine;* "The Quenching Crystals: Granite" was first published in *Vogue;* "The Magnificent Mussel" originally appeared in *Holiday Magazine.*

Manufactured in the United States of America

98765432

FIRST EDITION

Illustrations by Linda Kosarin

For my father, who made me want to be a writer.
And for my mother, who made me want to be a cook.

My thanks to . . .
Gourmet *and* Woman's Day *magazines*
for permitting me to include recipes
which appeared in their pages
in a slightly different form.
And thank you . . .
David, Benjamin, Dinah, Amanda . . .
Rheta . . .
Emmy, Charlotte, Jean . . .
Mother, M.F., Alice Vinegar, Daddy, Grandma, Rose, JoEllen,
Olga, Claire, Julia, Dorris, Tina, Florence, Paul, Jean,
Marcella, Ellen, Maibelle, Tina, Dickie, Art, Zena, Marion,
Glenna, Jeanne, Marilyn, Perry, Geranium . . .
and my darling Papa . . .
for everything.

This is a collection of recipes from all over the world.
I love them. My family loves them. Our friends love them.
They just happen to be among the cheapest things you
    can cook.
And, to my mind, among the best.

S.V.T.
Malibu

Contents

Hors d'Oeuvres and Good Things from the Icebox

Classically and in almost every other corner of the world hors d'oeuvres—or *antipasti, zakuski, Vorspeisen, mezethakia, smörgåsbord*—comprise the carefully chosen first course of a dinner. In this country, we stuff ourselves before dining with what are euphemistically called "appetizers"—peanuts, clam puffs, *guacamole* dip, sausage rolls—anything to keep us from keeling over our cocktails.

A dinner party is above all a matter of balance and timing. *Every* dish must be considered part of the whole. The first course—the hors d'oeuvres—states the theme of the meal to come. Then, the second and third courses develop the theme with variations.

After many years, I think we have solved the what-to-serve-with-drinks problem at our house. We ask our guests for seven-thirty, assume everyone will arrive by eight, and sit down to dine around nine o'clock. In that leisurely time, people have a chance to get the temperature of the room, and guests ease into one another's moods and conversations.

For something to nibble on, to keep nervous people occupied and thirsty people sober, I offer a splendid composition of *crudités*—raw vegetables—with a sauce for seasoning. About 20 minutes before dinner is to be served, when guests are beginning to be honestly hungry, I hand around plates of a simple hors d'oeuvre. A wedge of gingered melon. Some homemade bread and *kajmak* with *ajvar*. Or a slice of the house pâté. Then when plates are empty and appetites are keen, we move to the dinner table and continue with the next course. Wonderfully easy beginning.

Budget notes

A budget is less a problem with hors d'oeuvres than with many another course in entertaining. So much may be made of good vegetables, interesting sauces, ripe fruits, potted cheeses, relishes, economical cold meats, fowl, fishes, pâtés, and so on.

Besides whetting appetites, the good things in this chapter are excellent stopgaps between meals. A see-through bag or box of *crudités*—see-through because *it's important to keep all things cheap and nourishing visible*—set front and center in the icebox should keep little (and large) hands off costlier food in the back. Place a jar of Dickie's Sauce for dipping beside it. And a jar of Peasant Caviar, for example, next to a loaf of dark bread will surely distract from the jam jar. At least, it's worth a try.

Garlic: press vs. knife: When even the merest speck of garlic in a dish is undesirable, a press forces an unpeeled clove of garlic into a fine purée. Very helpful. But some of the garlic's essence remains stuck in the press together with the skin. Therefore, I usually do this: Lay a whole unpeeled clove or two of garlic on a chopping board. Lay the flat of the blade of a chef's knife or cleaver on top of the garlic, then gently lean down on it with the heel of your hand until you hear the cloves pop open. Now the skin will pull right off. Holding the tip of the knife or cleaver down with one hand, use quick short strokes to finely mince the garlic with the other. The whole procedure really isn't more effort than cleaning a garlic press, and you don't waste one whit of the garlic (which isn't all that cheap!).

Milk, any sort: Whole, low-fat, or nonfat milk either fresh or reconstituted from powder. It does not include buttermilk.

Vacuum-bagging: This is a simple but invaluable way to wrap food for the refrigerator or freezer free from the deteriorating properties of air. Use one very strong or two weak plastic food storage bags (some of them can be counted upon to break open). Fill with food no more than two-thirds full. Have a deep pot of tepid water in the sink. Gather the neck of the bag above the food with a firm grip. Push the food all the way under water in the pot, making sure that the opening stays above water at all times. You will see that the water pressure forces all the air from around the food, out of the bag, creating a vacuum. Keeping it under water, twist the bag around a few turns to seal out the air, then double the top over onto itself and secure it tightly with a rubber band or wire twist. If for freezing, double the bag over as high as possible at the top, to give ample space for the food to expand.

NOTE: *The keeping times in recipes in this chapter are only for food stored in tightly covered jars in the refrigerator.*

Crudités

(Raw vegetables)
COUNT A GOOD HANDFUL PER PERSON

Choose the freshest, youngest vegetables that taste good raw—nearly all do. For a party, build a composition in your mind's eye: Look for dramatic colors—purple cabbages, ochre crookneck squashes, flame red bell peppers; amusing shapes—skinny asparagus, fat round radishes, ruffly broccoli; refreshing textures—crunchy carrots, slippery cucumbers, juicy tomatoes; and varied tastes—sweet peas, earthy mushrooms, nippy turnips.

Keep the vegetables as natural as possible—do not peel, and leave tops, tails, stalks, and a few leaves on when possible. Gently scrub, then pat your vegetables dry; vacuum-bag separately and chill. If you have room in the refrigerator, early in the day you can arrange your *crudités* in several bowls or baskets or on one big platter. Cover with plastic film, then a terry cloth towel, and then with a handful of ice cubes. Refrigerate, and then just before the doorbell is due to ring, unwrap and set out the *crudités*.

The only seasoning you really need is salt—I like coarse (kosher) salt, and sometimes, seasoned salt. But a dipping

sauce or two (see following) gives the *crudités* character—
it can be different every time you entertain, as you change
the sauce. Simpler still, the French offer a softened bar of
sweet butter smoothed into a crock for a contrast with their
crisp *crudités*.

To make the vegetables a complete hors d'oeuvre, pass
plates and forks to your guests, then serve dishes of cold
sliced meat or pâté, a few drained chunks of tuna, black
olives, small sour pickles or sweet gherkins, halves of hard-
cooked eggs, and hunks of good bread for sopping up.

Real Mayonnaise

1¼ CUPS

Homemade mayonnaise is altogether a different sauce
from store-bought—and often it's even cheaper! (It takes no
time to make, and these instructions will make it foolproof.)

> *1 whole egg or 1 egg yolk, according to mixing*
>   *method, at room temperature*
> *1 tablespoon vinegar or lemon juice*
> *½ teaspoon powdered mustard*
> *Scant ½ teaspoon salt, or to taste*
> *Pinch of white pepper*
> *1 cup light-tasting oil*

NOTE: A heavy-tasting oil can ruin mayonnaise and put
you off making it ever again. The best oil, I think, is virgin
olive, and the finest (apart from costly French) comes from
Lucca, Italy. Save up and buy a large tin of it from an Italian
grocer (ask his advice about the brand), then store, tightly
closed, in a cool dark place. If you can't find this, then mix
corn, safflower, or your favorite oil with what olive oil you've
got, until the flavor of the mayonnaise is pleasing.

In the blender: Warm the blender jar with hot water, then
dry it well. Place egg, vinegar or lemon juice, mustard, salt,
pepper and ¼ cup of the oil in the jar. Cover and turn on

lowest speed and at once lift cover. Begin pouring in *a very thin drizzle* of oil, aiming straight for the blade. Turn off motor the moment all the oil has been incorporated.

Every so often, when the gods are mad at you, the mayonnaise won't thicken. In that case, pour the mixture into a small pitcher, wash the blender jar thoroughly with hot water and soap, rinse well, and dry. Now, place an egg yolk (not the white) in the warm jar. Turn motor on lowest speed and add the mixture ve . . . ry slowly. It will pull itself together and thicken nicely. (And if it doesn't—it's only happened to me once—repeat the above with one more yolk.) You may add a little more oil and vinegar or lemon juice for this extra yolk, if you wish, but it isn't necessary.

Sometimes, the finished mayonnaise is thinner than you'd like it. Simply drizzle in more oil at lowest speed until it's the texture you want; taste for seasoning when you've finished.

On the other hand, if the mayonnaise looks too thick for your taste, simply stop adding oil when it's ready, even if it's less than the 1 cup called for.

You may also adjust the seasoning to your taste—more zip with added vinegar or lemon juice, more snap with extra white pepper, and so on.

By hand: (The Old Guard, of which I am not a member, says that this mounts to much greater volume.)

Rinse a small bowl with hot water to warm it, and dry thoroughly. Add 1 egg yolk (not the white) to the bowl, together with the vinegar or lemon juice, mustard, salt and pepper as above. Now use a whisk to beat the oil in drop by drop. As the emulsion thickens, add the remaining oil in a *slow*, steady drizzle, whisking constantly. You may add a bit more vinegar or lemon juice and pepper, too.

Your mayonnaise will keep at least 10 days.

Fines Herbes Mayonnaise

(Mayonnaise with fresh herbs)
   1¼ CUPS

If plain mayonnaise looks pale, this gives a verdant contrast.

> Scant 3 tablespoons chopped fresh herbs or greens:
>   parsley, spinach, sweet basil, tarragon, dill, thyme,
>   green onion
> 1 recipe Real Mayonnaise (see preceding recipe)

Bring a small pot of water to boil and drop in the greens. Count to 30, then drain them in a sieve (save the water for soup!). Press excess water from greens, and chop them finely. Whisk them into the mayonnaise. It will keep at least 1 week.

NOTE: Do not add greens in blender; a speckled-green sauce—achieved only by adding greens after blending—is much more appealing.

Dickie's Sauce

Good with everything, fast, and cheap. God bless Dickie Hendler.

> 1 part mayonnaise
> 1 part Super Yogurt (see p. 77)
> Some part buttermilk, for a thinner sauce
> Chopped fresh or dried herbs, optional
> Garlic, minced, optional
> Salt and white pepper, optional

Whisk together in a bowl, adjusting to your taste. It will keep until eaten.

Aioli: The Butter of Provence

(Garlic mayonnaise)
2 CUPS

The true *sauce aioli* complements just about any cold meat, fowl, fish, egg, or vegetable dish you can think of—but it requires the company of very good friends! (It's also much easier to make than it sounds.)

16 peeled cloves of garlic, or to taste
3 egg yolks, at room temperature
¼ teaspoon salt, or to taste
2 cups light-tasting oil
2 tablespoons warm water
4 teaspoons lemon juice, or to taste

Use a mortar and pestle if you have them, or the back of a sturdy wooden spoon and a bowl if you haven't. A blender or a mixer won't go slow enough for proper control, and will result in a terrible texture.

Crush the garlic cloves thoroughly until puréed. Blend in the yolks and a pinch of the salt. Now, drop by drop, using the pestle or spoon, steadily beat in the oil. When half the oil has been absorbed, you may change to a whisk and continue adding the oil in a very fine drizzle; also beat in a little of the warm water every now and then. When all the oil and water have been added, whisk in the rest of the salt and the lemon juice. If there are any lumps of garlic, force the *aioli* through a fine sieve.

NOTE: This sauce tends to curdle. If it does, use the same method as for thickening mayonnaise. Keeps at least 1 week.

Mock Aioli

For a quick mild sauce, press a few cloves of garlic into real or top quality store-bought mayonnaise. It's not at all the same, but it's good.

Salsa Tonnata

(Creamy cold tuna sauce)
1 CUP

A piquant sauce that's cheap, easy, and versatile. For hors d'oeuvres, spoon a little over cold platters of one or several of these: quartered hard-cooked eggs; quartered or sliced tomatoes; drained cooked white beans (the larger beans are best); whole tender-crisp cooked green beans; boiled whole, halved or quartered potatoes in their jackets; grilled sweet peppers; or pass simply as a dip for chunks of good bread.

Drained capers, thin lemon quarters, and parsley furls are the classic garnishes; choose one or all.

> *1 egg or 2 egg yolks according to mixing method, at*
> *room temperature*
> *Pinch of salt*
> *½ cup light-tasting oil*
> *3½ teaspoons lemon juice*
> *½ cup (4 ounces) drained tuna, any sort*

In the blender: In the pre-warmed jar, drop the egg, salt, ¼ cup of the oil, and 1 teaspoon of the lemon juice. Cover, turn to lowest speed, lift cover, and at once add remaining oil in a very slow, steady drizzle. Turn off motor the moment all the oil has been incorporated. Add the tuna and remaining lemon juice and turn again to lowest speed; blend until it is a smooth, creamy sauce (you may have to stop the motor and stir it in occasionally).

By hand: Follow directions for whisking homemade mayonnaise by hand, substituting the proportions listed above. Rub the tuna to a purée in a bowl with a pestle or the back of a wooden spoon; whisk it gradually into the stiff cream you have made. If sauce isn't perfectly smooth, rub it now through a sieve.

Cover and chill until needed; it keeps 2 or 3 days.

Chile con Queso

(Southwestern melted cheese)
8 TO 10 SERVINGS

This is the sort of dunk that people at a bash won't leave until they've cleaned the bottom of the pot—a delicious first course or supper if served over toasted French bread in the manner of a cheese rarebit—a sit-up-and-take-notice new way of making macaroni and cheese (just stir it in to 1 pound of steaming macaroni)—terrific.

2 pounds American cheese, diced
1 large tomato, skinned and chopped medium fine
2 tablespoons finely chopped canned "California mild
green chiles," or to taste (I make it with 5!)
2 cloves of garlic, minced
Merest bit of a hot jalapeño *chile; minced; or chile*
powder, to taste
¼ cup any sort of milk, or more

NOTE: Should the price difference not be that much, half-Cheddar, half-American cheese gives better flavor (and nourishment, if this is dinner). And chiles are cheap, but they may be hard to find—ask the local fancy grocer.

In chafing dish pan, or any heavy large pot, melt cheese over low heat, stirring occasionally (it takes a while). Stir in tomato, chiles, garlic, and *jalapeño* or chile powder. When smooth and blended, add just enough milk to make it of dipping consistency. Refrigerate, tightly covered, overnight if you like, then warm up slowly. Serve in a chafing dish or other keep-hot arrangement, with corn chips or chunks of French bread for dipping. And beer for drinking.

Peasant Caviar

(Roasted eggplant relish)
   6 SERVINGS

The Turks call this *Imam Bayeldi* ("The Bishop Fainted"
—probably from eating too much of it).

1 large eggplant
¼ cup light-tasting oil, more or less
1 generous tablespoon lemon juice
Lots of salt and fresh ground pepper
3 to 4 tablespoons finely chopped onion
3 to 4 tablespoons finely chopped green pepper,
   optional
3 to 4 tablespoons finely chopped tomato, optional

Set the eggplant on a baking dish in the center of the oven.
Turn heat to 250°F. and roast overnight, or for at least 6
hours. (This long roasting time is crucial to the texture of
the dish.) When the eggplant has shriveled and the meat
inside feels plump and soft, remove it from the oven and cool
slightly. Scrape every last bit of meat and juice from the skin
into a bowl.

Use a fork to whip the eggplant to a fluffy texture (a few
lumps are fine). Whip in oil, lemon juice, salt, and pepper,
tasting with each addition. Add the onions. The green
peppers and tomatoes are nice too, but not necessary. Cover
and refrigerate, and wait until the next day, if possible.
Serve with dark bread. This will keep for a week, if no one
can find it.

Ajvar

(Serbian sweet pepper relish)
   1 SWEET PEPPER PER 2 TO 3 PERSONS

One of the handsomest and most delicious combinations imaginable on dark bread is this gaily colored relish over *kajmak*, a snowy Balkan-style cheese.

> *Grilled sweet green and red pepper, in season;*
> *off-season, buy a jar of red sweet peppers packed in*
> *brine or vinegar (usually found with the pickles*
> *or kosher products)*
> *French Dressing, to taste (see p. 46)*
> *Minced garlic, to taste*
> Kajmak (*see p. 76*), *optional*

If you are using the jar peppers, slit them open, scrape out seeds, rinse under cold water, blot dry, then run them beneath the broiler for a few minutes until they blacken here and there, to absorb a taste of grilling.

Chop peppers fairly fine, and season with just enough dressing to give them a light, moderately loose, relish consistency. Add garlic, cover, and refrigerate to ripen. To serve, pile over *kajmak*-spread dark bread. It will keep for a week.

Gingered Melon

   1 WEDGE PER PERSON

In summer, when melons are in season, this is my favorite hors d'oeuvre. An English custom, it is easy, refreshing, and complements almost every menu.

Use ripe honeydew, Cranshaw, casaba, cantaloupe, or Persian melon (it should smell as it will taste, and should also have a little give to it when pressed with a thumb). Slice stem to blossom end into wedges; remove seeds. Now, *leaving them in place,* use a small sharp knife to cut out bite-size cubes; run the knife the length of the wedge to free cubes. Wrap cubes on their melon shells in plastic film and chill up to 8 hours. Remove from the refrigerator about 15 minutes before serving.

Sprinkle each wedge with finely chopped preserved (candied) ginger, which you can usually buy at a reasonable price in boxes at an Oriental market and store indefinitely in the freezer. If preserved ginger is costly, simply sprinkle with powdered ginger.

Remember the principle of not serving the same sort of food twice in a menu, so plan a non-fruit dessert.

Soups

The beautiful soups of this world are as dazzling in their variety as their ingredients—the vegetables, beasts, and seasonings—and the cooks who combine such makings in their soup pots. In these pages you'll find marvelous and inexpensive French, Finnish, Greek, American, Canadian, Creole, Jewish, Russian, and Italian soups. The great thing is to taste from everybody's pot. So be an adventurous—and thrifty—gourmet. Stir up these soups in *your* pot!

Budget notes

Soup is a fine filler-upper. A bowlful as a first course, whether for family or for guests, means that the courses to follow can be in smaller portions. And soup can serve a double function in a meal: fresh vegetable soup, for example, is all your vegetables for dinner, as cream of bean soup could be the starch.

But the best soup of all is the whole-meal soup—easy economical, and comforting. Nearly every soup here can serve as luncheon or supper; I've given suggestions for accompaniments which would balance out the meal. Also think of soup for breakfast. On a chilly working morning, let the family come into the kitchen to find a pot of soup warming for them. It's less effort than cooked cereal, and more fun.

After you've made your lovely soup, be careful how you keep it. *Always refrigerate soup the moment the meal is over.* Simmer it up about 5 minutes every 2 to 3 days (depending on the perishability of its ingredients), to keep out unfriendly bacteria.

Food mill: An inexpensive stainless steel hand-grinder quickly purées cooked or soft raw food through a fine, medium, or coarse blade—and holds back seeds, strings, skins, and so forth which a blender would grind into the whole. Mine is French-made, 15 years old and going strong.

Simmering: Means maintaining liquid at a temperature which sends up just one bubble at a time. That can be tricky. I set an asbestos pad with a metal bottom between pot and burner, and handle it carefully (particles of asbestos, if ingested, are unsafe). If you'd rather not use asbestos, then do check the pot every so often to make sure the temperature hasn't crept up and the liquid isn't boiling away. Cheap cuts of meat and fowl must have very gentle heat to render them tender and succulent.

Soup bowls: Throughout the book I mention "very large soup bowls." Mine are about 14 inches across and 2 inches deep, and were purchased very reasonably from a large Oriental grocery. They are invaluable for 1-dish meals. See if you can't find some—they don't at all have to match.

Vegetable shredder: An inexpensive stainless steel hand-grinder which can grind raw vegetables and fruits into anything from super-fine wisps to large, thin rounds—in seconds. Mine is French-made with five blades, and will probably last forever, like my food mill. But shredders are also available in other forms, such as attachments to various small kitchen appliances. Not a luxury, really, but a good investment in time and labor savings.

My Vegetable Soup

6 SERVINGS

Based on what the French call *à la bonne femme* ("a good woman's"). Use this recipe only for the method—invent your own combinations. That's the pleasure, and practicality, of soup making.

> *3 fat bulbs of green onions or 1 small onion, coarsely chopped*
> *1 clove of garlic, minced*
> *2 tablespoons oil*
> *2 peeled potatoes, thinly sliced*
> *¼ cup (2 ounces) margarine*
> *1 to 2 cups of raw or leftover chopped vegetables (carrots, broccoli, green beans, spinach, tomatoes, cauliflower, asparagus, turnips, anything)*
> *Chicken or beef broth, to cover*
> *Milk, optional*
> *Salt and fresh ground pepper, to taste*
> *An herb you like*
> *Squeeze of lemon juice, optional*
> *A spoonful of Super Yogurt (see p. 77) or Crème Fraîche (see p. 73), optional*
> *Chopped parsley, optional*

In a large soup pot, over medium heat, sauté the onion and garlic in oil until golden. Add the potatoes and margarine and stir to blend. Sauté 1 minute or 2, then add your vegetables and stir again. Cover generously with broth, cover the pot, lower the heat, and simmer gently until everything is tender, about 20 minutes.

You can purée this if you like—or purée part of it, to make a thick base for the vegetables—using the medium blade of a food mill, or in the blender. Or you can simply enjoy it lumpy. Heat again, thinning with more broth, if need be, or a little milk. Season with salt, pepper, a complementary herb, and lemon juice if it needs point. Serve topped with a

THE BUDGET GOURMET 20

bit of yogurt or *crème fraîche*, if suitable, and chopped parsley if it needs color.

To make a meal, add cole slaw, homemade whole wheat bread, a light dry red wine, and a dish of poached apples for dessert.

Fast Fresh Pea Soup

3 SERVINGS

If you keep peas in the freezer, you can whip up this beautiful soup for friends in no time.

2¼ cups (10 ounces frozen or 2¼ pounds fresh) peas
1¾ cups (14 ounces) light chicken broth
1 small clove of garlic, pressed
2 bulbs of green onions or ¼ small onion, coarsely
  chopped
1 lettuce leaf
Few fresh or pinch of dried thyme leaves
Dash of white pepper
Salt to taste
Super Yogurt (see p. 77) or Crème Fraîche (see p. 73)

In a medium-sized covered pot over medium heat, bring peas, broth, garlic, onion, and lettuce to a simmer. With petite-sized peas, turn off heat now; larger frozen or fresh peas will need to simmer just until tender. Lift out with a slotted spoon and set aside a handful of the peas; purée the rest of the soup in the blender or through the medium blade of a food mill. Return purée to pot and gently reheat with the thyme and white pepper. Heat just to the simmering point, the color must keep bright green. Ladle into flat soup bowls, garnish with the reserved whole peas and a dollop of yogurt or *crème fraîche.*

Serve with lettuce and tomato salad, hot French rolls, black olives, chilled Chablis, and for dessert, orange sherbet sauced with strawberry preserves.

A Soup of Summer's Squashes

4 TO 6 SERVINGS

This is fast, cheap in season, marvelous—no guest you serve it to will have tasted anything like it before.

> 8 *medium unpeeled summer or pattypan, or 5 to 6 medium-small zucchini or crookneck squashes*
> ¼ *cup oil*
> 2 *onions, finely chopped*
> ¼ *cup (2 ounces) margarine*
> 3 *cups (24 ounces) light chicken broth; more, if necessary*
> *Salt and white pepper, to taste*
> *Lemon juice, to taste*
> *Chopped parsley*
> *Thin slices of lemon*

In a large soup pot over medium heat, sauté the onions in the oil until golden. Top, tail, and dice the squash; add with margarine to the onions, and stir to blend. Add broth, bring to a simmer, cover, and reduce heat to let the soup simmer gently until vegetables are tender, about 15 minutes. Stir occasionally. Purée in the blender or through the medium blade of a food mill. Cover and chill, if you like, up to 6 hours. Or freeze it for another day.

Reheat slowly, adding more broth if too thick. Taste for salt and pepper and heighten flavor with a bit of lemon juice, if necessary. Serve sprinkled with parsley and a float of lemon.

A mixed salad with Dickie's Sauce (see p. 8) flavored with dill, dark bread, a brisk cheese, a glass of Chablis, and one or two pieces of shortbread with the tea or coffee would make a pleasant luncheon for friends.

Olga's Mother's Cream of
Fresh Tomato Soup

4 SERVINGS

This has an extraordinarily pure flavor. Save it for the height of tomato season, when tomatoes are real and ripe and scented—and reasonably cheap.

7 good-sized ripe fresh tomatoes, coarsely chopped
1 teaspoon lemon juice
½ medium onion, chopped
¼ cup margarine
¼ cup unbleached unsifted flour
2 cups low-fat milk
⅛ teaspoon nutmeg
1 teaspoon salt, or to taste
Dash of white pepper
Croutons, optional

In a medium-sized pot over low heat, covered, stew the tomatoes, lemon juice, and onion 15 to 20 minutes. At the same time, make a béchamel sauce by melting the margarine in a small pot, stirring in the flour over low heat, then whisking in the milk, nutmeg, salt, and pepper. When thickened, whisk another minute or two, then set over lowest heat. Purée tomatoes through the fine blade of a food mill or a coarse strainer into a bowl. Whisk the sauce into the tomatoes—the soup won't curdle this way. Return to the larger pot and gently reheat. Serve with a float of croutons, if you like.

With cold glasses of milk, some whole-grain crackers, wedges of a mild cheese, and for dessert, a thick slice of melon, this makes a fine hot-weather supper. Or serve this splendid soup as the first course of a dinner party, with a good braised beef perhaps.

Tzatziki

(Greek cold yogurt and cucumber soup)
4 SERVINGS

Yogurt soup may sound unlikely, but this couldn't be more refreshing. Make it for a summer night when it's too hot to eat, really, and cucumbers are in season.

The Persians embellish this soup—which they call *cacik* —with raisins plumped in ice water and chopped hard-cooked eggs; then they float ice cubes (as the Spanish do in their *gazpacho*) in the bowl just before serving.

3 cup Super Yogurt (see p. 77)
2 cloves of garlic, minced
1 medium peeled and grated cucumber
1 generous tablespoon olive oil
1 generous tablespoon lemon juice
Salt to taste
Chopped fresh or dried mint or dill

Stir together all ingredients but the mint or dill. Cover and chill all day. Stir again, then serve in glass bowls, if you have them, sprinkled with the herb. (If you're using homemade yogurt, and it's very thick, thin with a little water.) This soup keeps for several days.

Sesame crackers are suited to this, and a tingling cold beer, then fresh ripe peaches out of hand for dessert.

As a delightful first course for company, you might serve it to precede moussaka or a cooled grilled chicken with fresh fruit for dessert.

French Vegetable Bouillon

6 SERVINGS

A beautiful-looking soup, of inexpensive ingredients. Regard this recipe merely as the basic rule for soup of vegetables on hand.

4 unpeeled carrots
1 large, leafy stalk of celery
1 medium peeled turnip
1 small onion
*2 medium fresh tomatoes or 1 pound can of firm
   tomatoes, drained*
1 whole green onion
2 dark green lettuce leaves
1 clove of garlic, minced
7 cups water
1½ teaspoons salt, or to taste
Fresh ground pepper, to taste

If your kitchen is quiet and you can work without inter-ruption, then you can set the water in a large covered pot over high heat, and prepare the vegetables while it comes to a boil. But if you're frazzled, have each vegetable ready in a separate heap before the water goes on. Do follow the cutting directions precisely—the shapes are what make this soup special. Put the carrots through the ⅛-inch (number 3) of a vegetable shredder or cut into very fine, long shreds. Cut as *thinly as possible:* celery in crescents; turnips in slices then halves; onion and tomatoes in slices then quarters; green onion all the way up; lettuce in shreds.

Reduce heat so pot simmers; waiting 2 minutes after each addition, add carrots, celery, turnip, and onion; then —together—the tomatoes, green onion, lettuce, and garlic. Cover and simmer a total of 20 minutes, or just until vege-tables are tender-crisp. (If you wish to make this ahead of time, simmer the last 10 minutes just before serving.) Sea-son and serve with French or brown bread, mild cheese, a cold rosé, and vanilla-scented applesauce for dessert.

The soup is marvelous reheated, thinned with tomato juice —but do not let it simmer again lest it go soft.

Kaläkeitto

(Finnish fish and potato soup)
4 SERVINGS

A handsome way to stretch a few filets of fish—and to fill the eye as well.

1 pound filets of any lean fish
2 cups (16 ounces) light chicken broth
1 cup dry white wine
3 medium peeled potatoes
1 large ripe peeled tomato
3 green onions, bulbs only
1 teaspoon chopped fresh or ⅓ teaspoon dried dill
½ red Bermuda or sweet yellow onion, chopped
¼ cup margarine, melted
Yogurt, optional

Cut the fish into large pieces to fit into a 2-quart pot. Pour any juices from the fish package into a measuring cup, and add chicken broth to make 2 cups. Pour this and the wine over the fish, cover and bring to a simmer over medium heat. The moment the broth simmers, lift out the fish with a slotted spoon and set aside. Prepare the other ingredients while you wait.

Cut potatoes into ½-inch dice, chop the tomato, cut onion bulbs in thin rings. Add vegetables to the broth, cover and simmer gently until the potatoes are tender. Meanwhile, cut the fish into 1-inch dice. Put fish back in the soup when potatoes are ready. Add the dill, and heat (or reheat) only until the soup begins to simmer around the edges. Serve with a sprinkling of chopped onion and a drizzle of melted margarine in each bowl. A dot of yogurt is nice, too.

A tossed green salad and a cut of warm coffee cake would make a lovely supper.

Minestrone San Michele di Pagano

(Thick vegetable soup from the Italian Riviera)
ABOUT 6 SERVINGS

Making minestrone (wonderful way to pass a rainy afternoon) has an everything-in-handfuls feeling about it, even though it is a thrifty sort of soup. Don't fuss with precise measurements or ingredients here. Add what's available and cheap.

1 handful each of 3 or 4 sorts of dried beans, rinsed
½ bay leaf
¼ cup oil
1 large onion, thinly sliced then halved
3 large whole green onions, thinly sliced
2 cloves of garlic, minced
2 unpeeled carrots, diced
2 peeled potatoes, diced
¼ cup raw brown rice
8 ounces tomato purée
3 fresh or drained canned tomatoes, chopped
*1 tablespoon fresh chopped or 1 teaspoon dried
   sweet basil*
2 beef stock cubes or 1 can undiluted beef broth
Handful chopped parsley
Handful chopped celery sprigs
Handful chopped fresh spinach or other greens
Handful chopped red or white cabbage
Handful sliced zucchini, in season
Handful cut green beans
Handful peas
Handful small pasta
Salt and fresh ground pepper, to taste
1 recipe Pesto (see p. 216)
Lots of grated Parmesan

Combine dried beans and bay in a large pot and cook according to directions for making Memphis Beans (see p. 95). In a medium-sized skillet over medium heat, sauté the onion, green onions, and garlic in the oil for about 5 minutes. Add the carrots, potatoes, and rice, and sauté for 10 minutes more. Stir in the tomato purée, tomatoes, basil, and beef cubes or a little of the canned broth. Blend all thoroughly.

When the beans are tender, remove about one-third of them and pass through the medium blade of a food mill, or mash well. Stir the sautéed vegetables into this paste, then return it all to the bean pot, adding the parsley and celery sprigs. Add the rest of the canned beef broth, if used, and enough water to make a little less than double the volume. Cover and simmer over very low heat for about 2½ hours, stirring occasionally so it doesn't stick. Now add the remaining vegetables and pasta, season to taste, and simmer another 15 or 20 minutes, stirring occasionally until the pasta is *al dente*. Just before serving, blend in the *pesto* to taste. Ladle soup into heated bowls, top with Parmesan, and pass hot Italian or French bread on the side. For an occasion, a cool Chianti is good to drink. No need for salad or cheese at all, just a creamy coffee ice cream for dessert.

Filé Gumbo

(Creole fish-and-other-good-things soup/stew)
4 TO 6 SERVINGS

Everyone loves a gumbo. I've seen a pot of it fill an entire Little League baseball team and their families for dinner. This recipe is just the beginning; you can add pieces of sautéed chicken, chunks of cooked turkey, sausage links, ham (if you've a mind to), any shellfish, should it ever be cheap enough, lots more vegetables and rice—whatever the purse and the season provide.

Do look in a fancy grocer's for a jar of *filé* powder—the pounded leaves of sassafras and thyme—which will make your Creole gumbo authentic. It ought to be reasonably priced and it does keep.

*1 generous pound lean filets of any fish (Louisiana catfish
    is traditional)*
*1 cup chopped green pepper (if it's out of season, add
    more celery and onion instead)*
1 cup chopped celery
¾ cup chopped onion
1 large clove of garlic, minced
3 tablespoons oil
1 cup raw converted white rice
½ cup undiluted canned beef broth
2 pounds canned tomatoes, best quality, juice included
1 pound fresh or 2 packages frozen okra, in 1-inch cuts
1 bay leaf, crumbled
Tabasco, taco, or any hot sauce, to taste
1½ teaspoons salt, or to taste
Hot fish or chicken broth, optional
*1 tablespoon gumbo filé powder, or powdered thyme,
    to taste*

In a large heavy pot over medium-high heat, sauté the green
pepper, celery, onion, and garlic in oil until tender, stirring
often. Following package directions, start the rice cooking.
When vegetables are tender, add the beef broth, chop the
tomatoes and add them with the okra and bay. Bring to a
simmer and simmer, uncovered, over medium-low heat, 15
minutes; stir occasionally.

Cut the fish into thin slices, if necessary, then 1-inch
squares. Add them now to the pot and simmer gently another 10 minutes. (If you're increasing this recipe to serve a
crowd, add hot cooked chicken and so forth now.) Take off
the heat; gently stir in the hot sauce and salt. If you want it
soupier, to stretch further, thin with broth. Add the *filé*
powder, then turn into a heated tureen if the cooking pot
isn't suitable. Bring to the table at once. Serve in large bowls
—a spoonful of rice, and then a good ladleful of gumbo
over it.

The gumbo may be made ahead and reheated only before
the *filé* powder has been added—do not add the *filé* over the
heat or the gumbo will become stringy. Serve with a tossed

salad, French bread, a cool light red wine or beer, and cottage pudding with hot lemon sauce.

Doukhobor Borsch

(Light cabbage, potato, and tomato soup)
4 TO 8 SERVINGS

The Doukhobors are a religious sect who fled persecution in Russia at the end of the nineteenth century. My friend, Olga Matson, grew up near their settlement in Canada, and enjoyed this soup often as a child. The directions sound complicated, but they're not; they simply assure that each vegetable is cooked perfectly.

6 small (1 pound) unpeeled red or white new potatoes
4 cups cold water
1 bunch small new beets and their greens, optional
¼ cup margarine
1 medium onion, chopped
4 fresh or 2 cups drained canned tomatoes, chopped
2 cups (1 pound) chopped cabbage
½ cup Crème Fraîche (see p. 73), or Super Yogurt
(see p. 77)
1 tablespoon fresh chopped or 1 teaspoon dried dill
2 teaspoons salt, or to taste
Fresh ground pepper, to taste

Cut potatoes in 1-inch dice, then set in a large soup pot with 1 quart water over high heat. Bring to a boil, lower heat and simmer, covered, until tender. If you're using them, cut leaves from beets and place unpeeled beets in a pot with water to cover; bring to a boil, lower heat and simmer, covered, until tender. In another pot over medium heat, sauté the onion in the margarine until golden. Add the tomatoes to the onion pot and simmer over low heat a few minutes, stirring occasionally. Add 1 cup of the cabbage to tomatoes and simmer 2 or 3 minutes more. Chop the beet greens coarsely, if used; slip skins off beets and cut into 1-inch dice.

Lift out about half the potatoes from their water with a slotted spoon, and set aside in a dish. Add the other cup of cabbage and the beet greens to the potato pot, and simmer 2 or 3 minutes—just until the cabbage is tender but still crunchy. Meanwhile, with a fork, mash the potatoes set aside (skins and lumps are fine), and blend in the *crème fraîche* or yogurt. Since yogurt is tarter, you can add more later, to taste.

When the cabbage is tender-crisp, gently stir in the tomato and potato mixtures and the beets; turn off heat. Stir in the dill, salt, and pepper, and serve at once. Best not reheat this soup, because the cabbage must stay crunchy.

To make this a meal: Rye bread, homemade cream cheese and a light rosé are lovely with this, and for dessert, a plum crisp.

Old-Fashioned Chicken Soup

3½ TO 4½ QUARTS

If you weren't raised with it—have never tasted it—then homemade chicken soup will be a whole new world for you. The flavor is pure poetry, the broth is wonderfully versatile, but more than that, chicken soup is one of the great tonics for what ails you.

Once, stewing hens were the cheapest chickens and the stuff this soup was made of. Now they are nearly extinct. But you can still make the soup economically by buying just chicken backs and necks. Or when a big package of mixed chicken pieces, heavy on backs, necks, and whatnot is cheap, save the meaty pieces for other dishes and make soup with the rest. Too, if you freeze necks, giblets, tails, wing tips, skin, and cushions of fat from fryers as you use them, a great heap of these trimmings makes savory soup. (If you have a pet, here's a further saving: simmer the soup over lowest heat until the fine bones cook soft—then all that's left in the colander can nourish Fido or Pussy.)

And it is still economical to use plump fryers in soup. The chicken simmers gently to succulence while making a dividend of broth.

This is from Claire Calof, who has been making incomparable chicken soup for more than fifty years.

> *5 to 6 pounds of chicken in any form ("trimmings" means*
> *necks and backs, giblets, fat, and so forth)*
> *Seasonings:*
> *3 large unpeeled carrots*
> *3 leafy ends of celery*
> *1 peeled parsnip*
> *1 large unpeeled onion*
> *3 cloves of garlic, smashed and peeled*
> *12 leafy stalks of parsley*
> *4 parsley roots and tops, scraped, optional*
> *12 whole peppercorns*
> *2 teaspoons salt, or to taste*
> *A little fresh chopped or dried dill, optional*
> *Chopped parsley*

Place chicken in a 2-gallon soup pot. Add cold water to cover by 1 inch or so and set over medium heat. (If you're using just trimmings, add the salt now.) Cover and bring slowly to a simmer; turn heat to lowest maintainable and let simmer about 1 hour. For a clear broth, skim off the foam every 20 minutes until it bubbles clear; for the family, the foam is nourishing, leave it. Simmer about 1 hour.

NOTE: If you're using a roaster or fryer, add the seasonings together with the chicken. Then depending on what you'll use the meat for, remove chicken when it's tender.

With stewing chicken or trimmings, add the seasonings (cut the onion down but not through in 3 or 4 places) and continue simmering one bubble at a time until the stewing chicken tests tender with a cooking fork, about 2½ hours. With trimmings, you can simmer the soup all day if you like.

Place a colander over a large bowl and carefully pour the soup into it, gently pressing the vegetables to glean every drop.

To remove fat from broth: It's easiest to chill the broth and simply lift off the congealed fat. Or let the fat float to the top; put the tip of a bulb baster near the bottom of the pot and suction the lean broth up, releasing it into another pot or jar; pour the last of the broth into a tall glass jar so you see where the fat begins, and stop. Or you can carefully spoon the fat off the top and blot up the last specks with paper towels.

Add salt to taste, and a touch of dill, if you like. Chopped parsley over each bowlful is a must. The soup keeps 3 or 4 days in the refrigerator, or many months in the freezer. Serve it hot, alone or with egg noodles, fluffy kasha, or the ephemeral matzo balls of the next recipe.

Matzo Balls

ABOUT 30 BALLS

¼ cup (2 ounces) margarine, chilled
2 eggs
½ teaspoon salt
⅛ teaspoon nutmeg
2 tablespoons minced parsley
½ cup matzo meal, more or less
8 cups (64 ounces) simmering broth

In a small bowl with a wooden spoon, stir the margarine, eggs, salt, nutmeg, and parsley together. I know, it's an exercise in frustration; just do it. Stir in as little matzo meal as you can in order to make a thick, creamy paste too thin to handle (about the consistency of a light drop cookie dough). Cover and refrigerate from 1 to 24 hours.

Shape the balls: Wet your hands and take just enough paste to make 1-inch balls; roll them lightly in the palms of your hands and set on an oiled baking sheet or platter. Cover airtight and chill again, from 1 to 24 hours.

To cook, have a deep pot of chicken broth (or beef, if you like) simmering over lowest heat. Drop in the balls ever so gently, cover the pot, and simmer 15 minutes without peeking. Then taste one to see if it's tender. Serve, or remove pot from heat, cool in the broth, cover tightly, and refrigerate up to 2 days. Reheat gently to serve. Count 4 or 5 per person.

Chicken or beef soup with matzo balls makes a marvelous first course, or it can be dinner, with a hearty mixed salad thick with vegetables and beans and a glass of cold Chablis. For dessert, Pour Custard (p. 273) over warm poached apples.

Stracciatelle

(Roman egg and Parmesan soup)
4 TO 6 SERVINGS

This is very special. And there's nothing to making it, provided you begin with great broth. An incomparable quick light lunch or supper.

> *4 cups chicken broth; simmer 5 or 6 cups down*
>   *for extra richness*
> *2 eggs*
> *2 tablespoons grated Parmesan cheese*
> *Small pinch of nutmeg*

Put the broth on to simmer over high heat. Whisk the eggs, Parmesan, and nutmeg together in a measuring pitcher until thoroughly blended. When the broth boils, stir with spoon or whisk—a spoon makes a coarse shred, a whisk a finer one—while you pour in the eggs in a thin stream. At once turn off heat and ladle into hot soup bowls.

Really, don't make this unless your broth is very, very rich. The flavor must be clear chicken coming through a delicate nutty edge of cheese and nutmeg, which you can't quite taste.

Make a light meal of it with good bread, *salade de saison,* a glass of cool light red wine and for dessert, perhaps a dish of drained canned whole apricots sprinkled with Triple Sec or other orange-flavored liqueur.

Glorious Chicken in the Pot

(Chicken, vegetables, matzo balls, and noodles in broth)
8 SERVINGS

There are few dinners as welcoming as chicken in the pot. And there are few recipes as foolproof as this one of my mother's.

> 6 *pounds of plump frying chicken, in pieces, at room temperature*
> 20 *cups (160 ounces) light chicken broth (homemade or from good quality powder, cans, or cubes)*
> *Seasonings:*
> > *Add 1 bay leaf to the seasonings listed for homemade chicken broth; tie in a square of scrupulously clean cloth*
> *Garnishes:*
> > 2 *recipes Matzo Balls (see p. 32); cooked, or formed and chilled*
> > 12 *young peeled carrots, in thin rounds*
> > 20 *ounces fresh or thawed frozen green beans, Frenched (put through the double-bladed end of a vegetable peeler)*
> > 20 *ounces fresh shelled (buy 2½ pounds) or thawed frozen peas*
> > 8 *ounces quick-cooking broad egg noodles*
> *Salt and fresh ground pepper, to taste*
> 1 *bunch parsley, finely chopped*

NOTE: You can use the matzo ball broth for cooking the chicken, but strain it through a fine cloth first.

About 1½ hours before serving: Remove all skin from the chicken while the broth comes to a simmer in a 2-gallon soup pot over high heat. Keep it simmering gently while you drop in the seasonings and then one piece of chicken at a time. Cover, turn heat to lowest maintainable, and skim foam now and then. Begin testing the white meat with a cooking fork after about 35 minutes; when the juices run clear, it is done and the dark meat soon will be. Remove seasonings and set pot half off burner. If matzo balls haven't been cooked, ladle out about 3 generous quarts of the broth into a large pot, set it over high heat, then cook balls as directed.

30 minutes before serving: Set a big covered pot of hot water over highest heat for the noodles. Set timer to remind yourself to cook noodles at the last minute, according to time on the package. Set chicken pot over medium heat.

15 minutes before serving: If you have cooked the matzo balls in advance, turn them into the chicken pot to warm up. Also add the carrots. If broth isn't simmering, raise heat slightly.

10 minutes before serving: Drop *fresh gr*een beans and peas into pot now; for thawed vegetables, add them for the amount of time the package directs.

Just before serving: Drain noodles and add them to pot. Add matzo balls and broth, if they've been simmering apart. Stir pot gently, taste for salt and pepper, then pull light and dark pieces of chicken to opposite sides of the pot so you can pick out a guest's preference easily. Rush pot to the table (if you like, tie a napkin to each handle, for flourish). Serve in large soup bowls, a bit of it all, well laced with broth and sprinkled with parsley. Offer homemade egg bread if you can, cold kosher dill pickles, and chilled beer. For dessert, a warm apple tart.

Purée of Disaster Soup

Soup can be a saving more ways than one. Next time you have a casserole or vegetable dish or meat or even a soup that just doesn't quite make it, do this: thin with broth or milk, season with a good bit of minced garlic, lemon juice, and sweet basil (garlic, lemon, and basil save anything, I think), purée it all in the blender or through a food mill, and heat it up. You may be surprised at how fast it's eaten.

Anyway, it can't hurt.

Turkey Broth

2 GENEROUS QUARTS

For basting and making gravy for a 16-pound or larger turkey. Cut ingredients proportionately for a smaller bird.

Giblets and neck from turkey
2 pounds chicken backs and necks
1 pound chicken giblets
⅔ the amount of ingredients for Old-Fashioned Chicken
  Soup (see p. 30)

Follow directions for making broth with trimmings; simmer all day or overnight for richest broth—but add water 2 *inches* to cover at the beginning. Cool and strain broth into jar—do not remove fat, refrigerate. Discard vegetables, chop giblets and neck meat medium-fine, vacuum-bag and refrigerate.

Boeuf Bouilli

(Beef, vegetables, and noodles in broth)
8 SERVINGS

A simple but perfect dinner in a single dish. To make it, follow the next recipe, for Pot-au-Feu, adjusting ingredients (noodles in broth; beef, chicken, sausage, and vegetables).

Same beef
Same beef bones
8 cups cold water
4 cups (32 ounces) light chicken broth
4 cups (32 ounces) light beef broth
Seasonings:
  ½ the amount of same ingredients
Garnishes:
  ⅔ the amount of same ingredients
1 scant tablespoon salt, or to taste
Fresh ground pepper, to taste
Lots of parsley, finely chopped

Follow pot-au-feu method, except serve meat, vegetables, and noodles in the broth all together in very large soup bowls. (If vegetables are cooked just tender-crisp and noodles *al dente*, the finished soup can wait over lowest heat up to 1 hour.)

For accompaniments, boiled beef wants pumpernickel bread, kosher dill pickles, beet horseradish, cold beer, and for dessert, cold baked pears with *crème fraîche.*

Pot-au-Feu

(Noodles in broth; beef, chicken, sausage, and vetgetables)
10–12 SERVINGS

For surprisingly little effort and expense, this is—to my taste—the great dish to serve special guests in winter, just as *le grand aioli* is the great dish for summer. It is foolproof, as long as you don't overcook.

4 *pounds chuck arm (shoulder round-bone) roast; or use
beef simmering cuts (see p. 113) and buy what's
cheapest of the meats in one piece; at room temperature*
2 *pounds beef marrow or meatless soup bones, in 2″ cuts*
2 *pounds meaty chicken backs and necks, or trimmings*
4 *pounds plump chicken, the cheapest sort, whole or in
pieces, skinned; at room temperature*
2 *pounds mild, smoked, uncooked (and unpreserved)
sausage; substitute cooked, if necessary; at room
temperature*
20 *cups cold water*
10 *cups (80 ounces) light chicken broth*
10 *cups (80 ounces) light beef broth*
Seasonings:
    12 *pods of peas*
    2 *ripe fresh or firm canned tomatoes*
    6 *large bulbs of green onions*
    2 *unpeeled onions, each stuck with 2 cloves*
    2 *leafy ends of celery*
    1 *small peeled turnip*
    1 *small peeled parsnip*
    4 *large unpeeled carrots*
    4 *cloves of garlic, smashed and peeled*
    Few sprigs of fresh or large pinch of dried thyme
    Few leafy stalks of parsley
    1 *bay leaf*
    12 *peppercorns*
Garnishes:
    14 *very small whole or 10 medium-sized halved
unpeeled red or white boiling potatoes*
    24 *small or 16 medium-small peeled boiling onions*
    12 *very small whole or 8 medium halved turnips*
    24 *small or 14 medium-sized whole unpeeled carrots*
    12 *bulbs of very large green onions*
    1 *large head of cabbage cut in thin wedges, then each
wedge cut in half*
    9 *ounces fine egg noodles or small pasta*
2 *tablespoons salt, or to taste*
Fresh ground pepper, to taste
Lots of parsley, finely chopped

The broth: Trim all visible fat from the meat and tie it snugly in a very clean cloth. Tie up marrow bones in another cloth. Lay beef, bones, chicken backs and necks, and giblets, tail, fat, skin, and wing tips from the chicken in a large preserving kettle. Add water and broths, set pot over medium-low heat and very slowly bring to a boil—give it at least 1 hour. Skim off foam every 20 minutes or so until the foam turns cream-colored, then stop skimming.

Meanwhile, on a baking sheet, roast the pea pods and quartered tomatoes for 20 minutes in a 375° F oven.

When the froth has turned creamy, add the seasonings, then cover the pot and turn heat to the lowest maintainable —if the broth can be kept just below the simmering point, the meat will be juiciest.

If you've found a whole stewing chicken, truss it and drop it into the pot 30 minutes after the seasonings; a roasting chicken goes in 1½ hours after the seasonings; and frying chickens go in about 2 hours and 20 minutes after.

Two hours after the seasonings, drop in the whole un-cooked sausages; cooked sausages go in after 2½ hours, just to warm up.

Continue to poach until the beef tests tender with a cooking fork and the chicken thigh juices run clear yellow when pricked; it will take from 3 to 4 hours. Keep the water at a mere tremble, and nothing should overcook. Turn off the heat and ladle the top inch or so of broth into a tall pitcher. When the fat floats to the top, remove it. Set the pot in a cool place or refrigerate if you are not planning to reheat within a few hours.

The meat and garnishes: Bring pot to room temperature, if chilled, removing any fat from the surface. An hour and a quarter before serving, lift out and set aside the meat, bones, chicken, and sausage, then pour soup through a colander, gently pressing the vegetables to glean every good drop. Return broth and reserved meats to the kettle and set over medium heat, covered, so soup will slowly come to a simmer.

Take out the meats 45 minutes before serving and keep warm in a covered pre-warmed dish at the back of the stove or in a 225° F oven. To the broth, add the potatoes, boiling onions, and turnips; if the carrots are not tiny, add them, too. Cover and return to a simmer, regulating heat so the vegetables simmer slowly. After 25 minutes, drop in the carrots if tiny, and the green onions. Also simmer the cabbage wedges in a separate pot in some of the broth, covered, over low heat until tender-crisp. Put on a covered pot of hot water for the noodles or pasta.

While vegetables cook, untie the cloth and slice the beef with the grain in about ⅜-inch-thick pieces, removing any fat and gristle; the slices may not be uniform, but they will taste marvelous, so don't worry. Lay slices on a very large heated platter or in a large heated casserole—or two, if need be—and moisten with some of the hot broth.

NOTE: It's a good idea to lay out all the meats and vegetables raw to see how they will fit on what serving dishes you have so you won't have a nasty last-minute surprise.

Gently pull the chicken meat from the bones, tearing or cutting it neatly into large pieces; arrange next to the meat. Cut the sausage into good-sized chunks and add them, too. Lay the wet cloth from the beef over all meats, cover with foil and a terry towel, and set in a 225° F oven.

When the vegetables are tender-crisp, lift them out with a slotted spoon and arrange them in a garland around the meats. Keep everything moist with hot broth, wet cloth, foil, and a towel; return to the oven. It will keep ½ hour longer than you'd planned, should that be necessary.

Serving the broth: While the garnish vegetables are simmering, boil noodles or pasta according to package time, then drain in a colander and set in a heated tureen or pretty pot. Taste the broth for salt and pepper, then ladle out simmering broth from the kettle over the pasta—count 2 generous ladlefuls per person. (By the time the vegetables are tender, you'll be ready to take the broth out—the timing here works marvelously.) If noodles are cooked *al dente,* they will wait in broth in a pot over lowest heat ½ hour longer than you'd planned, too.

Unwrap the marrow bones, if you've used them, and

either spread the marrow on hot toasted French bread, or simply drop a marrow bone into each bowl. Ladle the soup into very large soup bowls and serve, sprinkled with parsley.

Serving the garnished meats: After the soup course, stagger in with the platter of meats and vegetables, and serve them in the same large soup bowls. For accompaniments, the French like white horseradish, Dijon mustard (or use a cheaper domestic sort), coarse (kosher) salt, drained capers, sour gherkins, hot French bread, and dry red wine like a claret. For dessert, a delicate *crème brulée*.

You will have buckets of fabulous broth left over. Keep it in the refrigerator 3 days, or the freezer up to 1 year.

Salads

Cool greens dressed with delicate oil and vinegar are wonderfully reviving. That is why the canny French offer just lettuces after the main course—to cleanse the palate and refresh the diner before a serious cheese and dessert.

Salads are easy: toss, toss. And delightfully practical. They can be the vegetable in a meal, or indeed, the meal itself. And of course they are nourishing. More, raw salads are the vital roughage a healthy digestive tract needs every day. Usually, the makings are reasonably priced. Here are a few dressings and combinations to keep your salad bowl perky.

Budget notes

Remember, the deeper the green, the more vitamin A. Buy such as romaine, salad bowl, and red leaf lettuces rather than pale-faced iceberg. And don't forget spinach, cabbage, and wild greens free for the picking. Ask around your neighborhood about the edibility of native greens; I've seen people in vacant lots and on country roadsides gathering armloads of greens I never knew were there.

Bring salad greens home and wrap them loosely in light towels in a plastic box, bag, or crisper; let them breathe. Do not wash until just before using, but then rinse thoroughly, gently pat dry with an absorbent towel, and tear into large-bite-size pieces. For a party, however, it's helpful to wrap the torn pieces in a thick dampish towel in the refrigerator early in the day.

About the bowl: I used to imagine that, like a wok or an omelette pan, much of a wooden salad bowl's mystical virtue would be washed away if touched with water. I've learned better. Oil can turn stale in wood. Now I often swish the bowl beneath warm running water and dry it thoroughly, just to keep it honest.

NOTE: *It is important to refrigerate all dressings and salads containing eggs.*

Your Own Bottled French Dressing

2½ CUPS

Once I loved the verve of the classic dressing, three parts oil to one of vinegar—and garlic by the fistful. Now I prefer subtlety, and the flavor of the salad itself.

This is a bare-bones sort of dressing. It has nothing in it to turn stale, so it will stay fresh in a cool dark cupboard as long as the oil alone would keep. Always add one good accent to the salad just before you drizzle the dressing over: minced green onions, or a few fresh chopped herbs, or if you're in the mood, a passel of Parmesan and sesame seeds.

If you haven't found a way to keep oil in a cupboard any length of time, then make up only as much dressing as you'll use in a week. Cheaper, purer, and as easy as store-bought.

2 cups light-tasting olive or your preferred oil
6 tablespoons red wine or any vinegar
1¾ teaspoons salt, or to taste
½ teaspoon powdered mustard
½ teaspoon fresh ground pepper

Measure oil in a 1-quart-sized measuring pitcher, then mix in remaining ingredients with a fork. Pour from pitcher into a dark bottle or jar. Keep tightly covered in a cool, dark place. Shake well before using.

Silky Dressing

(French dressing lightened with egg)
½ CUP

Wonderful French creation which clings to greens like a veil. If you should be lucky enough to have a pot of sweet basil on your window sill, this is the place for some leaves.

1 teaspoon egg yolk, at room temperature
1 tablespoon vinegar, or to taste
7 tablespoons light-tasting oil
Small handful of fresh or ½ teaspoon dried sweet basil
¼ teaspoon salt
⅛ teaspoon powdered mustard
Fresh ground pepper

To the yolk in a small bowl, add a dash of the vinegar, and then, ve . . . ry slowly, use a fork to beat in the oil. When most of the oil is in, add the rest of the vinegar, crumble in the dried basil if you're using it, add the salt and mustard, then the last of the oil. If the dressing isn't as thick as un-whipped cream, put ½ teaspoon more yolk in another small bowl, and slowly beat this dressing in with the fork.

Cover and, especially if you're using dried basil, let the flavors marry about 1 hour in a cool place. With fresh basil, tear the leaves into 2 or 3 pieces, and add them to the greens. Grind black pepper over the salad before tossing.

Creamy Herbal Dressing

ABOUT 1 QUART

Keep a jarful in the fridge—it's popular, low-calorie, dresses all sorts of greens and vegetables, and cheaper than any store-bought dressing like it. The recipe is from our Great-Aunt Florence Auingier; if you haven't her selection of herbs on hand, substitute those you do.

1½ tablespoons chopped chives or green onion stems
1½ tablespoons fresh chopped or 1½ teaspoons dried dill
1½ teaspoons fresh chopped or ½ teaspoon dried
*   tarragon*
1½ teaspoons fresh chopped or ½ teaspoon dried chervil
1 teaspoon powdered mustard
1 teaspoon paprika
2 teaspoons salt, or to taste
½ teaspoon fresh ground pepper
2 large cloves of garlic, pressed
2 tablespoons vinegar
¾ cup light-tasting oil
2 cups Super Yogurt (see p. 77)
1 cup buttermilk

Place chives, dill, tarragon, chervil, mustard, paprika, salt, pepper, garlic, and vinegar in blender or mixer bowl with 2 tablespoons of the oil. Cover and blend or mix at low speed; remove cover and add rest of the oil in a slow stream. Keep motor on while you add the yogurt and buttermilk; stop when blended thoroughly. Keeps, refrigerated, at least 10 days.

Dickie's Dressing

This is simply Dickie's Sauce (see p. 8) thinned with buttermilk to the desired consistency.

Salade de Saison

(A simple salad of lettuces)
1 LARGE BUNCH MAKES 4 SERVINGS

Choose two or three contrasting colors and textures of lettuces, if you can. And if dinner is rich, try to include a wild green, such as dandelion or dock. Rub the salad bowl with a cut clove of garlic, then dress the large-bite-size greens with a perfectly simple French dressing or a silky one. No flourishes.

Fresh Spinach Salad

Tender young spinach has become the number-one salad at our house. Its flavor complements nearly every meat, fowl, or fish I might serve. It gives a lovely color and texture contrast on the plate. And it's incredibly nourishing; only carrots, parsley, kale, and a few wild greens have more vitamin A than raw spinach. Spinach leaves have as much vitamin C, ounce per ounce, as fresh orange juice; as much calcium as cottage cheese; and more potassium than tomatoes. And often it's the cheapest of all the salad greens. (As Charlotte might spin in her web, SOME SALAD.)

Sometimes I balance the sort of lemony taste of spinach with a creamy dressing. And sometimes I heighten it with a French dressing made with lemon juice. The addition of a few fresh chopped tomatoes and dill is marvelous. So are a few slivers of raw mushrooms. Or chopped hard-cooked eggs. And although I stiffen at the thought of phony food, the soy-based "bacon bits" aren't bad on the spinach now and then.

For a main-dish salad, thick slices of boiled potatoes, chopped tomatoes, and rings of hard-cooked eggs are great with Dickie's Dressing (see preceding page). Then good rough bread, homemade cream cheese, and maybe a plum-topped cottage pudding for dessert.

To rinse spinach quickly: Fill the sink with *lukewarm* water. Cut the stalks free at the roots, but leave tender stalks on leaves. Let the spinach soak a minute or two while you pick out anything past its prime; swish leaves gently, lift out, shake off excess water. Empty the sink, rinse away the sand in it, fill the sink again—half full this time—with lukewarm water. Soak and swish the spinach once more, then lift out, shake, and spread out on a terry towel. Pat dry with another towel gently, then wrap in the driest of the towels and chill briefly, if convenient.

French Tomato Salad

When the tomato season hits its peak and some are marked down because they're super-ripe, prepare tomatoes in this incomparable manner.

Remove stem scar, then slice unpeeled tomatoes with a sharp serrated knife as thinly as possible. Lay in a white or glass bowl; sprinkle copiously with finely chopped parsley, and lightly with oil (no vinegar), salt, and fresh ground pepper. Toss together gently with a rubber spatula, then set aside at room temperature for 1 or 2 hours before serving.

Salad of Grilled Sweet Peppers

In summertime, sweet peppers also happily are cheaper. Then take advantage of the season to make this delectable accompaniment to almost every meat, fowl, and fish.

Blanch whole peppers just until they lose their crispness. Dry them, then spread beneath a hot broiler or over hot coals (charcoal, if you have any sort of barbecue, adds immeasurably to the flavor). Turn peppers gently and often until their skins blister and some edges have caramelized. Remove to a plate, being careful not to lose any juices.

Cut a ring around the stem, then pull it out, hopefully with the seeds inside attached. Slice peppers in half lengthwise, scrape out any remaining seeds, then gently pull away the skin—if some skin doesn't come, leave it. Lay peppers in a dish and pour over a generous amount of French dressing; use a rubber scraper to lift the peppers gently so the dressing can sauce them underneath. Set aside at room temperature up to several hours, then drain well before serving.

Vegetables à la Vinaigrette

(Tender-crisp cooked vegetables in French dressing)

For hors d'oeuvres and as a combination vegetable-and-salad, this practical French notion is superb.

Simmer vegetables in light chicken broth in a large skillet, covered, over medium-high heat until they are tender-crisp, no more. Drain well (saving the broth for soup), then immediately lay in a flat, shallow dish. Season generously with French dressing, what the French call *sauce vinaigrette,* made with lemon juice or wine vinegar. If an herb or two would enhance the vegetable, or minced garlic, chopped green onions (or a combination of garlic and green onions to simulate shallots), or capers, then add them. Use enough dressing to cover the bottom of the dish ¼-inch deep, and spoon it over the vegetables several times to be sure of moistening them thoroughly.

The vegetables may be dressed ahead of time—some further ahead than others. Whole slender carrots or cut in fine julienne strips (⅛-inch wide or use number 3 blade of a vegetable shredder), julienne of red or green cabbage, whole thin green beans, baby brussels sprouts, flowerets of broccoli, thin lengths of young zucchini, and lightly blanched branches of spinach should be served while still bright and crisp and warm—within the hour.

But small potatoes in their jackets (splashed first with Chablis), slices or julienne of peeled parsnips, lengths of leeks (when reasonably priced), buds of cauliflowers, tiny or quartered peeled beets, quartered hearts of celery, julienne strips of peeled celery root, thin asparagus in spring, and kidney or white beans or lentils may be refrigerated for hours then brought to room temperature.

To serve, drain thoroughly, then garnish with strips of pimiento, or press a hard-cooked egg through a sieve over the vegetables, being careful not to move the egg once it's drifted down; this looks like tiny blossoms and is called mimosa. Or simply sprinkle with chopped parsley, green onions, or chives.

Cole Slaw at Our House

I LARGE HEAD MAKES 6 SERVINGS

. . . is cabbage cut into thin but rough shreds with a knife, tossed with Dickie's Dressing, a dash of lemon juice, lots of dill, a whiff of onion powder, and several turns of the pepper mill. The children, especially, enjoy it.

If I weren't so harassed at suppertime, I'd add finely shredded carrots and/or red cabbage. But I am and I don't.

Potato Salad at Our House

I OR 2 POTATOES PER SERVING

. . . is simply cool boiled potatoes and something creamy to dip them in. Very nice for casual dinners, buffets, picnics, lunchboxes, and stand-up meals in front of the icebox.

Choose the smallest boiling potatoes you can find; red-skinned ones are particularly good. Scrub them, then simmer whole until a cooking fork tests them tender—don't let potatoes start to break open. Drain (saving the water for soup-making or bread-making), then use a pastry brush dipped in light oil to coat the skin of each potato. Cover and cool at room temperature.

You can vacuum-bag them airtight and refrigerate up to 3 days. Bring to room temperature before serving. Sprinkle with coarse (kosher) salt and, if it complements the rest of the meal, chopped fresh or dried dill—but not too much of either; use a rubber spatula to turn the potatoes as you sprinkle. Heap the whole potatoes in a wooden bowl and offer a creamy dipping sauce, plain yogurt, or *crème fraîche* on the side. (*Aioli*, real or mock, is smashing.)

Greek Rice Salad

12 SERVINGS

This is my re-creation of a salad I once enjoyed at Zonar's, a sidewalk café in the heart of dusty Athens. There is something both of ancient Greece and modern Middle East in its flavor. It sounds more complicated than it is. Make it in summer, a day in advance, for a dinner party.

14 medium very firm fresh tomatoes, for stuffing; or
    3 large ripe fresh or firm-quality canned ones
¾ cup light-tasting oil
1 large onion, finely chopped
2 cloves of garlic, minced
2 ounces drained pimientos, finely chopped
2 cups raw converted long grained white rice
¼ teaspoon powdered cumin
½ teaspoon turmeric
1 teaspoon mushroom powder, optional
1 chopped sprig fresh or ¼ teaspoon dried mint
Pinch of ground allspice
Pinch of powdered thyme
4 cups (32 ounces) light chicken broth, simmering
2½ tablespoons vinegar
¼ cup mild taco sauce, or any hot sauce, to taste
Small handful of pine nuts, optional
Small handful of dried currants or chopped raisins
½ teaspoon salt, or to taste
¼ teaspoon white pepper, or to taste
2 bunches of parsley
Black olives, optional

Heat 3 tablespoons of the oil in a large heavy pot over medium-low heat; sauté the onion and garlic slowly until clear—do not brown. Stir in the pimientos, blending thoroughly, then the rice. Sauté a few minutes until the rice is clear, then sprinkle with cumin, tumeric, mushroom powder, mint, allspice, and thyme. Pour 1 cup of the simmering broth evenly over the rice without stirring. Raise the heat so the broth bubbles briskly. Cover pot at once, give it a shake, and after a minute or so, turn heat to the lowest maintainable.

In 5 minutes, add another cup of the broth without stirring; 5 minutes later, another cup—and so on, only adding broth as the cup before has been absorbed by the rice. After 25 minutes in all, each grain should be tender but still firm and separate. While hot, spread rice in a shallow dish and at once pour over it a dressing of the oil, vinegar, taco sauce, pine nuts, currants or raisins, salt, and pepper. Cover and chill 4 to 24 hours.

Now. You can heap the gold-colored rice in tomato shells —very handsome. Or simply mix chopped tomatoes into the rice for color. If you wish to make the shells, then while the rice chills, blanch the tomatoes a minute or two and slip off their skins. Cut a slice off the tomatoes at the top of their shoulders; remove the stem scar and put tops into a bowl. Use a spoon and gently scrape the seeds and juice from each tomato into another bowl; scrape the solids into the bowl with the lids. If a shell should tear (you have a safety margin of 2), add it to the solids. Gently set shells upside down on a terry towel to drain.

Chop the solids fairly fine, then use a rubber scraper to mix them into the rice. Add just enough strained juice to make the rice moist but not soupy. Taste; it must be highly seasoned.

When the rice is cool, gently spoon it into the shells, filling but not packing tightly. Mound the rice as high on top as it will stay. Arrange tomatoes on a platter, then spoon any remaining rice around them as a border. Decorate with parsley flourishes, set black olives about for accent if you like, then cover airtight. Refrigerate up to 24 hours; remove from refrigerator 1 hour before serving.

If you don't want to bother with the tomato shells, then after blanching, seed and finely chop 2 or 3 large tomatoes (or canned ones) and fold them into the rice as for the solids. This salad may be refrigerated up to 2 days. Serve garnished with parsley and olives, in a bowl which dramatizes the colors.

This salad is a splendid complement to cold slices of turkey, chicken, lamb, beef, fish, or chunks of tuna garnished with lemon. Also offer a choice of French bread and rough dark bread, and a block of *feta*, if you can find it. *Feta* is Greek goat cheese, white and salty and habit-forming; it is a bargain if you buy it canned—a pound will serve a dozen people. To drink, cold beer or light white wine; and for dessert several sorts of melon or fruits in season, perhaps arranged on a bed of crushed ice.

Salads of the Last Little Bits

Sometimes I forget that a handful of boiled beef, stewed chicken, or half a can of tuna—or chopped cooked broccoli, grated cheese, or the leafy tips of celery—can be excellently finished off in a salad. Don't you forget!

Afterthought: An especially good combination of leftovers is tuna or any light meat with cold boiled potatoes, diced cucumber, black olives, and Bermuda onion rings dressed with homemade mayonnaise.

Also try tuna with white beans, celery, and French dressing.

And anything with *Aioli* (see p. 9).

Salade Niçoise

(Mediterranean main-dish salad)

A lifesaver, because given an hour's notice and some inexpensive good things you've hidden away for emergencies, you can serve last-minute guests this beautiful main dish salad from the French Riviera.

Amounts are for 1 serving of the salad composed of the basic *Niçoise* ingredients and 5 or 6 flourishes.

Basic Niçoise makings:
  1 egg
  1 small fresh tomato
  Small handful black olives
  2 anchovy filets (1 flat tin should serve 6)
  French Dressing (see p. 46)
  Minced garlic, to taste
Any or all could be added:
  About 3 ounces drained tuna
  1 unpeeled whole small or 1 quarter of a large boiling
    potato
  Small bunch of whole thin green beans, fresh or thawed
  1 or 2 thin rings of green pepper
  3 to 4 ounces white, garbanzo, or kidney beans, cooked
    or canned, drained
Served over:
  1 large leaf of loose leaf lettuce
Substitutes:
  1 small whole or heap of julienne beets, cooked fresh or
    canned, drained
  1 artichoke heart, canned (often a bargain when
    imported from Spain)
  1 broad strip of pimiento
  1 or 2 thin rings of onion

How to make the salad fast: Put eggs and potatoes together in cold water in a covered pot over high heat; when water boils, turn heat to low and set timer for 15 minutes. Put on a pot of hot water for the beans. When timer rings, remove eggs with a slotted spoon and plunge into ice water to cool. Test potatoes for tenderness every couple of minutes from now on; when they are ready, drain, then pat dry and set them in the freezing compartment to cool (set timer for 15 minutes lest you forget them).

Meanwhile, blanch the green beans until tender but crunchy, about 8 minutes, then drain and add them to the eggs in ice water. When cool, lift out, pat dry, and wrap in a towel; set aside. If you're using frozen beans, run them under cool water to thaw, then pat dry and wrap in a towel.

Rinse and pat dry the tomatoes, green peppers, and lettuce leaves. Quarter the tomatoes, slice the green pepper in thin rings, and tear the lettuce into large pieces. Open and drain the cans of olives, anchovies, tuna, and beans. Whisk the French dressing, adding the garlic. Crack the eggs and quarter them. Line a broad, shallow bowl or platter with the lettuce. Turn the tuna out of the can into the center of the platter in a mound. Surround it with separate heaps of the garnishes, alternating colors; for example (clockwise): tomatoes, potatoes, green beans, kidney (or other) beans, eggs, and green pepper rings. Strew the olives in small piles here and there, then decorate here and there with crossed strips of anchovies.

If you're not pressed for time, the salad can be covered and refrigerated for a couple of hours.

At the table, drizzle lightly with French dressing. To serve, pick up a few lettuce leaves to line each plate, then repeat the large arrangement on an individual scale. Serve with French bread, cold Chablis, a light cheese to follow, should you have it, and for dessert, vanilla ice cream with melted currant jelly on top.

The basic *Niçoise* makings are a fine, simple hors d'oeuvre, by the way, with French bread and some sweet basil sprinkled over.

Eggs, Homemade Cheeses, and a Super Yogurt

An egg is, I guess, the most versatile ingredient in the kitchen. And surely the biggest bargain. An egg will help dishes rise up, get thick, hold together, look pretty, be breaded, emulsify—and although it can't cook the dinner by itself, an egg will provide it for you.

Well over a century ago, Thomas Moore numbered "six hundred and eighty-five ways to dress eggs . . ." Such staggering variety comes from a mere handful of cooking methods: Eggs are cooked in the shell (in water or steam), out of the shell (in butter, water, or the oven), or left completely uncooked. It's not as though you need learn countless techniques to cook eggs any number of ways.

Here is a clutch of my favorite egg recipes. And at the close of the chapter, a few homemade cheeses that cost little, but rival the finest fresh cheese made.

Budget notes

It's frustrating that when so much else is costly, the comforting Cheddars, Monterey jacks, domestic Swiss, and mozzarellas which once made a budget meal are ridiculously high-priced now, too. But for heaven's sake, *only buy such natural cheeses.* In the long run, they are not much more expensive than the seemingly cheaper processed cheeses in terms of nutritional value for money—and certainly natural cheese is superior in terms of purity and flavor. Process-blended, processed cheese foods, and processed cheese spreads can legally be composed of lots of things besides real cheese—the spreads are but 51 percent cheese! A passel of chemicals not listed on the label can be unnerving ingredients.

Fresh cheeses—cream, cottage, others in tubs—and yogurt should be purchased with a sharp eye on the *expiration date*. Wrap tightly in plastic film or keep the lid on snug; refrigerate on the top shelf of the icebox. Of fresh cheeses, only cream cheese may be frozen, and only up to 2 weeks.

Hard cheeses must also be refrigerated on the top shelf. If you buy hard cheese on special, and aren't sure how fast you will use it up, then wrap in a very clean cloth dampened in a solution of ½ cup water, 1 teaspoon vinegar, and ½ teaspoon salt. Keep the cloth damp and closely wrapped around the cheese. When you want some, cut just what you need and return the rest to the icebox—frequent changes of temperature can ruin good cheese. If, despite being careful, a few lumps turn very hard or bloom with mold, then simply scrape the mold off and grate the cheese into a jar—cover tightly, and the gratings will keep for cooking. Sometimes, however, the moldy scent pervades all the cheese, or some semi-hard cheeses, such as Teleme, go "off"—then, alas, they are lost.

Rather than lose good cheese, consider that Cheddar, mozzarella, Swiss, brick, Edam, Gouda, Muenster, Camembert, and Port-Salut—should you ever find a windfall of such lovely stuff—*may be frozen*. Cut into 1-pound or smaller chunks no more than 1-inch thick; vacuum-bag, then wrap in freezer paper. At zero degrees Fahrenheit, the cheese will keep up to 6 months; use the cheese the moment it has thawed.

If you use eggs at a steady rate in your kitchen as I do, then keep them, as I do, in a basket on the counter. Eggs should always be at room temperature for cooking, and this way—besides looking lovely—they never need warming in hot water. I've always kept my eggs this way, and in twenty years haven't lost one to spoilage yet (but of course it depends on your climate).

Always watch heat in cooking with cheese, whether fresh or hard. High heat will cause cheese to get stringy, an indication that you've destroyed some of the protein you've paid for.

Béchamel Sauce: The base for soufflés and at least a dozen other sauces, this is simply good old white sauce with a French name. But white sauce sounds so stark and béchamel so sumptuous. Here are the proportions for making it. (See Step 2 on p. 64 for directions.)

Key to making béchamel: Use 1 cup of any sort of milk; (the richer the milk, the creamier the sauce):

CONSISTENCY	MARGARINE	FLOUR
Thin	1 tablespoon	1 tablespoon
Medium	2 tablespoons	2 tablespoons
Thick	3 tablespoons	3 tablespoons

Cheapest natural hard cheese: Sometimes, I call for this in a recipe, rather than specify Cheddar or whatnot. In my experience, mozzarella is often the cheapest—a good thing, because it is lower in fat than most hard cheeses. It does have a tendency to string even at low heat, as you know, but that won't affect the character of the dish that much. But if it's to be layered through a dish for company and Cheddar or Monterey jack isn't frightfully expensive, however, use one of them.

NOTE: *Again, eggs must be at room temperature for cooking!*

Who's Afraid of a Big Soufflé?

4 SERVINGS

The only way to approach making a soufflé is not to be intimidated by all that glamorous show. A soufflé is nothing more than a béchamel sauce given substance with egg yolks, wrapped around a little chopped something for flavor, and lifted high off its base with air whipped into its egg whites. All sorts of delicious things can flavor soufflés. It's a superb way to finish the last cup of grated natural hard cheese, cooked ground or chopped beef, chicken, lean white fish, puréed potatoes, spinach, carrots, celery, summer or winter squash, turnips, eggplant, cauliflower, asparagus, tomatoes, sautéed onions, canned tuna or any savory combination thereof. The only qualifications for a soufflé filling are that the food be chopped, shredded, or puréed so that it can blend into the eggs, and that it have a certain substance so the soufflé won't be thin and watery.

The following recipe is infallible.

¼ cup margarine
3 tablespoons flour
1 cup milk, any sort
3 eggs, separated
1 cup filling (see preceding paragraph)
Parmesan, optional
Salt and pepper, to taste
An appropriate herb, to taste, optional
1 extra egg white

1.   Butter the inside of a deep 1-quart-sized baking dish with 1 tablespoon of the margarine. The dish may actually be any shape you please; I've seen soufflés served in shallow dishes. The soufflé will rise no matter what it's in. If it's a compatible flavor, dust the inside of the dish thoroughly with grated Parmesan.

2.   In a deep pot over medium heat, melt the remaining margarine, then whisk in the flour. As soon as the flour has been absorbed, begin whisking in the milk, little by little. (You may find it easier to take the pot off the heat as you do this; when all the milk has been blended in, return pot to the heat.) Continue whisking until the sauce thickens and there are no lumps.

3.   Remove from heat and whisk in the yolks one at a time, whisking to blend thoroughly after each. If you wish to prepare this a few hours ahead of time, run a lump of margarine over the top of the sauce, lay plastic wrap directly on top, cover and set in a cool place until needed.

4. Set oven to 375° F. Fold in the filling, using a rubber scraper to blend gently but thoroughly. Taste for seasoning. If this sauce isn't room temperature, warm it up, stirring over low heat just until tepid—do not let simmer!

5. Add the extra egg white to the rest in a scrupulously clean non-plastic mixing bowl. A large French balloon whisk will beat them best, but a smaller whisk or electric mixer (at low speed until whites are frothy, and then at medium-high speed until stiff) will do fine. When the whites will hold a peak that doesn't wobble when held out of the bowl by the beater, stop.

6. With a rubber scraper, lift out about one-fourth of the whites and fold them into the sauce, using a smooth down, under, up and over circular motion. Turn the pot with every stroke so you'll hit every bit of the contents. Fold just until the mixture is uniformly spongy.

7. Now turn the remaining whites onto the top of the sauce, and gently but quickly fold them in the same way, being certain to reach to the bottom of the pot with every stroke. This time, do not blend in thoroughly, but stop while there are still some bits of fluff here and there.

8. With a rubber scraper, smooth the soufflé mixture into the baking dish. It should just fill the dish; if it doesn't, smooth into a smaller dish. Run a fingertip an inch down inside around the rim; this will make a little top hat when the soufflé rises (and keep the soufflé from overflowing). Sprinkle a bit more grated Parmesan on top, if appropriate.

NOTE: At this point before baking, you may actually set the soufflé dish in a warm place, free of drafts, and cover it with a big pot (that won't touch it) for protection. If left undisturbed, the soufflé will hold up for 1 hour, but, of course, it's *best* to bake it as soon as possible.

9. Place the soufflé on the lowest rack of the hot oven and bake from 25 to 40 minutes. You can peek briefly after 25 minutes. The length of baking time depends on the texture you like. If you like the center a bit runny, as the French do —this way, the soufflé provides its own sauce—bake just 25

to 30 minutes. However, it will be trembly and fragile and will sink almost before you can dash it to the table. If you like it firm all through, after 35 minutes a long thin knife thrust to the center from the side should emerge clean (as in a custard). At this point, you can turn off the oven and let the soufflé stand 5 minutes while you make certain everyone is seated.

For a 2-quart dish, serving 4 to 8 people, double the proportions given above and bake an extra 5 to 7 minutes.

For luncheon or supper, almost any soufflé would be enhanced with garlic-buttered French bread, a mixed green salad, crisp carrot sticks, a cool light red wine and Persian red pears for dessert.

For individual soufflés—an impressive and delightful hors d'oeuvre—pour the soufflé mixture into 4 buttered and Parmesaned (is that a word?) 1-cup-sized baking dishes set on a baking sheet. Or use tomato cases; blanched well-drained green-pepper shells; blanched scooped-out fat zucchini shells (cut the long way); or why not potato soufflés in baked potato shells? Fill two-thirds full and bake about half the usual time.

The Incomparable Omelette

Some of the tenderest omelettes in this house come from the children's hands. All of them have mastered the art. If they can, you can. Omelettes are a matter of practice, and even the failures taste good.

NOTE: About the pan—you'll give yourself a running start if you have just the right pan and reserve it for omelettes only. It should be slope-sided, of a heavy material that can be set empty over highest heat a minute or so without harm. My pan is steel, 8¼ inches at the top, sloping down to 5¾ inches at bottom. This size makes a perfect, thin, 1-egg or 2-egg omelette. You don't want the omelette, which is really an egg crêpe, at all thick. And this size, when folded into an oval, fits handsomely on a breakfast plate or luncheon plate.

Perhaps you have heard that one should never wash an

omelette pan. That is not affectation. Like the Chinese wok, when the steel has been properly seasoned with heat and fat over a period of time, something that I don't understand happens to the metal; the result, I do understand—nothing sticks. To clean the pan, even if some of the sticky filling has spilled out, simply heat the pan empty, and rub with an oiled paper towel.

An omelette for each person: Individual omelettes are much nicer in appearance, and much more flattering to those being served. They cook so quickly that there is no reason to make a big overstuffed many-egg matter that needs slicing—the filling falls out, and the whole sleek oval is ruined.

> *1 lump of sweet butter the size of a walnut (it can be margarine for the family, but unfortunately sweet butter makes a big difference in flavor)*
> *1 to 2 eggs (I prefer 1)*
> *Pinch of salt*
> *Dash of white pepper (even in sweet omelettes)*
> *½ teaspoon light-tasting oil (just a quick thin glug)*
> *2 to 4 tablespoons filling*
> *Drizzle of melted sweet butter or margarine*
> Crème Fraîche (*see p. 73*), *or sifted powdered sugar*

1.   Have everything ready: a small bowl, a fork, all the ingredients, a heated dish to receive the omelette, the pan, and the omelette-eaters in their places.

2.   Set the pan over a burner at its hottest. Break the egg into the bowl, add the salt, pepper, and oil, and beat with a fork just enough to blend the yolk and white.

3.   Drop the butter in the pan—it should sizzle at once; tilt the pan all about to spread the butter evenly over the bottom. When the butter turns the color of a hazelnut (pale brown), give the egg one or two last quick beats, then dump in the egg, tilting the pan so it completely coats the bottom like a crêpe.

4.   At once use the tip of the fork to pull the cooked edges

toward the center—at the same time, tilt the pan in that direction to fill the empty space with runny egg. Stop when there is no more runny egg—if the pan is hot enough, it should take no more than 30 seconds for the bottom to be sealed and the top to be set but still moist.

5.   Turn off heat at once, or remove the pan, and use the fork to spread the filling evenly over the center third of the omelette. Give the pan a little shake, and the omelette should detach itself from the pan; if not, run the fork along the rim to loosen any part that's stuck.

6.   To fold the omelette into an oval, use the fork to flip the third of the omelette nearest you over the filling; now hold the pan just over the plate and slip the open third opposite you out of the pan, close to the center of the plate. With a quick tilt and a flip of the wrist, turn the omelette over onto itself and the plate. Drizzle over a light glaze of melted butter, garnish as you like, depending on the filling—*crème fraîche* for savory omelettes, powdered sugar for sweet ones. Or perhaps you can give a hint on top of what's inside, with thinly sliced sautéed zucchini, shreds of cooked chicken, rings of brown onions, and so on.

Because an omelette is a subtle matter, it can mantle an abundance of fillings. There are books and even restaurants devoted exclusively to omelettes. One easy classic is the following recipe.

David's Fines Herbes Omelettes

Nothing more complicated than a few favorite fresh minced herbs (parsley, green onion bulb and stalk, and a speck of garlic for gourmets without herbage) beaten into the eggs, and then strewn through the center. Garnish with *Crème Fraîche* (see p. 73) and an additional sprinkling of herbs.

For luncheon, have green beans *vinaigrette*, light wheat bread, radish flowers, a glass of zinfandel perhaps, and for dessert, drained whole canned apricots dashed with kirsch. Our eldest son David makes this to perfection.

Country Omelettes

4 SERVINGS

A super last-minute luncheon or dinner in itself—a sunny peasant combination.

If you have different proportions of these ingredients on hand—or other country things such as a few scraps of turkey, or white beans, or celery, or olives, or eggplant—then by all means vary them. The precise amount of each vegetable isn't important, and one or another flavor can predominate.

2 large onions, thinly sliced
2 cloves of garlic, minced
2 large peeled potatoes, thinly sliced
1 green pepper, in strips, optional
½ cup oil, or less
1 whole pimiento, in strips, optional
4 large fresh or firm canned, drained tomatoes
Lots of fresh chopped or dried sweet basil
Lots of chopped parsley
Salt and fresh ground pepper, to taste
4 omelettes (see p. 66)
Crème Fraîche (see p. 73) or Super Yogurt (see p. 77)

In a large skillet over medium heat, sauté the onions, garlic, potatoes, and green pepper in only as much of the oil as is needed to keep vegetables from sticking. Stir occasionally with a wooden spoon. When the onions and potatoes are translucent, add the pimiento. Chop the tomatoes coarsely and add them with the herbs; season lightly. Keep the filling warm while you make and fill each omelette. Serve them the moment each is finished—dollop with *crème fraîche* or yogurt and sprinkle with more herbs.

If you have fresh or canned sliced peaches on hand, make a crisp and bake it while the vegetables are sautéeing. You don't need a salad, really, just some good bread and cold cider or a cool light red wine.

Papa's Fuffled Eggs

6 SERVINGS

My husband can cook only two things. Hot chocolate as the French nuns made it for Alice B. Toklas and Gertrude Stein during World War I, and this. The children dearly love both. Here, in his own words, is Papa's recipe.

Count 1½ eggs per person. If you are not sure how many people are coming, ask. Add an extra egg for the pan.

Break eggs in dish. Break yolks with fork. Lightly beat eggs for 1 minute by the clock, using the fork.

Pour in half a cup of half-and-half for 10 eggs. Lightly beat eggs and half-and-half for a minute more.

Open a can of Cream of Mushroom Soup and add 3 heaping tablespoons to eggs. Beat with fork another minute.

Add a pinch of each of the following: parsley, tarragon, thyme, garlic powder, onion powder, salt. Grind in fresh pepper. Beat in bowl for another half-minute.

Melt 2 tablespoonsful of sweet butter [or margarine. Ed.] slowly in a large pan. Pour in the mixture, stirring constantly.

While continuing to beat eggs in pan over a low flame, make toast.

Get out plates.

Yell for children, napkins, and forks.

Make sure bacon (which you forgot) has been made by someone else.

Do not overcook.

Hint: Do not invite more people because the recipe won't work. Or make it in batches, and invite guests in a multiple of six.

All Sorts of Omelettes

Then there are cream cheese omelettes—lumps of Neufchâtel or your own homemade low-fat cream cheese tucked in, with chopped green onion stalks and a pressing of garlic.

And chicken or turkey or beef or sausage omelettes—the meat in shreds, with cooked complementary vegetables as well; a whole dinner, there. Mushroom omelettes, with just a few mushrooms when they're on special sale (actually, mushrooms cost a lot per pound, but a few, thinly sliced, add so much), sautéed with green onions, creamed with *crème fraîche* and dashed with paprika. For breakfast, jelly omelettes—apricot, blackberry, and raspberry preserves especially, with powdered sugar on top. And for dessert, a scented sautéed apples omelette, laced with domestic brandy, maybe even lit up with it.

In restaurants, omelettes are costly. Whipped up in your kitchen, they only look and taste extravagant!

Oeufs Florentine chez Madame

(Poached eggs in a creamy spinach bed)
6 SERVINGS

This is an easy, cheap, marvelous dish that can be luncheon for guests, dinner for the family, or a first course for a dinner party if the main course is simple. Children love this, because it is a splendid moment indeed when the golden yolk of egg pops and spills over the soft white, then down the dark mountain of spinach.

1 recipe Florentine Bed (see p. 98)
6 or more very fresh eggs
1 recipe Sauce Mornay (see p. 73)
Parmesan
Melted margarine
Grated nutmeg, optional

Have the hot creamed spinach spread in a shallow buttered baking dish which is large enough to accommodate your poached eggs. With the back of a spoon, make little impressions in the spinach bed according to the number of eggs to be used; cover with foil and keep warm in a 225° F oven.

To poach eggs: In a large flat pan over high heat, bring to a simmer enough water to cover your eggs generously. Add 1 tablespoon of vinegar for each quart of water (more or less won't hurt). Turn heat to low; the water mustn't even bubble once. Break each egg in its turn into a saucer; hold the saucer over the spot in the pan where you want it, then carefully slide the egg into the water. Immediately slip a thin spatula beneath the egg to keep it from sticking to the pan— it should float free. As the yolks set, constantly spoon water over them so they will cloud over and form a milky skin. In about 3 minutes, the whites should be set to a firm but custard-like consistency, and the yolks should be veiled with white. It may take 4 minutes, depending on lots of things. Lift one egg up with a slotted spoon and see how firm the white is; when ready, transfer it to its spinach bed, shaking off excess water on the way. Continue with the other eggs, as they become firm. Heat the broiler to its hottest.

Have the Mornay sauce ready and spoon some of it over each egg—leave the spinach a deep green contrast. Sprinkle lightly with more Parmesan, and drizzle with melted margarine. Slip the dish beneath the broiler for a moment or two— but don't leave it—to brown lightly. A fresh grating of nutmeg now gives a handsome finish. Serve at once, spooning up the spinach and egg all together (a pancake turner is useful).

For the family, you can skip the cheese sauce, and just sprinkle with grated Parmesan, if you wish. Drizzle lightly with melted margarine to moisten before browning.

This dish was a favorite of mine when I was a student in Paris. Madame Galetti made it superbly for her *pension* guests—and served it with a fresh tomato salad, French bread, plenty of Beaujolais, and one fine Algerian orange for dessert. It's a splendid meal which we enjoy often in Malibu, with California burgundy and oranges instead.

Sauce Mornay

(Delicate cheese sauce)
1 CUP

A very useful sauce for creaming cooked vegetables or meat, as well as garnishing poached eggs. In fact, *oeufs Mornay* is a simplified version of *Oeufs Florentine* (see p. 71)—simply lay poached eggs in a flat baking dish covered with Mornay sauce, moisten with more sauce, then sprinkle with Parmesan and melted margarine and brown lightly as for *Oeufs Florentine*.

1 cup thick Béchamel Sauce (see p. 63)
1 egg yolk
1 tablespoon Parmesan, or to taste

When the béchamel has thickened, remove from heat and whisk in the yolk and Parmesan. Set sauce over low heat and whisk continually just until the sauce coats the whisk—about 2 more minutes. Do not cook longer, or it will curdle. Set over hot (not boiling) water and film lightly with melted margarine if necessary to keep this; do not hold more than 10 minutes for best texture.

Crème Fraîche

(Homemade sour cream)
1 QUART

Some unknown genius has worked out this formula to enrich our lives. It bears a close resemblance to French thick cream, which isn't really sour, but has a delightful edge.

The original formula calls for whipping cream. I can afford neither the extra pennies nor the fat. I make mine with half-and-half (half milk, half cream, if your dairy doesn't know about it) and use it just like sour cream. A great saving, this—only 60 percent of the calories and the fat of store-bought sour cream, for 50 percent of the price.

1 quart half-and-half
3½ tablespoons buttermilk

Shake together in a covered jar about 1 minute. Set in a warm place undisturbed until it sets, from 5 to 24 hours. Keep refrigerated; it will stay fresh almost 1 month!

Pure and Simply Perfect Cream Cheese

1½ POUNDS

Ever since I was eight, I've tried to make cream cheese. Scouring books and following a dozen different methods, I always ended with a sour rough curd that stuck in my throat. Until this.

½ gallon 2 percent fat milk
¼ cup buttermilk, at room temperature
¼ teaspoon salt, optional

Heat the milk to 100° F (a drop on the wrist feels just a trifle warm). Pour into a warmed bowl and whisk in the buttermilk. Cover with plastic film, then wrap the bowl in a few layers of terry cloth or a blanket. Set undisturbed in a cozy corner. After 24 hours in summer, or perhaps 48 hours in winter, the curdled milk, clabber, will look very much like yogurt—a white custard.

Then set a colander in the sink and line it with wrung-out cheesecloth or a scrupulously clean cloth. (And I mean clean! Otherwise, the cheese will taste of no-phosphate washing powder, which is not exactly a plus. Sweeten a cloth for cheese-making by boiling it briefly in water with baking soda, rinse very well, then let dry in the sun.) Gently pour in the curd, fold the cloth over to cover it, and let drain about 15 minutes. Now set the colander over a deep bowl, seal the cheese from odors by wrapping the whole thing with plastic film, and set in the refrigerator to finish draining.

Although I've never done so, I've been told you can use the nourishing whey in place of water in making yogurt with powdered milk, in making bread, or as broth for an appropriately flavored soup.

You can take your cheese out after 36 hours if you like a creamy, almost whipped texture; if you want it firmer, leave it for 48 hours. Scrape cheese from the cloth into a crock or bowl. The French fresh cheeses—the only rival for this cheese—are unsalted, but I like to salt mine lightly. Refrigerated, very tightly covered, it will last 5 days.

For company, line a basket with damp cheesecloth—or fresh leaves from a nut tree, scented geranium bush, or any delicately perfumed leaves—and smooth the cheese in. Cover with cloth or leaves and chill. Unmolded, it has a lovely shape—and incomparable flavor of leaves, as well.

Don't forget that served with fresh strawberries or raspberries (have you ever eaten as many raspberries as you wanted to in one sitting?) and a light sprinkling of sugar, this cheese is a classic dessert.

After tasting the glory of your own homemade cream cheese, you may want to go on to greater triumphs: Farmers' Bulletin Number 2075 from the United States Department of Agriculture will tell you how to make your very own rat cheese.

Poor Man's Fines Herbes Cheese

ABOUT 1 POUND

One of the inspired creations in French cheese-making has been the addition of garlic and fresh herbs to fresh cheese. But what it costs! Then my mother had an inspiration of her own. Here is her fines herbes cheese at a fraction of the cost of the imported.

There is one catch; you must have fresh herbs. The following blend is sensational, but seasonal—tarragon and basil grow only in summer, although you can try to bring them inside. If you can't get my mother's herbs, then create your own house fines herbes cheese. Even with parsley alone, it tastes good.

1 cup (8 ounces) homemade (see preceding recipe) or Neufchâtel (low-fat style) cream cheese, at room temperature
½ cup (4 ounces) butter, at room temperature
2 4-inch sprigs pineapple sage, or 1 sprig any sage
2 4-inch sprigs tarragon
2 4-inch sprigs oregano
2 4-inch sprigs sweet basil
1 4-inch sprig rosemary
4 sprigs parsley
2 tablespoons dry white wine
1 large clove of garlic
⅛ teaspoon white pepper
A bit of salt, to taste

Pull leaves from stems of herbs and chop very fine; you should have about ¼ cup in all. Blend with other ingredients, creaming well by hand or mixer. Pack into small crock or bowl. Let ripen, tightly covered in the refrigerator, at least 8 hours before serving. Serve cool, not cold, with crackers or dark bread. Keeps 5 days.

NOTE: This is one place where real butter is wanted; however, if you've a margarine whose flavor you enjoy, you can try substituting it here.

Kajmak and Brinza

(Serbian and Rumanian salty fresh cheese)

The Serbs' traditional white cheese, *kajmak*, brought to market in big wooden tubs, has the salty edge of *feta* and the texture of Devonshire cream. You can approximate its flavor —absolutely marvelous with *ajvar*, the sweet pepper relish— like this:

1 measure feta
1 measure sweet butter
¼ measure cream cheese, homemade or Neufchâtel

Have all three softened; whip *feta* and butter until smooth in the mixer. Add enough cream cheese to give a creamy base. If the *feta* stays lumpy, press the cheese through a sieve.

Rumanian *brinza* is very much like *kajmak* without the cream cheese. Instead of cream cheese add:

> *Pinches of chopped parsley, chives, paprika, caraway seeds and sometimes fennel seeds*

With both fresh cheeses, proportions really may be what pleases, since few of us will ever have the original to taste against (more's the pity!). Pack into crock or bowl, then serve at room temperature with rough dark bread. Keeps 5 days.

Super Yogurt

1 QUART

This just may be the best yogurt you've ever tasted—it will surely be the creamiest. It's half the cost of the cheapest store-bought, with at least 2½ times the nourishment! It's also wonderfully easy, quick, and foolproof to make. In case you haven't noticed, yogurt—especially this yogurt—is a superb replacement for sour cream as a topping, in cooking, and in baking. And as a snack or dessert, it couldn't be more useful (my favorite is a sprinkling of brown sugar and a few drops of vanilla mixed in).

You can double or triple this recipe (it's a nice gift for a friend, as a starter), saving fuel. In making it, use the cheapest evaporated milk and extra grade milk powder, but buy the very finest plain yogurt for the first starter—from then on, use your own. You may want to refresh the strain occasionally, as the culture tends to grow progressively more puckery. But there are cultures in Europe more than a century old, as there are a number of people who thrive on yogurt—it has mysterious healthful properties.

*1 13-ounce can evaporated milk, whole or skim—try it
   both ways*
13 ounces hottest tap water (just fill the empty milk can)
*2 cups nonfat milk powder, or amount on box for 1½
   quarts*
¼ cup plain yogurt, whole or low-fat, it doesn't matter

Set jar or jars on one large or on individual trivets in a deep
pot (canning jars set on their upside-down sealing rings are
ideal). Fill jars and pot with hot tap water; adjust water
from tap until it measures 110° F with a candy thermometer. Set pot over lowest maintainable heat.

In a pot, whisk evaporated milk, water, and milk powder
together; measure the temperature. If it's between 100° and
115° F, whisk in the yogurt starter, then empty the jars in
the water bath and fill almost to the top with the milk. If
mixture measures below 100°, set pot of milk over low heat
and warm it up to 110°; then fill the jars as above. If there's
much froth, just spoon it off. Cover the jars with plastic film
or their lids. Adjust level of water bath so it is just below the
rims of the jars. Hook candy thermometer to pot. Let the pot
rest undisturbed 5 hours, or until the yogurt has set like custard. Refrigerated, the yogurt will keep at least 10 days.
Ideally, your starter should be less than 5 days old. But that
is a purist's notion; it just gets tarter, that's all.

The first time you make this yogurt will be the only time
you'll have to give any attention to the pot. But until you find
the exact burner setting or stack of this and that which will
hold the water at 110° F, you'll have to check the thermometer every 20 minutes or so (my arrangement is the lowest
flame, 2 asbestos pads, a 9-inch cake pan, an 8-inch cake
pan, and *then* the pot! but an electric range I work with
needs no covering when set at the next to lowest heat, so it's
an extremely variable matter).

Vegetables

The following pages were written with love and optimism in the hope that you will enjoy cooking the beautiful vegetables they describe. In season, vegetables are great buys for gourmets on a budget. There's a world of superb eating in the vegetable bins.

Budget notes on buying vegetables: Buy them fresh. Buy them young. Buy them in season. Cook them as soon as you can.

If you work the seasons, you will do best both financially and gastronomically. And if you invest a small amount of time, you can have the great satisfaction of putting up summer produce at its peak for lean winter months. When sweet green and red peppers are abundant and even a small soft spot gets them marked down, buy passels. Then simply core them, cut out the blemish, and slice in smallish pieces. Vacuum-bag and freeze—absolutely invaluable for cooking. When tomatoes are also coming in so fast that the ripest go for a song, can them with leaves of sweet basil—they'll taste as though from Italy (follow directions in an all-purpose cookbook). And some abundant but tender vegetables, like tomatoes and zucchini, which don't freeze well whole, can be cooked, puréed, and frozen for winter sauces or soups.

The same saving advice goes for fruits too, of course. Because fruits, like tomatoes, are acid, home-canning poses no potential problems. If you've never had the experience of opening a jar of your own honey-packed apricots in January, try it. Or simply cut the good parts of marked-down fruit straight into syrup and freeze. The fresh flavor, color, and texture is remarkably preserved.

Have you ever bought produce wholesale? In most urban centers, there is a large wholesale marketplace, where your produce man buys his wares. In my community, a group of friends have had a bright idea: every week, one of them gets up in the dark of early morning, goes down to the market, and loads up the car with boxes of staples like oranges, apples, onions, potatoes, carrots, and so on—things that will keep until the next week. Then, the cooperating families distribute the vegetables and fruits, at a delicious saving. Perhaps you might form a marketing co-op with four or five other friends, which really brings fun and profit!

What about organic vegetables? After my own costly binge of buying what I wanted to believe were the purest vegetables and fruits obtainable, I came to the sadder but wiser conclusion that if you want to gamble with your money, the odds are better at Vegas. Until someone finds an ironclad way of guaranteeing produce is organic, just wash your supermarket vegetables well—or grow your own, even in pots!

Frozen vegetables are, in theory, excellent—*if* they have been picked at their peak, rushed to the plant, frozen immediately, and kept frozen from plant to market to freezer. That's a tall order. Even if it has been met, frozen vegetables have inevitably left some of their goodness back at the freezing plant in the blanching water tossed out. So buy frozen vegetables only when you especially need those unavailable fresh.

Canned vegetables barely belong to the vegetable kingdom —in fact, most of them taste like an utterly different breed. Too, much of their nutrients end up in the canning liquid which is usually drained down the sink.

Two cautions about both frozen and canned vegetables. You'll get better value for money nutritionally if you buy whole vegetables rather than "cuts." And do check the label for preservatives. There are chemicals involved in the canning process of many vegetables which are not mentioned on the label; so certainly buy another form of the vegetable you want if chemicals *are* listed.

Do some comparing of labels, if you must use a lot of canned or frozen produce. Brand name and price aren't at all an index of what's inside. I recently bought two cans of purple plums for the same price, one a house label and the other a little-known brand. To my astonishment, there were something like six big fat plums in the house label can, and ten small firm plums in the other. Both were good quality, but they would have served entirely different purposes; big plums for eating in a dish, smaller ones for putting in a jelly. I never would have noticed the difference had I not opened both together. It's important to suit quality to purpose; you can use rag-tag bits for soup and sauce, moderately firm vegetables for casseroles, but sometimes you need first-class stuff in a dish and it may or may not cost more. Even if you have to keep a list, it's worth it. I've read that intelligent shopping for canned and frozen produce can save hundreds of dollars for a family over a year.

Budget notes on cooking vegetables: Do not peel vegetables unless absolutely necessary. Precious vitamins lie close to the skin and are easily whisked away. Just scrub well. The rough green pot-scrubbing fabric squares are excellent for vegetables, because they lift up the dirt but not the skin.

Eat vegetables raw when you can; see notes elsewhere in this book about the value of indigestible fiber in the modern diet. Root vegetables are a particularly good source.

Cook vegetables whole whenever possible; every cut releases some of its precious nutrients into the air and cooking medium. If you must cut them, then make sure the pieces are even, for even cooking, and rather small, for fast cooking. Vary the shapes occasionally, to refresh the eye.

Once vegetables have been cut, cook immediately, and never soak in water—out go nutrients with the water. (For entertaining, sometimes soaking is helpful, however, and unlike when cooking for the family, you are not responsible for nourishment!)

The best vessel for cooking nearly every sort of vegetable is a broad, shallow sauté pan with a heavy bottom. Enameled cast iron is the best material for cooking with liquid, cast iron is best for most sautéeing (although, unless well seasoned, it can discolor acid foods). Iron gives a startling nutritional bonus: the food absorbs a little from the pan (so that most fish, for example, which hasn't natural iron, comes out of the skillet iron-fortified!).

A broad, shallow pan is essential because the heat can reach every morsel simultaneously with equal force. So don't crowd the vegetables; if you're cooking lots, use two pans. And always use a tight-fitting lid to seal in nutrients.

A squeeze of lemon juice in the cooking pot not only complements the flavor of most vegetables, but helps preserve color. Never use baking soda to set colors; it dissolves some vitamins.

When to add salt? Salt draws juices from anything it touches, thus toughening the fiber somewhat. Those who add salt while cooking reason that this slight toughening helps set color and flavor. I prefer to rely on careful cooking and a little lemon juice for maximum color and flavor; thus I always salt vegetables after cooking.

How to test vegetables for doneness? Always cook vegetables the least possible amount of time, so their flavor, color, and nutrition stay intact. Some vegetables need be cooked only until tender enough to chew, but still crisp enough to remind you of their origins. *Cook tender-crisp:* flower heads (broccoli, cauliflower); shoots (asparagus); pods (green beans, pea pods, okra); stalks (celery); heads (brussels sprouts, cabbage); tender fruit (summer squash, sweet peppers, tomatoes); tender leaves (chard, spinach); tender roots (beets, carrots, turnips); and fungi (mushrooms).

Other vegetables, however, must be cooked until tender— but no longer—to be at their best. *Cook just tender:* flowers (artichokes); seeds (corn, peas, shelled beans); sturdy fruit (chayote, eggplant, winter squash); tougher leaves (kale and beet, mustard, or turnip greens); larger roots (celery

root, kohlrabi, parsnips, rutabagas); tubers (Jerusalem artichokes, potatoes, yams); and bulbs (leeks, onions).

Always save vegetable pot liquor and use it later in a soup
or for cooking another, compatible, vegetable. There appears
to be no perfect method of vegetable cookery—some nutrients are inevitably lost both in the air and in the cooking
medium. You paid for the nutrients; save what you can.

NOTE: I have arranged these vegetable recipes by techniques of cooking, so you can learn to prepare your zucchini
or broccoli or new red potatoes in the way that suits them
best.

Butter-steaming vegetables: This method of cook-
ing probably retains the most flavor and nutrition of the
greatest variety of vegetables. In "butter"-steaming (we
mean margarine), the vegetables are cooked over quick heat,
tightly-covered, with a small amount of margarine or oil and
water or broth. Properly done, most if not all of the cooking
liquid is absorbed into the vegetables, leaving just a bit of
buttery sauce for serving.

Butter-steaming takes attention. "Mommy, you've burned
the peas again!" is not an uncommon cry in this house.
Perhaps locking the kitchen door is the answer, so you won't
mindlessly walk away.

Proportions of margarine or oil and liquid vary with the
vegetable. Soft vegetables like potatoes sop up great
amounts. Firm green sorts like beans require very little.

Begin with 1 tablespoon margarine or oil, 2 tablespoons
water or broth, and ¼ teaspoon lemon juice for each serving
of vegetables; then just check the pot after a few minutes to
see if more is necessary.

Summer Squashes Just Off the Vine

One of the most delightful vegetables I've ever been served
came from a friend who was just teaching herself to cook.
Because she didn't know it wasn't the accepted fashion, Tina

Crane simply butter-steamed whole untrimmed baby zucchini, yellow crookneck, and pattypan squashes together until tender-crisp (with margarine, water, and lemon juice for about 10 or 12 minutes). Tina presented them in an earthenware bowl, looking as brightly colored and tasting as true as if they had just come off the vine.

Sautéeing vegetables: Sautéeing is actually butter-steaming with the "butter" and no added liquid. The principle is the same—the nutrients are locked into the vegetable by the seal of fat (especially if the lid is kept on). The sauce which results isn't so creamy; rather, the vegetables end with a gloss.

Buttersilk Carrots

6 SERVINGS
This is a company vegetable—probably the best carrot dish you'll ever taste.

8 young unpeeled carrots
1 teaspoon lemon juice
6 tablespoons (3 ounces) margarine
Pinch of sugar
Pinch of salt
Dash of white pepper
Generous handful of chopped parsley

Cut carrots in half across the middle, then carefully cut them lengthwise into very thin matchsticks. (You can prepare them a few hours ahead of time, vacuum-bag, and refrigerate them.) In a large, heavy sauté pan, add lemon juice to margarine and heat over low heat until margarine has melted. Add carrots, shake pan to coat each stick, cover tightly, and sauté about 15 minutes, shaking pan gently often. You may need a bit more margarine and a dash more lemon juice to finish, depending on the age of the carrots.

When just tender-crisp, sprinkle on the sugar, salt, and parsley. Shake pan to mix, then serve at once.

Italian Greens

ABOUT 3 SERVINGS PER POUND

Bitter wild greens and rough tops of root vegetables can be deliciously tamed, as follows.

Rinse turnip, collards, chard, kale, or any other greens and cut off tough stems. Shake off excess moisture, then chop fine. For each good-sized bunch of greens you've prepared, heat 2 generous tablespoons of oil in a sauté pan over medium heat. When the oil is hot, add 2 mashed and peeled cloves of garlic and sauté the cloves until they brown; remove them. Add the chopped greens, cover, turn heat to low, and sauté until tender, stirring occasionally—it will take about 25 or 30 minutes. Add salt to taste and serve.

A handsome thought: Cut tender young peeled turnips in eighths, then butter-steam them in margarine and beef broth. (Since they get woody and watery if at all large, don't buy large turnips.) Serve turnips on a heated platter encircled with their steamed greens. Garnish with lemon rounds for color.

Paillasson

(French potato straw cake)

5 TO 6 SERVINGS

The brave and constant potato has provided nearly every cuisine in the world with an extravagance of dishes. But it was not considered fit for human consumption by the French until the late eighteenth century. (Imagine. Louis XV, who used to faint between courses, never tasted one.) It was then that an agronomist named Parmentier, convinced of their value, cultivated a field of potatoes during a period of famine. But how to get the suspicious Parisians to eat them?

Parmentier knew his people. He called upon the French Guard to watch over his potato field by day. At nightfall, all the Guards went home. In no time, potatoes were on everybody's table.

Paillassons, like many country things, are elegant in their simplicity. Fun to make, and marvelous for a dinner party as a crispy complement to grilled chicken, fish, or any roast meat.

> *About 7 to 8 large (2½ pounds) peeled boiling*
>   *potatoes*
> *1 cup (8 ounces) margarine*
> *1 to 2 large cloves of garlic, peeled and halved*
> *Lots of coarse salt and fresh ground pepper*

Make this with care. Pass the potatoes through the number 3 (⅛-inch) blade of a vegetable shredder. Or you may cut the potatoes into fine, long matchsticks with a knife, but I'll admit it's a chore. As you go, place the shreds in a bowl of ice water (since this dish is for pleasure, not nourishment). When all the potatoes are finished, drain the shreds, or you may leave them there up to 2 hours, rinse well under cold running water, and pat thoroughly dry on thick towels.

About 45 minutes before serving, rub the inside of your largest cast iron or other heavy skillet with halves of 1 clove of garlic. If you haven't a very large pan, use 2 9-inch or 10-inch pans, 2 cloves of garlic, and divide the ingredients between them. Leave the garlic in the pan while you melt 6 ounces of the margarine over medium heat; swish the margarine about so it moistens the sides of the pan. When the margarine is melted, give the garlic a good last mash, then remove it.

Add the potato shreds, and use a fork to settle the shreds gently, arranging them into a flat, even cake—do not pack down, but let light and air through the straws. Sprinkle lightly with salt (you will add more later), grind on pepper, then dot over half the remaining margarine. Cover the skillet and let the straws cook undisturbed. After about 20 minutes, use a long, thin spatula to slip down the sides and underneath the cake, carefully loosening it and freeing any stuck little straws. Look to see that it is all nut brown beneath.

When it is, give a sharp rap of the pan against the burner

or whatever won't be bashed, to free the entire cake. Lift it up with a very wide pancake turner—and a stout heart— slip the rest of the margarine under, swirl it quickly around the bottom of the skillet, then lay a spatula or your hand on the top of the cake to steady it. And—flip! (If you can't bear the thought, then before adding the margarine, place a plate on top and turn the skillet over, turning the cake out onto the plate. Now add the margarine to the pan and slide the cake from the plate into it.)

Sprinkle with more salt and pepper, then continue cooking uncovered another 20 minutes, or until the other side is crisp and nut brown too. When ready, serve at once on a hot dish (it can keep in a 225° F oven 10 or 15 minutes, if necessary). Cut in wedges to serve.

Pommes Chip

(Warm potato chips)

1 POTATO PER PERSON

I read that Maxim's in Paris serves these as a vegetable accompaniment—so can we! Warm ruffled (and unpreserved, if possible) potato chips on a cookie sheet in a 350° F oven for about 10 minutes. Serve in a napkin-lined basket as an unexpected but delightful crisp contrast to fish, grilled chicken, luncheon soup, and so forth.

Of course, to be really elegant, make your own chips— soak thinnest possible chips or julienne potatoes in ice water 2 hours, drain and dry thoroughly, then deep-fry in shortening or oil at 380° F until golden. Blot on brown paper, sprinkle with salt, and serve hot.

Chinese stir-frying vegetables: The French consider the Chinese their only rivals in the kitchen. (The Chinese, I imagine, never look over their shoulder.) *Chow* is the Chinese word for stir-fry, a lightning quick technique wherein red-hot heat and a veil of oil capture the essence of

a vegetable. In all of cookery, there is nothing more fascinating—nor more economical. The Chinese have made an
art of stretching modest ingredients to feed as many mouths
as there are at table, and a stir-fry—threads of this and tid-
bits of that, all tossed together with light and air—is the
heart of such graceful economy.

The wok is at the heart of *chow.* A wok is the bowl-shaped
pan ingeniously designed for cooking with the smallest
amount of oil (you can sauté a whole fish in 1 tablespoon of
oil!) and the smallest amounts of fuel and time. Chinese
cooking implements are refreshingly cheap, especially if you
buy them from an Oriental market. The wok should be of
iron, and 14-inches is a practical size for most families. Buy
a lid as well, and a ring for the wok to rest on.

Also ask about a *wok chan* (pancake turner with a tip
curved to fit the wok), a *siou hok* (a large, shallow ladle
which is used together with the *wok chan* in stir-frying), a
choy doh (a large Chinese cleaver, very useful), and a *chow
lee* (a large brass wire one-handled strainer that can lift
everything from the wok—or from a pot of spaghetti or
blanching peas—in one stroke). Be sure you inquire about
how to season and care for your iron wok—and find a basic
wok cookbook—before you begin to use it.

Any good skillet, however, can be used to stir-fry if it's
heavy and large enough.

Chinese Spinach Branches

6 SERVINGS

Toss this together in a twinkling for spinach fresher than
you've ever tasted.

2 *pounds fresh spinach*
2 *tablespoons light-tasting oil*
1 *teaspoon sugar*
2 *tablespoons soy sauce*
2 *tablespoons toasted sesame seeds* (*if you have them*)

Rinse spinach carefully, but leave the branches attached to the roots. Drain thoroughly. In wok or large skillet over highest heat, drizzle in the oil and at once add the spinach and then the sprinkling of sugar. Stir with a pancake turner, or a *wok chan,* in one hand and a big kitchen spoon, or a *siou hok,* in the other, and gently keep the spinach moving while it wilts—about 1 minute. Turn off heat.

Sprinkle on soy sauce and the seeds, mix lightly and serve. Delicious with rice and almost any meat, fish, or fowl.

Stir-Fry

3 OR 4 SERVINGS

This makes a marvelous dinner. Not only is it entirely put together in less than ½ hour, but you can use scraps of vegetables, and vegetables your family might otherwise disdain. The only rule is that colors, shapes, flavors, and textures of any mix give contrast—an important principle in Chinese cookery.

A pleasant stir-fry combination is celery, cabbage, carrot, spinach, peas, and water chestnuts. For a more substantial dinner, slip in shreds of leftover meat, fowl, or fish. From an expert *chow* cook, Connie Chin, comes the trick of steeping uncooked meat or chicken shreds in soy sauce or soy sauce and dry sherry 20 minutes before adding them to the wok.

6 cups or so of prepared raw vegetables
2 penny-sized slices fresh ginger root or ¼ teaspoon
  powdered ginger
1 clove garlic, minced
1 tablespoon oil
Thickening sauce:
  2 tablespoons soy sauce
  1 tablespoon sherry, gin, or vodka
  1 teaspoon sugar
  ½ tablespoon cornstarch
Salt, if necessary

1.   Prepare vegetables for cooking:

Shred: bamboo shoots (canned and inexpensive).

Slice diagonally $\frac{1}{16}$-inch thick, and then in matchsticks, if desired: carrots, celery, spring onions (bulbs and tender stalks as well), asparagus (leave young tips whole), broccoli, or cauliflower stems (cut their flowerets into 3 or 4 pieces), or other long, thick vegetables.

Slice across or lengthwise $\frac{1}{16}$-inch thick: sweet peppers, mushrooms, water chestnuts (also canned—buy the cheapest), and any other round vegetables.

Slice diagonally $\frac{1}{2}$-inch thick: Chinese cabbage (*bok choy*), any leafy greens, heads of cabbage, and lettuce; green beans (string them first, if necessary), and any other long, thin vegetables.

Slice in half diagonally only if very large: Chinese pea pods. Also string them first, if need be.

2.   Arrange vegetables separately in little heaps by the stove, those which need most cooking closest to you, those which need least cooking farthest down the line. Prepare ginger: Peel and smash the "pennies"—or add the powdered ginger to the thickening sauce. Have ginger, garlic, and oil ready by the burner. Mix ingredients in the thickening sauce together in a small bowl and set at the end of the line.

NOTE: Ginger roots are costly, but you use very little, and they keep well if wrapped airtight and refrigerated.

3.   Set wok on ring (or if you have a gas burner, try setting the wok directly upon it—for vegetables, the hotter the heat, the better) and turn heat to hottest. Now be prepared to move smartly. When the wok is smoking hot, add the oil with a quick thin streak around the top perimeter of the wok so it will run down and oil the pan. At once drop in the ginger and garlic and stir with *wok chan* or pancake turner while you dump in the first vegetable. Toss with *wok chan* or turner in one hand and *siou hok* or a big kitchen spoon in the other, rather as you would mix a salad—keep everything moving. Add the next vegetable and the next, according to their need for time in the wok. Cover the pan a few moments for faster cooking between additions and when everything has been

added—but use potholders to shake the wok frequently to toss the vegetables.

Light, thin vegetables will *chow* in 2 or 3 minutes. The longest any vegetable should take is about 8 minutes (shreds of carrots, for example). Raw shreds of meat or fowl take about 2 or 3 minutes.

4. When vegetables are still brightly colored and crisp, make a well in the center of the wok and pour in the thickening sauce. Toss gently but thoroughly with the vegetables and *chow* covered, 1 minute, or until the cornstarch has thickened—shake the pan once or twice. Taste for salt (it rarely needs it) and serve at once.

A stir-fry wants steamed rice, cups of China tea, and for dessert, almond ice cream with fortune cookies, if you can buy them.

Steaming vegetables: Vegetables cooked in hot steam without water ever touching them do retain their flavors and many vitamins and minerals—particularly if they are cooked whole and unpeeled. But you will find that the steaming water has the flavor and some of the color of the vegetable above it, an indication that it has absorbed some of the nutrients as well. So save that water for soup.

Steaming devices are almost all inexpensive. A small collapsible steamer is usually available wherever cookware is sold, and fits into most quart-sized pots with the cover on— the pot's cover, of course, traps the steam and is essential. A sieve or colander can sometimes be fitted into a pot with a lid or sheet of heavy foil to capture the steam, as long as it clears an inch of boiling water beneath. The Chinese are old hands at steaming—a very economical use of fuel. If you stack two or three round bamboo trays (available in an Oriental market) over a source of steam (water in a wok), you can cook a complete meal on one burner. I bought a huge two-tiered aluminum steamer from a Chinese grocery —marvelous for warming up food for lots of people, and the price was unbelievably low. Investigate.

Simmering vegetables: Plopping vegetables in water, bringing them to a boil, simmering until ready, and draining out the water—easiest of all vegetable cookery, and inexcusable! Unless, of course, you're conscientious about *saving the simmering water for soup.* But there *are* a few vegetables which may only be simmered, and dried beans are one of them.

Memphis Beans

6 SERVINGS

From Dorris Johnson, beautiful woman, beautiful cook.

1 pound (about 2½ cups) pinto or any beans
2½ quarts water
2 to 3 chicken broth cubes
1 large onion stuck with 3 cloves
2 large unpeeled carrots
1 large leafy stalk of celery
1 "palm-sized" piece of salt pork, ham, or bacon rind,
  optional
Salt to taste

Rinse beans well. Put them in a large pot with the water, bring to a boil, boil 2 minutes, turn off heat, cover and let soak 1 hour or longer. Add all remaining ingredients except salt, bring to a simmer again and simmer over lowest heat, covered, until tender. Salt to taste.

Use these beans in chili, or serve in combination with grains, nuts, or seeds (corn bread would be good) to make a complete protein for dinner. Round the meal out with tender-crisp cabbage *à la vinaigrette* as a change from cole slaw, radishes for color, and for dessert, perhaps drained canned peach halves sprinkled with brown sugar, margarine and if you have it, a little bourbon (or rum or Southern Comfort) warmed beneath the broiler and set alight.

Broth-Simmered Brussels Sprouts

3 SERVINGS PER POUND

Simmer strong-flavored vegetables in delicate chicken broth—something quite marvelous happens.

Grilling vegetables: Lightly oiling or buttering vegetables and then grilling them beneath the broiler or over coals emphasizes the earthy savor of many vegetables—especially the Mediterranean sort. Sprinkle well with oil, lemon juice, pepper, and perhaps a light mince of garlic—split zucchini, halved tomatoes, eggplant rounds, whole leeks (they are much cheaper in some parts of the country than in others), and pre-steamed potatoes. Here's a good place for using snail butter as baste.

Grilling Mushrooms (Instead of Meat!)

4 SERVINGS PER POUND

Mushrooms are expensive compared to other vegetables. But they compare favorably with ground beef in price, and are full of minerals with hardly any calories. Then when you see really large ones at the market, broil them and eat them as meat for dinner. (Chico, a Sicilian wizard up the road, grows mushrooms the size of the palm of his hand—like eating small steaks!)

Stem and moisten mushrooms with light olive oil and lemon juice, sprinkle with coarse salt and fresh ground pepper, then broil briefly on both sides. Spoon their juices from the broiling tray into the hollow of the mushroom caps, and dash on a bit of dill and paprika. Best at room temperature. Chop up the stems and sauté with a bit of margarine and lemon juice, then sprinkle over cream cheese spread on crackers, as an accompaniment. Add a big chef's salad—julienne strips of cheese, some leftover vegetables in small dice, torn leaves of spinach, romaine—and while the mushrooms are cooling, you can bake an apple crisp for dessert.

Baking vegetables: One of the most ancient methods of cooking vegetables is in an oven. All root vegetables take especially well to this, potatoes first and foremost. But have you ever baked little red new potatoes? Gorgeous. And don't forget that yams are rich in nutrients, are usually cheap, and are great just baked then puddled with margarine.

And beets—at their very best when baked. Scrub them, trim off greens, but leave on roots and tops. Bake in a 350° F oven (as with all these) for an hour or two, depending on size. When tender, slip off the skins (cold running water keeps fingers cool), then quarter or eighth them. Serve with dill, a dash of lemon juice, and margarine. Really special.

And onions. To save fuel, set some whole peeled onions in a dish, dot with margarine, and bake while pot-roasting the Sunday meat; onions take about 2 hours to cook tender, and are wonderfully sweet. I've not yet roasted turnips, parsnips or whole carrots, but I intend to.

Frijoles Negros Oaxacan

(Mexican baked black beans)
4 TO 6 SERVINGS

Black beans are shiny black when dry, but they cook up a magnificent rich chocolate brown. Also called turtle beans, if they're not in your market, you can buy them from Spanish-speaking or Oriental grocers. This is one of the purest bean dishes imaginable.

> *1 pound dried black beans (substitute pinto beans,*
> *if necessary)*
> *1 grated onion*
> *2 cloves of garlic, minced*
> *6 cups water*
> *Salt and fresh ground pepper, to taste*
> *Powdered cumin*
> *Parsley or fresh cilantro*

Heat oven to 275° F. Rinse beans well. Put everything into a 2-quart pot, earthenware, if possible. Cover and bake about

10 hours, or overnight, stirring when convenient. Season to taste before serving, and dust lightly with cumin. Garnish with fresh greens. This will keep, refrigerated, 3 days.

A superb Black Bean Soup that tastes richer than the most elaborate recipe is made by simply chopping some tomatoes and adding them, in any proportions you like, to some beans. Thin with water or light broth of any flavor (here's a place for a delicate pork broth), and garnish with chopped parsley or cilantro. The colors are beautiful. Serve with homemade bread, cream cheese, beer, and fruit.

Puréeing vegetables: Even finicky grownups can be tempted with a fluffy whip of the vegetable they might not otherwise touch. Purées are a good idea also because they may be prepared ahead of time if you add an egg or two; then, ½ hour or so before serving, simply slip into the oven, and it will puff up deliciously. And any leftover purées may be thinned with milk and heated up as soup. (See Index for more uses.)

A word about whipped potatoes. Hot fresh whipped potatoes are one of life's treats. They are not anything like the musty stuff whipped up in an instant from a box. With a food mill, you can purée unlumpy potatoes in no time (and for much less money). If you haven't tried it lately, by all means, do so.

Whipped Carrots ... Parsnips ... Potatoes ... and ...

Whipped carrots are sweet, creamy, with a color that's pure razzle-dazzle. Dice unpeeled carrots and sauté as for Buttersilk Carrots. Cook until thoroughly tender, pass with juices through the fine blade of a food mill or a sieve. Lighten with margarine, milk (half-and-half for company), season with salt and white pepper and a dash of nutmeg, then beat in 1 egg for every 6 or 8 medium-sized carrots. Turn into a buttered baking dish, dot with margarine, cover with plastic film, and set aside in a cool place until needed. Bake un-

covered on the bottom rack of a 375° F oven until puffed—
about 30 minutes or more, depending on amount and how
cold they were. Count 3 medium carrots per person.

Whipped parsnips are superb; follow directions above, but
peel first. Count 2 medium parsnips per person. Never call
them "parsnips"; make up a name and everyone will love
them.

For pure whipped potatoes, simmer 1 large peeled and
diced baking potato per person in water to cover (reserve
the water to make bread or soup). Add lots of margarine,
milk or half-and-half (about 1 tablespoon each per potato),
and salt and white pepper. They don't need an egg, but for
maximum lightness, serve them as soon as possible after
puréeing.

Now, if the whipped carrots or parsnips on their own
didn't get past your finicky eaters, here's my plan: slip in
new vegetables with whipped potatoes. One part purée of
carrots, parsnips, celery root, turnips (especially good, that),
rutabagas or Jerusalem artichokes, and so forth, and 3 or 4
parts purée of potatoes is sneaky—and delicious. Finish as
for pure whipped potatoes.

A Florentine Bed

(Purée of creamed spinach)
6 SERVINGS

This is a very tasty, easy, inexpensive, and useful dish.
The spinach may be served on its own, or as the foundation
for poached eggs, filets of fish, sautéed scallops of chicken,
and so on.

NOTE: *Very important.* If you have had only cooked frozen
spinach lately, you'll be amazed at the flavor fresh leaves
have to offer. There is no comparison. But one of the things
that separates fresh spinach from frozen or canned is *under-*
cooking. Be very careful with every step of this or any cooked
fresh spinach dish—take it off the burner or out of the oven
as soon as you possibly can.

2 *pounds fresh spinach*
1 *tablespoon oil*
1 *small onion, chopped, optional*
2 *to 3 tablespoons flour*
1 *cup milk (rich or half-and-half for company)*
1 *teaspoon salt, or to taste*
⅛ *teaspoon white pepper*
2 *chopped fresh leaves or a pinch of dried sweet basil*
¾ *teaspoon fresh chopped or ¼ teaspoon dried dill*
2 *teaspoons lemon juice, or to taste*

Rinse spinach as instructed elsewhere in this book. For the family, use tender stems; remove them for company. Place in pot with just the water that clings to their leaves; set over low heat and cook *just* until they wilt. Place spinach in a sieve over a bowl and press out most of the juice, saving it for soup.

Meantime, while the spinach wilts, sauté the onion in oil in a medium-sized skillet over medium heat until tender. Turn off heat. Sprinkle the onion with 2 tablespoons of the flour, and stir to mix. Turn spinach, onion, and milk or half-and-half into the blender. Press whatever button will *only chop it;* you want a coarse purée, not all the texture taken out of it. Or chop on a board with chef's knife or cleaver.

Return spinach to the onion skillet and stir over medium heat just until thickened. If the purée is too thin for your taste, sprinkle a little more flour over it and stir with a fork until thickened. Take off heat and taste for salt and pepper, then add the herbs and lemon juice. Serve at once, or turn into a bowl, cover tightly, and chill. Reheat very gently. Reread very important note above.

A drift of Parmesan over this is lovely.

You can make a handsome Spinach Tart with this recipe. Just whisk in 2 beaten eggs and ¼ cup Parmesan after you've thickened the purée, *before* you add the flavorings; add salt and lemon juice only to taste. Smooth into a 9-inch baked pie pastry shell (in a dish or a flan ring) and bake in a preheated 350° F oven 30 minutes. Sprinkle with nutmeg and paprika, slip onto a platter, and serve at once as a main luncheon dish with crisp colorful raw vegetables, white wine, hard-cooked eggs to dip in Salsa Tonnata (see p. 10), and lemon ice with chopped preserved ginger for dessert.

Saucing vegetables: Rarely, rarely do I make a sauce for vegetables—not because it's a nuisance, but because vegetables carefully cooked taste best *au naturel.* There are a couple of simple sauces, however, which do give point to particular flavors.

Beurre Noir

(Brown butter sauce)

Let margarine cook over low heat in a heavy skillet until brown. Add finely chopped parsley and perhaps a few drained capers, and a mere trickle of vinegar at the last. Pour over vegetables—particularly the strongly flavored ones such as broccoli, brussels sprouts, cabbage, and cauliflower—and serve.

Beurre à la Bourguignonne

(Garlic and herb butter)
½ CUP

Best known as snail butter, but it can be a sunny sauce for potatoes, zucchini, mushrooms, tomatoes as well. An elegant touch for little money.

½ cup (4 ounces) margarine at room temperature
1 tablespoon minced green onion bulb
3 large cloves of garlic, minced
2 tablespoons minced parsley
Pinch of fresh-chopped or dried sweet basil
Squeeze of lemon

Cream all ingredients together and drop in little golden plops over whipped, grilled, baked, or steamed vegetables. This will keep, well covered and refrigerated.

Blanching vegetables: Except for those stir-fried (an entirely last-minute operation), there are no vegetables as crisp, bright, and flavorful as those blanched in advance, then lightly tossed in butter or margarine just before serving. The French do it routinely, and that's why their vegetables always taste better than everybody else's. For entertaining, it's the only way.

Blanching means to drop vegetables into boiling water and boil them briefly until their color has set and they have tenderized—almost to the eating point or just a bit, depending on use afterward. The former technique is called "parboiling." Then they are whisked from the kettle and sunk in ice water to stop the cooking instantly, then dried and refrigerated (or frozen—all frozen vegetables must first be blanched) until needed. The process essentially halts the aging process and suspends the vegetable at its prime state (would that there were a blanching process for us all!).

An appalling amount of nutrients is lost forever in the boiling and ice water. But the following recipe is, I daresay, the *sine qua non* of fresh vegetable eating. Try it.

Della Robbia Wreath of Vegetables

Della Robbia was a family of sculptors in fifteenth and sixteenth century Florence, noted particularly for their exquisite faïence wreaths of vegetables and fruits, which decorated walls and doorways all over the city.

Imagine, then, an enormous platter wreathed with heaps of fresh whole spring vegetables—the rouge of red potatoes, cream of cauliflower, leaf green of broccoli, marigold of carrots, chrysoprase of green beans, ivory of turnips, vert of zucchini, crimson of beets, and meadow green of peas—glistening with butter, the flavors sweet and true.

It takes a bit of vigorous last-minute action over the stove (perhaps 10 minutes in all), but for a dinner party of people who care about fine food, for not that much expense, nothing you could present would entrance them more.

Save the spectacle for spring or summer, when tender young vegetables spill from the bins at the market. The morning of the party, shop for the tiniest vegetables in the most colorful selection you can buy. And if vegetables aren't tiny and perfect, then buy what you can that's cheap and colorful, and trim large pieces into attractive smallish cuts.

Theoretically, once blanched and wrapped airtight in the refrigerator, vegetables will keep up to 2 days and still taste fresh when revived in butter or margarine. But for this masterpiece, absolute freshness is required.

> *For each guest: count 1 pound trimmed vegetables,*
>   *which should be something like:*
> *½ pound unshelled peas*
> *¼ pound broccoli*
> *¼ pound cauliflower*
> *3 baby carrots*
> *1½ tiny turnips*
> *2 baby beets*
> *6 skinny green beans*
> *2 baby zucchini*
> *2 baby potatoes*
> *Cherry tomatoes or tomato quarters*
> *Butter or margarine (about 2 ounces per person)*
> *Lemon juice*
> *Coarse (kosher) or plain salt*
> *Parsley or watercress branches*

Wash vegetables. Shell the peas. Cut broccoli flowers of even size with stems as long as possible; peel the tough outer skin down to the soft flesh. Cut cauliflower into flowers with shorter stalks, all the same length; their meat is brittle and the stems might snap. Cut green stems off carrots, turnips, and beets, and trim their roots without cutting tips too short. Peel only the turnips. If green beans have strings, snap one end and pull the string down the side; repeat with the other

end and string. If beans are stringless, leave them as is—
just as you should not touch a knife to the zucchini.

Over highest heat, bring your largest kettle ¾ full of unsalted water to a furious boil. Now you may blanch in any
order you please. Since the process requires a lot of water
and heat, it's most economical to use the same water for as
many vegetables as you can get away with. A huge kettle
can absorb peas, then green beans, then carrots, then maybe
zucchini, and then perhaps even cauliflower the first water.
The next water could start with potatoes (they absorb other
flavors the fastest), then broccoli, turnips, and beets last,
depending on how the water tastes. Taste the water after
each vegetable, and change it when any has left strong
traces.

To the rolling boiling water, add the vegetables by the
handful, slowly, so the boil will keep alive. Cover and listen
to the pot until it is boiling again; count the time from that
moment. Taste or test at the minimum time. There is no
sure way of knowing the age of your vegetables (unless
you've raised them!); therefore the absolute times for
blanching are uncertain. Judge the larger vegetables with a
sharp cooking fork or skewer, and taste the smaller vegetables: when they are on the *brink of tenderness, take them
out.* Pay close attention. Catching the vegetable at its
moment of truth is crucial to the success of this dish. Here
are the *approximate* times for blanching:

> *Peas: 3 to 8 minutes*
> *Broccoli: 4 to 8 minutes*
> *Cauliflower: 6 to 12 minutes*
> *Carrots: 8 to 10 minutes*
> *Green beans, zucchini: 8 to 12 minutes*
> *Turnips, beets, potatoes: 8 to 15 minutes*

Scoop vegetables out with a large long-handled sieve—a
chow lee is ideal (see p. 90)—and plunge into a ready sink-
ful of ice water.

Let the vegetables cool there a few minutes until they are
tepid. Then lift out and pat dry on terry towels. Slip skin
from beets. Line a separate bowl for each vegetable with

paper or terry towels to absorb any juices; turn each gently
into its bowl. Cover carefully with plastic film and set in a
cool place (the refrigerator if the day is very hot).

Bring vegetables to room temperature and pat them quite
dry. About 15 minutes before you plan to serve them, have a
big serving platter or casserole hot (if you can choose, use
the richest-looking dish rather than the plainest), and the
oven at 225° F. Also have a large square of foil cut for each
vegetable.

Have as many skillets over moderate heat on as many
burners as your stove has. Drop enough butter or margarine
into each skillet to cover the bottom copiously. When the
butter is just hot, gently add one kind of vegetable. Squeeze
on a bit of lemon juice—not enough to taste. Cover and give
the pan a shake—gently but with ardor—to distribute the
butter through the pieces. It shouldn't take more than a few
minutes to heat up each vegetable.

If your skillets are large, you can probably sauté two vegetables at once—but don't let them get mixed up. For example, sauté the whole green beans, 1 or 2 minutes, then
move them over in the pan, add the peas, and continue 2
minutes more. Begin by sautéeing those vegetables which
take longest to heat through—anything thick through the
middle—and count about 6 or 7 minutes for them. Toss the
cherry tomatoes or firm tomato quarters just a few moments
in butter to warm up. When the butter beneath each vegetable has turned nut brown, and a vegetable, tasted, is hot,
then turn each sort onto a square of foil, twist corners at
top, and keep warm in the oven until all are ready. (Or
simply cover the sauté pan, if it is oven-proof and you can
spare it.)

To arrange your Della Robbia wreath, have a little map
of each vegetable's place written down, so you can work
quickly. The colors should set one another off—you might
try potatoes in the center, then a circle of separate heaps of
beets, zucchini, cauliflower, peas, carrots, broccoli, turnips,
and green beans again next to the beets. Stud little clusters
of tomato here and there for dash, and tuck bunches of parsley or watercress around the perimeter for a lacy frame.
Nasturtium blossoms—or any country flowers, really—may

be added. Rush to the table! Serve everyone a bit of every-thing—including flowers.

This is a dish the guests won't mind waiting for. Just explain you'll be a few minutes in the kitchen, and let them work away at their first course of melon and ginger. This is the night, too, for the chicken you grilled that morning and serve now piled in a pottery bowl or basket. A *salade de saison* afterward, and then scoops of half-lemon/half raspberry sherbet sprinkled with grated orange peel for dessert. A memorable dinner.

NOTE: Blanched whole tiny boiling onions, whole thin asparagus, whole button mushrooms (these not blanched, but quickly sautéed), when in season, are other possibilities.

What About Vegetable Leftovers?

If they are cold and not stuck with congealed margarine, dice them nicely and add them to a salad, or fold them into mayonnaise to garnish a cold fish. If they have been cooked in margarine, then dice them and drop into soup or fold them into an omelette, or make them the base of a soufflé. Sprinkle them in casseroles. Toss them hot with pasta, a bit of oil, and Parmesan and garlic. Or just stand in front of the icebox and swipe them through yogurt or Dickie's Sauce (see p. 8) for your lunch. A cold vegetable can always find a good home.

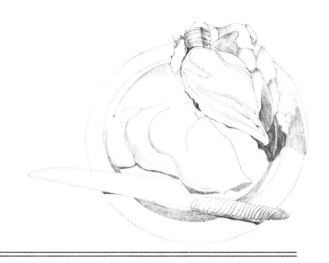

Meats

Time was when red meat on the dinner table was as much a necessity as salt. No more. Now we know that it makes much better sense—nutritionally, gastronomically, and financially—to draw upon all of nature's sources of protein, all of the time.

At our house, we eat lots of chicken, fish, and turkey. And lots of soups, pastas, beans, and pasta–bean combinations. In winter, we have mostly-vegetable stir-fries. In spring and summer we enjoy dinner of a della Robbia wreath of vegetables (butter-steamed, not blanched). And there are always lots of casseroles with half as much meat, fowl, fish, or cheese layered through. And now and then, a savory pastry. And every so often, A Roast.

When you do buy red meat, it's essential to know how to get the best value for money. These notes should take the mystery out of meat for the gourmet on a budget.

Budget notes on buying meats

As the United States Department of Agriculture will tell you, when it is free of fat, bone, and gristle, *all meat from the same animal has the same food value.* Costly filet mignon is not more nourishing than cheap chuck blade steak.

Then, for very best value for your money, *buy according to cost per serving of edible meat*, not the simple price per pound on the label. You don't eat bone, fat, and gristle, but you do pay for it. Sometimes, however, that just plain takes too much cash. So here is an exception to the rule: bones are "wasty" cuts, but they are always flavorful and cheap. Some nights, it's fun to gnaw on an oxtail stew bone or marinated breast of lamb—the dish is filled with other good things, so no one goes away hungry, and you've saved some money.

Try to buy meat "on special." Advertised meat specials are often at or below the butcher's cost; they're the best way to stock up the freezer. Don't confuse "specials" with outdated "mark-downs"—which can be bargains, if you trust your butcher, and if you can cook it or freeze it that day. But I would never buy marked-down pork, poultry, fish, or processed meat.

For slow-cooked and ground meats, buy U.S.D.A. Good Grade. It is always cheaper. Some markets carry it under their house name, or a euphemism such as "bonded" or "guaranteed" meat. Good Grade is simply meat with less fat marbled through it; therefore cuts are higher in protein, lower in calories and hidden fat than the identical cuts of Choice Grade. Good Grade is subject to the same government inspection as Choice and Prime grades. Good Grade meat has less moisture and flavor, but careful cooking can compensate for that. I've made countless dishes of braised beef from Good Grade, and nobody knew the difference.

If the meat counters at your market have never stocked a shin of beef, a breast of veal, or a calf's foot, then get yourself to a butcher whose patrons talk to him in Italian, German, Chinese, or what have you. His display case will surely be full of every sort of meat from head to tail, and he will happily tell you how to cook it all.

What is chuck? Where's the round? What's the most economical grind of ground beef? Across the country, names and cuts of meats vary. So do relative prices. That's why it's important to memorize where the primary cuts come from on an animal, and what characterizes each location.

How much meat to buy? In the following lists the numbers indicate servings (of approximately 3½ ounces of cooked boneless meat) from each pound of meat purchased. Cuts are with the bone in, unless otherwise specified.

Beef: For young beef, look for bright, rich red meat with creamy white fat. A whole carcass of beef is first divided into two sides, then each side is divided into two sections: the forequarter and the hindquarter. Generally, beef from the *fore*quarter has the best flavor. The forequarter and hindquarter are next divided into seven primary cuts.

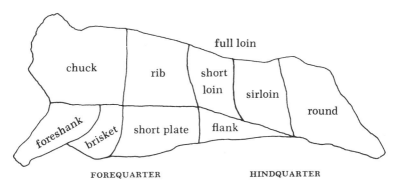

FOREQUARTER   HINDQUARTER

The four primary cuts of the forequarter are as follows:

1) CHUCK—the shoulder and the neck of beef. Many feel that chuck cuts have the best flavor of all. But because it is muscle much used, chuck can be tough if not tenderly treated. Carefully cooked, it will be tender and juicy.

2) BRISKET—the cut directly beneath the chuck. Like chuck, it has fine flavor, but it is fibrous and requires moist heat. Short ribs (*flanken*) come from this area. The foreshank is the foreleg or shin in front of the brisket. Not counted as a primary cut. It is also tasty and also requires moist heat.

3) RIBS—next to the chuck. The tenderest meat of the forequarter. Costly.

4) SHORT PLATE—breast meat below the ribs, the short end of the brisket. Flavorful, but bony and fat, it needs moist heat.

The three primary cuts of the hindquarter:

5) FULL LOIN—back of the ribs. The tenderest meat of the animal. Expensive.

6) WHOLE FLANK—a triangular piece beneath the full loin. It runs wide back of the short plate, mostly suet, to a

narrow point at the round. This point is the lean and sinewy flank steak, which may be braised or broiled.

7) ROUND—the rump and back leg of the beef. The leanest cut of the hindquarter. The round is divided into seven cuts: a) the rump, which contains the pelvic bone—for roasting; b) the side of round called "top sirloin," because it is next to the sirloin; c) top round (inside); d) bottom round (outside); e) eye of round; f) shank (hind shank, and less wasty than the fore shank—needs moist heat); and g) heel of round (back of the lower leg, and cheap, boneless, but stringy—needs moist heat).

Ground beef is sold under names permitted by the United States Department of Agriculture (at this writing) on the basis of fat content. "Ground sirloin" can have 15 to 18 percent fat; "ground round," 20 to 23 percent fat; "ground chuck," 25 percent fat; and "ground beef," 28 to 30 percent fat. The leanest grind is 15 percent leaner than the fattest grind; but it can cost up to 50 percent more. Therefore, *always buy the cheapest grind of beef* unless the price is proportionate to the fat content. Cook it slowly in a skillet without added fat until still a bit pink, then drain thoroughly in a strainer before proceeding with further cooking in casseroles or sauces. For hamburgers, pan-broil in a skillet with ridges, and pour the fat off as meat cooks, or broil on a broiling pan so the fat drips down.

NOTE: Despite legislation to the contrary, I sometimes have the impression that one market's "lean ground beef" is another market's "hamburger" (a label you shouldn't buy, because it describes nothing). If you don't trust the butcher or his ground beef, buy a piece of cheapest boneless chuck and ask him to grind it for you—then shop elsewhere in the future.

Lower-cost ground beef and vegetable protein mixes: The sort you buy are not all that cheap in terms of value for money, and they are mixed with ingredients you wouldn't add in your kitchen. Stretch ground beef yourself with protein boosters: ground cooked soy beans, brewers' yeast, sesame seeds, Parmesan cheese, nonfat milk powder, cooked whole grain cereals, or crumbled whole grain bread.

Our best buys of Good or Choice Beef Grade for braising, simmering, or pot-roasting:

Chuck arm (shoulder, arm, or round bone) steak or roast; a luscious piece of meat, 2 to 3½ servings

Center-cut chuck (7-bone) steak or roast, 2 to 3 servings

Chuck blade (1st cut) steak or roast, 2 servings

Chuck shoulder (cross rib, Boston, English, or clod) roast, boneless, 3 to 4 servings

Short ribs (*flanken* or English ribs), 2 servings

Shank (shin); hindquarter is meatiest, forequarter is best for soup, 1½ to 2 servings

Neck-end chuck (neck); fibrous but lean, 2 servings

Plate, 1 to 1½ servings

Our best buy of Good or Choice Grade beef for dry roasting:

Chuck shoulder (cross rib, Boston, English, or clod) roast; the first 3 or 4 pounds of the shoulder closest to the ribs are best; boneless. Ask the butcher to tie a sheet of fat on top, to help self-baste. 3 to 4 servings

Our best buys of Choice Grade beef for steaks:

Chuck blade (1st cut) steaks, 2 servings

Center-cut chuck (7-bone) steaks, 2 to 3 servings

NOTE: As the cuts get closer to the ribs, the "7" bones become a thin "1" of white cartilage, and you have especially juicy steaks; ideally, they are cut about ¾-inch thick.

Our best buy of Good or Choice Grade beef for ground meat:

The cheapest; 4 servings, or up to 7 in a casserole

Calf or baby beef: Somewhere from never-neverland comes an animal whose meat is not pearly white and delicate as veal nor brick red and robust as beef. Rather, it is a soft rose color and neither here nor there in flavor. Its name is calf (or baby beef), and the only reason for buying it is that you are seized by a craving for stuffed breast of veal but can't afford it. Otherwise, I wouldn't pay calf's higher-than-beef (albeit lower-than-veal) price.

Our best buy of Choice Grade calf for oven roasting:
    Breast, 1 to 1½ servings

Veal: Really young veal has velvety pink-gray-white meat with firm white fat and soft small reddish bones. It is likely to be most reasonably priced in winter. Veal, being young, is also likely to be relatively free of additives. Veal is divided into the foresaddle and the hindsaddle, and into essentially the same cuts as its older brother, beef.

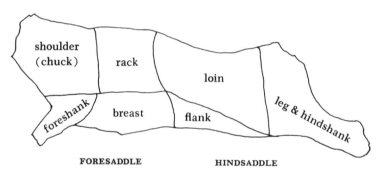

    The foresaddle of veal is always least expensive; some butchers won't even bother handling it. In larger cities, however, there are still specialty butcher shops which carry the whole carcass and whose prices for breast and shank won't make you shudder.

    BREAST *and* FORESHANK—stuffed breast of veal is superb; the tender bones also make delightful stew; foreshanks cut up are braised into marvelous dishes.

    SHOULDER—may be roasted; boned, rolled and braised, or stuffed. Once, it was reasonably priced, but no more.

    And that's it, for veal. There is less and less of it, and as demand increases for what there is, gourmets on a budget get crunched out.

Our best buys of Choice Grade veal for braising and sim-
mering:

Breast, 2 servings
Foreshanks, 1½ to 2 servings
Riblets from the breast, 2 servings

Our best buy of Choice Grade veal for dry roasting:

Breast; stuffed, 2 to 3 servings

Lamb: The youngest lamb has firm, bright pink meat,
pure white fat, and soft, pinkish bones of comparatively
small size. If there is any season in which lamb is going to be
a bargain, it is early summer—the lamb is still young, but
not so much a delicacy as the first lamb of spring. Watch,
then, for specials, and buy what you can for the freezer.
Lamb will keep there from 6 to 9 months. Like veal, young
lamb is relatively free of additives. Lamb is also divided into
the foresaddle and the hindsaddle.

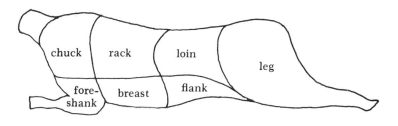

FORESADDLE   HINDSADDLE

The foresaddle includes:
1) CHUCK—the neck, shoulder, and some of the foreshank. Flavorful for braising.
2) FORESHANKS—underneath the chuck, meaty and
very tasty. Not the value-for-money buy of the leg, but you
can buy fewer shanks for a small dinner, more cheaply.
3) RACK—comparable to the ribs on beef in every way.
4) BREAST—beneath the rack; flavorful, but needs long,
slow cooking to render out the fat.

The hindsaddle includes:

5) FLANK—comparable to the flank of beef—not a speck of fat on it, so when it's cheap, it's great.

6) LOIN—Comparable to the short loin on beef.

7) LEG—all the rest of the lamb, often divided into two roasts, the shank end, which is the best value, and the rump end. Leg is the best value-for-money buy of lamb, but it's usually a lot to pay at one fell swoop.

NOTE: A felicitous buy—always cheaper—is frozen lamb from New Zealand. New Zealand permits no adulterants in its meat, and the lamb always tastes young, tender, and sweet.

Our best buys of Good or Choice Grade lamb for braising and simmering:

Foreshanks, 2 servings
Shoulder, 2 to 2½ servings
Neck, 2 servings
Breast or riblets, 1½ to 2 servings

Our best buys of Good or Choice Grade lamb for dry roasting:

Shoulder, 2 servings
Breast or riblets, 1 to 1½ servings

Our best buys of Good or Choice Grade lamb for chops:

Shoulder; blade cuts nearest the rack, 3 servings
Shoulder; arm (round bone) chops, 3 servings
Square-cut shoulder roast; look for the round bone on one side and the long blade bone on the other—ask the butcher to slice it into chops; you'll have both blade and arm chops at a saving. 3 servings

Pork: To determine younger, leaner, more delicate pork, choose firm gray-pink meat with pure white fat and soft, slightly pink bones of comparatively small size. Pork is divided into seven primary cuts.

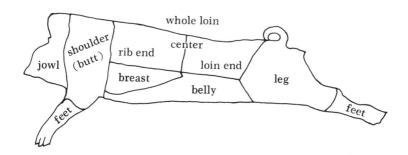

Back to front:

1) LEG—a fresh or cured ham, divided into 2 roasts: a full butt end, which is leaner and meatier, the better value; and a full shank end, which is easier to carve but less meaty.

2) LOIN—divided into rib and loin cuts; look for smaller cuts indicating younger animals. Meaty country-style spareribs from the rib end are the best sparerib buy.

3) BELLY—cured into salt pork and bacon.

4) BREAST—"slabs" of spareribs.

5) SHOULDER—flavorful and comparatively cheap; divided into the fresh Boston butt and the fresh shoulder roast.

6) JOWL—for bacon (a meat packer friend once recommended against it for hygienic reasons).

7) FEET (TROTTERS)

Our best buys of available grade* of pork for braising, simmering, and dry roasting:

Fresh shoulder of pork (picnic, arm, or calia); fat and "wasty," but still a good value, 2 to 3 servings; if the butcher will bone it for you (and roll it, for an oven roast), you're way ahead of the game, 3 to 3½ servings.

* U.S.D.A. 1, 2, and 3, graded according to proportion of fat. Generally, unlike beef, there is little difference between grades.

Boston butt (shoulder or blade butt); distinctive flavor; depends on how your butcher cuts the shoulder which of these two roasts are meatiest, 2 to 3 servings; boned and rolled. 3 to 3½ servings

Our best buys of available grade* of pork for chops and steaks:

For bargain cuts, remember the word "end":

Loin end chops (sirloin or hip), very good buy on special, 2½ to 3 servings

Rib end chops (shoulder), 2½ to 3 servings

Fresh shoulder or Boston butt: ask the butcher to cut these roasts into steaks for a substantial saving. Fine for sautéeing, broiling, or barbecuing. 2 to 3 servings

Do not succumb to the "bargain" offer of a sliced quarter pork loin. My advisors tell me that you will get some center-cut chops, but the end chops included will be "wastier" than those you would carefully select for yourself from smaller packages and buried where you can't see them.

Insides and outsides: These are not meats for every day—they are, as a class, quite rich, and some are exceedingly high in cholesterol. But also, as a class, they are the cheapest of meats, very nourishing, and in many cuisines of the world, considered gourmet fare. So as valuable relief for a pinched purse, when you see a package of something heretofore uninviting, invite it home, and turn it into one of the classic dishes I've included.

KIDNEYS, HEART, TONGUE, TRIPE, SPLEEN, LIVER, SWEET-BREADS, and BRAINS (the last three should be eaten the least frequently)— always buy the filtering-sort of innards of the

* U.S.D.A. 1, 2, and 3, graded according to proportion of fat. Generally, unlike beef, there is little difference between grades.

youngest of the species; they are more likely to be free of additives, 3 to 5 servings per pound.

FEET (TROTTERS), HEAD, EARS, TAILS—these are "wasty" cuts, but excellent European and Oriental dishes emphasize their silky nature, 1 to 1½ servings per pound.

Processed meats:

HAM—until nitrates/nitrites are no longer used to preserve it, ham should be off our list for family cooking. I do love and buy an infrequent center slice for a company dish, 5 servings per pound. But if you want your ham no matter what, then the best value for money is a whole butt half, 3 to 3½ servings.

FRANKFURTERS and LUNCHEON MEATS—also preserved, but also off our list because they are very poor values, both nutritionally and economically. (See the Index for good cold meat alternatives.)

BACON—preserved, and wildly expensive, 80 percent of your good money is drained from the pan! Slab bacon, if you've a slicer, is cheaper than sliced. But Canadian bacon comes from the lean loin, and is a far better value for money buy, 5 servings.

SAUSAGES—only buy freshly made ones, not preserved, from a butcher or delicatessen you trust. But they, too, are very fat and wasteful, 4 servings.

NOTE: Make friends with your butcher. Seek his advice— he may know even better than you do what you need for a dish, or remember a special one-of-a-kind piece tucked away in his fridge that would be perfect. Most butchers are proud of their trade, and nothing is too much trouble for a friend who appreciates what he or she is getting. Proof: One day, I asked a butcher at an unfamiliar market if he would be good enough to bone some chicken breasts for me. He would—for a dollar more the pound! Later, I asked my butcher if he would do it. "No problem, Mrs. Thompson. Just give me a little time." (A glass of Paradise Jelly at Christmas can be a thoughtful thank-you for extra kindness.)

Budget notes on cooking meats

The economical cuts of meat we use *must be cooked slowly*. Slow heat helps keep shrinkage to a minimum. How slow is slow—200° F, 275°, 300° or 325°—depends on the cut, the cook, and the cook's whim. Moist-cooked meats can take protracted cooking, but dry-cooked (roasted and broiled) meats must be cooked only until tender, otherwise they will go dry and tough.

A good meat thermometer is cheap insurance for the inexperienced meat cook. Be sure its tip is in the center of the meat (measure first on the outside, mark with your fingers, then slip it in only to that point), not touching a bone or fat.

How to test meats for doneness if you haven't a meat thermometer? By touching it: press it gently but firmly with a finger when it goes into the oven, and remember that feeling. Then, if you want it roasted rare, the meat will test fairly close to that softness. Medium rare, it will be soft yet pliant. Medium, it will be less pliant; and well-done, the meat will be firm when pressed. You can also slip a very sharp cooking fork or skewer into it. (Although you do lose juices this way, it is a true test.) If juices that follow the fork run rosy, the meat is rare; if they run pink, it is medium; if the juices run clear, the meat is well-done. You can also cut near the bone to see how it looks.

Fresh ground turkey meat: It has all the virtues: delicate flavor, about as much protein but only half the fat of lean ground beef, and in terms of value for money, ground turkey is cheaper than ground beef because there is scant shrinkage. If fresh ground turkey hasn't turned up in your part of the country yet—believe me, the turkey growers are working on it—then ask your butcher about it. To cook, just combine the very lean meat with something juicy, and be sure it is fully done; use the recipes in this book as models, then invent from there.

Servings of meat: Appetites for meat so differ. To simplify things, I've given the number of 3½-ounce servings of cooked meat which you can expect to dish up from each recipe. They are modest portions (we really eat more meat

than we need to, you know), but if it says, "Makes 6 servings," and you can count on your teenage son to eat three of
them, at least you'll know where you stand.

For entertaining, if you don't know your guests' appetites,
count on each man to eat 2 servings of most dishes, and
each woman to eat about 1¼ (women are always dieting).
Better leftovers than not enough. However, when a recipe
says, "Serves 8," it means I've served it to that many with
plenty for seconds—and I imagine our friends aren't that
much hungrier than yours.

To help with cuts of meat I don't mention specifically, the
average number of servings from 1 uncooked pound of boneless meat is 3 or 4; from bone-in meat, 2 or 3; and from very
bony meat, 1 or 1½.

NOTE: *All meat must be at room temperature before cooking to prevent shrinkage and toughness.*

Casserole Dauphinoise

(French baked meat and potato dish)
6 SERVINGS

This traditional recipe can be regarded as the model for
building succulent, flavorful casseroles with modest ingredients. When you make it, memorize *the principle of casserole
layering:* bottom layer is a bed of a starch which will soak up
the casserole's juices; middle layer is a fairly thick cover of
cooked meat (or poultry or flaked fish) in small bits; top
layer is a light blanket of a flavorful vegetable which will
moisten the meat. In between are seasonings—salt, pepper,
sautéed onion and garlic, herbs, and grated cheese, with perhaps a shower of flour if it needs thickening. Poured over is
milk, buttermilk, juices, gravy, or sauce, which will help bind
the ingredients together. And over all, a blanket of grated
cheese or seasoned crumbs to make the top crisp and golden.
Of course some or all of the layers may be repeated as suits
the shape of the dish.

Casseroles are splendidly convenient. You can put them together in advance because they generally improve when given time for flavors to marry. And on days when you can't get your family to the table in one sitting, you can divide a casserole into individual baking dishes and bake them when needed for ¾ the given time.

I've outlined the method step by step, so if you have good cooked pasta instead of potatoes, chopped spinach instead of tomatoes, and pot gravy instead of milk, you can make your own superb casserole combination with this recipe.

1 pound uncooked ground beef, lamb, pork, or turkey; or
    2 to 3 cups diced cooked meat or poultry, no fat
4 medium-sized peeled baking potatoes
1 large onion
1 clove of garlic, minced
3 large fresh or 16-ounce can of firm, drained tomatoes
2⅓ cups coarsely grated (7 to 8 ounces) cheapest
    natural hard cheese
Oil
Salt and fresh ground pepper, to taste
Fresh chopped or dried appropriate herb
3 generous tablespoons flour
2 cups milk, any sort
Paprika

1.   In a medium skillet over medium heat without fat, sauté the raw meat, if using meat. When mostly cooked but still a bit pink, turn into a sieve and drain off fat (juices will come too, but not enough worth retrieving).

2.   Oil a shallow 2½-quart baking dish (if it's deep, the potatoes will be underdone or the meat overdone). Grate 2 of the potatoes on the wide blade of a grater as for scalloped potatoes directly into the dish; spread evenly, and season lightly with salt, pepper, an appropriate herb, and 1 tablespoon of the flour.

3.   Cover with the meat. Grate the onion on the coarse blade of a grater and mix with the garlic; sprinkle half the mixture over the meat and season again with salt and pepper.

4.   Chop 1½ of the tomatoes and strew them over; sprinkle on half the grated cheese, then 1 more tablespoon of flour.

5.   Grate the remaining potatoes as you did the others and lay them over; sprinkle with remaining onions, a bit of salt, pepper, herb, and the last of the flour.

6.   Very thinly slice the remaining tomatoes and make a lid of them over the casserole.

7.   Now pour over the milk—it should not quite cover the potatoes.

8.   Finally sprinkle on the remaining grated cheese. Add a few decorative dashes of paprika and herb, then drizzle over a bit of oil to moisten. If making ahead, cover and refrigerate. Preheat oven to 400° F before baking.

9.   Bake loosely covered, at 400° F for 1 hour, or until a cooking fork tests the potatoes tender. If chilled, add about 30 more minutes to the time.

A delicious seasoning fillip is the combination of chopped fresh spinach (or chard), parsley, and onion listed in the turkey pâté. Sprinkle the mixture over the potatoes as you go.

A salad of mixed lettuces with creamy herbal dressing, a light red wine, and a dessert of whole green apples, their hollowed-out cores filled with honey, lemon juice, margarine, and cinnamon (called Dinah's honey apples in this house) baked with the casserole would make a satisfying dinner.

A Very Light Moussaka

(Greek baked meat and eggplant dish)
   8 SERVINGS

Moussaka is a savory layered baked dish, generally made of meat and vegetables. This combination, from the ancient Greek province of Thessalonika, is the result of years of

refining, and I must say it's super. It's an ideal dish for entertaining, and can easily be doubled or tripled—just fit it in a
larger baking pan.

 2¼ pounds eggplant
 About ½ cup oil
 2 large onions, chopped medium fine
 1 pound ground lamb or beef
 1 8-ounce can tomato sauce
 ½ cup less 1 tablespoon plain dry bread crumbs, and
     more for top
 Merest dash of cinnamon
 1 teaspoon salt
 ¼ cup (2 ounces) margarine, and more for top
 6 tablespoons flour
 2½ cups milk, any sort
 Dash of nutmeg
 Dash of white pepper
 2 egg yolks
 Parmesan
 Chopped parsley

The eggplant: Preheat broiler, and oven too, if you can, to
very hot. Brush the broiler pan and a large baking sheet each
with oil. Peel and slice eggplant in ¼-inch-thick rounds.
Divide the rounds of eggplant between pans, and brush
lightly with oil. Now, if your oven will work this way, brown
the eggplant in relays: broil one panful and bake the other.
Keep an eye on the broiler pan, as the eggplant will begin
to brown quite suddenly after some time—and being this
thin, it can burn. When nicely browned, turn rounds over,
brush lightly with oil and brown on the other side. Remove
pan from broiler to cool and slip pan from oven into broiler.
When these rounds are also browned, remove them to cool.
Reduce oven heat to 350° F. If your oven won't work this
way, simply broil and brown first one pan of eggplant, then
the other.

NOTE: Usually eggplant is browned in oil in a skillet—but it soaks up oil like a Greek sponge that way. This method uses much less oil, and as a result, the dish is far less rich.

The meat: Meanwhile, heat 2 tablespoons of the oil in a large heavy skillet over medium-high heat. Sauté the onions, stirring frequently, until lightly browned. In another heavy skillet, over medium heat, sauté the meat without fat until still a bit pink. Turn into a sieve and drain off all fat. Add meat to the onions, together with the tomato sauce, crumbs, cinnamon, and ½ teaspoon of the salt. With a fork, toss lightly to mix thoroughly. Turn heat to low and let it sauté gently, stirring now and then while you prepare the sauce.

The béchamel: Make a thick sauce in another smaller pot by melting ¼ cup margarine over medium heat, then whisking in the flour. When blended, slowly whisk in the milk, nutmeg, and white pepper. Turn heat to medium-low, and continue whisking until the sauce thickens. Turn heat to lowest, and whisk now and then as the sauce ripens.

The moussaka: Oil a 2½-quart baking tin or dish (typically, it should be a square or rectangle). Stack the eggplant rounds in twos, matching sizes. Now cover the bottom of the tin with all the top rounds of the stacks. Cover them with half the meat. Arrange remaining eggplant evenly over this, and then spread on the rest of the meat.

Remove béchamel sauce from heat and whisk it as you beat in the yolks. Pour the sauce evenly over the moussaka. Sprinkle a light blanket of dry crumbs over it, then a heavier blanket of Parmesan. Cover and chill if desired. Bake in a 375° F oven about 45 minutes; 75 minutes if chilled. Dot with margarine and slip under the broiler to finish browning. Cut in squares from the tin and dust with parsley.

Serve with *bolillos* or French rolls, a fresh spinach salad with dressing of olive oil and lemon juice, cold beer, and for dessert Persian Red Quinces, in season, or Persian Red Apples, with yogurt.

Pastitso

(Greek meat and macaroni dish)
8 SERVINGS

This dish has a special character I find extraordinary. Everything melts into everything else, resulting in a delicate, light, unique, and glorious flavor. Make it in tubfuls for a party. The recipe is easily increased.

1½ pounds ground beef
1 chopped onion
1 clove of garlic, minced
2 tablespoons oil, and more for dish
1½ teaspoons salt
2 dashes cinnamon (and that's it!)
1 8-ounce can tomato sauce
7 tablespoons (3½ ounces) margarine
¼ cup flour
2 cups milk, any sort
Dash of white pepper
Dash of nutmeg
⅓ cup Parmesan
8 ounces small elbow macaroni
2 eggs
2 cups shredded (8 ounces cheapest natural hard)
    cheese

In a large skillet over medium heat, sauté the onion and garlic in the oil until they are soft. Crumble in the beef and stir until the meat is mostly cooked but still a bit pink. Turn into a sieve and drain off fat. Stir in 1 teaspoon of the salt, the cinnamon, and tomato sauce, and set aside.

In a small saucepan over medium-low heat, melt 3 tablespoons of the margarine, then whisk in the flour. Add milk and whisk until thickened. Add ½ teaspoon salt, the pepper, a pinch of the nutmeg, and the Parmesan. Set this Mornay sauce over very low heat to mellow.

Cook the macaroni in boiling salted water 10 to 12 minutes, or until *al dente*—but no longer. Drain well and return to pot. Break the eggs into the macaroni and add 2 tablespoons of the margarine. Beat with a wooden spoon until well mixed.

Oil a shallow 2½-quart baking dish and layer ingredients as follows: half the macaroni, all the meat, half the hard cheese, the remaining macaroni, then the Mornay sauce (whisk again before pouring). Shake the dish gently to settle the sauce. Sprinkle on the remaining hard cheese, dot with the remaining margarine, and sprinkle with a bit of nutmeg.

Cover and refrigerate if desired. Bake uncovered at room temperature in a 375° F oven for 1 hour. If chilled, bake 25 to 30 minutes longer.

For company, a salad of roasted green peppers or green beans *à la vinaigrette* would be handsome, and a light dry red wine. For dessert, boughten sponge cake and sliced oranges in winter, or fresh strawberries on pretty leaves in summer to dip into a mound of powdered sugar.

Dorris Johnson's Dave Chasen's Chili

14 SERVINGS

This is one great cook's "down-home" interpretation of another great cook's legendary restaurant chili.

1 recipe Memphis Beans (see p. 95)
5 cups (from about 70 ounces) canned tomatoes, drained
1 cup diced salt pork
1 pound green peppers, seeded and chopped
1½ pounds onions, chopped
2 to 3 cloves of garlic, minced
½ cup chopped parsley
½ pound lean raw bacon, finely chopped, optional
2½ pounds ground beef, ground just once
1½ pounds lean pork, chopped
½ cup chili powder: 6 tablespoons mild, 2 tablespoons
    hot, or your favorite, to taste
2 tablespoons salt, or to taste
1½ teaspoons fresh ground pepper
1½ teaspoons ground cumin (comino)

Dorris says: "I use about four different chili powders; Texas (hot and dark), New Mexico (mild and sweet), Mexican (a mix), and Californian. . . . All growing things have a flavor variable, and I depend on my taste buds to bring things to a certain point . . ."

Hold the lid on the bean pot and drain the beans (save broth for soup!). Add the tomatoes, and simmer uncovered over medium heat 5 minutes. Set aside. In a medium skillet over medium heat, sauté the salt pork until it oils the pan, then add the green pepper; sauté 5 minutes. Add the onions, lower the heat, and sauté until onions and peppers are tender. Add garlic and parsley, stir and set aside.

If you're using it, slowly render the bacon in a medium skillet over low heat, pouring off the fat as it melts. When limp, sauté the beef and pork with the bacon 15 minutes. Add meat to onions and stir in chili powder. Cook together 10 minutes over medium-low heat, stirring occasionally.

In your Dutch oven or a large top-of-the-stove-proof earthenware casserole, mix the meat and beans. Add salt, pepper, and cumin; cover and simmer very slowly for 1 hour, stirring frequently. Simmer uncovered another 30 minutes. Cover and refrigerate until needed—or to serve the same day, keep in a cool place until ready to warm up. This tastes even better a couple of days later. Skim fat from top before heating 1 hour in a 325° F oven.

Dorris says: ". . . serve with very crunchy cole slaw or a broken crisp lettuce salad and French bread." And lots of cold beer. And Danish caramelized custard for dessert.

Then everybody lie very still on the floor.

Benjyburgers

(Hamburgers at their best)

Speaking of chili, my son Benjamin and I found the best hamburgers imaginable at a street-side stand owned by Greeks. The Greeks have long since sold the stand, but in this house, Benjy keeps their creation alive and well.

After pan-broiling the hamburgers on an iron skillet with ridges, Benjy sets out all the ingredients in bowls on the dinner table, and everyone constructs his own hamburger. Amounts vary with the builder, but this is the order we like best, from bottom up:

Warm whole-grain hamburger-bun bottom
Spoonful of thick hot chili without beans (canned)
½-inch slab of fresh tomato
3 or 4 dill-pickle chips
¼-pound patty of medium-rare ground beef
Slice of Cheddar cheese
Mountain of shredded lettuce
Thousand Island dressing (bottled)
Warm whole-grain hamburger-bun top

For dessert, we have a fresh fruit compote creamed with plain yogurt—a marvelous dinner!

Fleischklösse in Frolic Sauce

(German featherlight meat dumplings in a piquant sauce)
8 SERVINGS

A dear friend, after discovering a delicacy, returned to the store for a second jar, was told they did not carry such things as "frolics," became indignant, quarreled, refused to yield, and finally found for herself, on a shelf behind the defeated grocer, a jar of capers.

These are miraculous meat balls, with a sauce to match. Particularly good idea for a big buffet.

Meatballs:
2 *pounds ground beef*
2 *tablespoons oil*
2 *large onions, finely chopped*
4 *large slices day-old home-style white bread*
1 *cup rich milk*
2 *teaspoons anchovy paste*
2 *eggs, beaten*
½ *teaspoon salt*
½ *teaspoon fresh ground pepper*
3 10½-*ounce cans concentrated beef broth diluted with*
    4 *cups water* or 8 *cups homemade beef broth* (*left*
    over from making Pot-au-Feu, *p. 37*)

Sauce:
3 *tablespoons* (1½ *ounces*) *margarine*
⅓ *cup flour*
2 *cups beef broth from meatball pot, or as needed*
3 *tablespoons lemon juice*
2½-*fluid-ounce bottle of capers, drained*
Chopped parsley

Fleischklösse: In a heavy skillet over medium heat, heat
the oil and sauté the onions until very lightly browned; stir
often. Meanwhile, trim crusts from bread and soak bread in
the milk in a mixing bowl. Break up the crumbs with clean
fingers, then add milk and bread to the onions in the skillet
with the anchovy paste. Stir lightly with a fork to blend. Add
seasoning, eggs and pepper, then work this mixture into the
meat with your fingers; return to the bowl if easiest. When
all is well blended, wet your hands to keep the mixture from
sticking, and form into rounds no bigger than walnuts. Set
balls on waxed paper. Pour diluted canned or homemade
broth into a deep saucepan and bring to a simmer over
medium heat. Drop the *Fleischklösse* gently into the simmering broth, cover, turn heat to low, and simmer for 10 minutes, or until one dumpling tests cooked (eat just one!).

Frolic sauce: Meanwhile, melt the margarine in a small
saucepan over medium heat, then whisk in the flour. Measure 2 cups of beef broth from the meatball pot and whisk

in a little of it, then pour in the rest of the 2 cups slowly, beating continually. Add the lemon juice and capers and whisk until the sauce thickens—gently—you don't want to mash the capers. Add a bit more broth if you like a thinner sauce, or a sauce less tart. Don't forget, the meatballs will thin it down somewhat.

Simmer sauce over very low heat 15 minutes, then lift out the meatballs with a slotted spoon or *chow lee* and turn them into the sauce. They may be kept in the sauce a few hours in a cool place, then warmed up very gently.

Serve, dusted with parsley, over whipped potatoes or buttered noodles—there's plenty of sauce to sop up. Sautéed slices of zucchini or buttersilk carrots would do nicely as a vegetable, and so would a fresh spinach salad with Dickie's Dressing. Have Chianti or cold beer to drink. And for dessert, a big pear crisp, perhaps à la mode with vanilla ice cream.

You can make a delicious soup of beef dumplings just by serving the meat balls in their poaching broth without thickening it; strew with lots of chopped parsley.

Julia Samuels' Hungarian Stuffed Cabbage

AT LEAST 24 SERVINGS

This is a great party dish—cheap, foolproof, and men, especially, are mad about it. The cabbage is marvelously flexible, it can be reheated two or three times without harm, and it freezes beautifully. It's such an ideal make-ahead dish that once, with the help of a friend, I made it for 90 people for a Christmas party! The recipe is from one of the most gifted cooks I know.

5 *medium-sized firm green cabbages, heavy for their size*
4 *large onions*
2 *28-ounce cans sauerkraut*
5 *pounds ground chuck beef (a fatter grind would make*
    the dish too rich—the fat has nowhere to go)
3 *cups raw converted long-grain white rice*
2 *eggs*
Handful of chopped parsley
2 *cloves of garlic, minced*
2 *tablespoons salt, or to taste*
2 *teaspoons fresh ground pepper*
1 *to 2 cups of hot water*
2 *teaspoons paprika*
1 *to 2 large cans tomato juice*
1 *to 2 cups diluted canned beef broth*
2 *to 3 pints* Crème Fraîche (*see p. 73*) *or sour cream*

NOTE: Do not let anything aluminum—neither foil nor pot
—touch the cabbage. The acid of the sauerkraut will eat
holes in the foil, and be discolored by the pot.

The cabbage: Put a big covered kettle of hot water on to
boil over highest heat. With a sharp knife, cut out the cores
of the cabbages, leaving the heads intact. Put the cabbages,
one by one, in a deep bowl or pot and pour the boiling water
over them, to soften and loosen the leaves. Use tongs to pull
off all the large leaves—don't tear them—and set them aside
on a terry towel. Lift out the rest of the head and chop it
coarsely.

Also chop 2 of the onions coarsely. Drain the sauerkraut
in a colander and rinse a minute or so under cold running
water; shake off excess water. In a bowl, mix the chopped
cabbage, onions, and sauerkraut together with clean hands.

The meat: Grate on medium blade of a grater the remaining 2 onions and turn them into a large bowl with the beef,
rice, eggs, parsley, garlic, about 2½ teaspoons of the salt,
and ½ teaspoon of the pepper. Mix well with clean hands,
then mix in 1 cup of the hot water. If the mixture is not
moist but still very thick, add a little more hot water. Cook a
small bit in a pan to see if the seasoning is right.

The rolls: Now use a sharp knife to trim off the back spine of each cabbage leaf so it will be supple. To fill, turn the base of the leaf toward you, hollow side up. Place a 1-inch-thick roll of meat at the base, with a 1-inch margin at either side. Now fold the right margin over and roll up the leaf loosely, because the rice will expand. Tuck the left end into itself, thereby closing the opening. Use all the stuffing; chop any remaining leaves and add to the sauerkraut mix. Set oven to 500° F.

The baking: In your turkey roaster, cover the bottom of the pan with a layer of the sauerkraut mix. Season with a sprinkling of the remaining salt, pepper, and the paprika. Arrange a layer of cabbage rolls, seam side down, not too tightly packed, over it. Make another layer of the sauerkraut, season lightly, then another layer of cabbage rolls. Continue to the top. Portion the sauerkraut out so you'll have enough to cover the top layer of rolls—the sauerkraut should come to about 2 inches below the top of the pan, no more.

In a large pitcher whisk together 1 large can of tomato juice, 1 cup of diluted beef broth, and 1 pint of crème fraîche or sour cream. Pour it evenly over the cabbage, and use a rubber scraper to nudge the rolls so the juice is well distributed all through the layers. There should be enough juice to be seen just beneath the top layer of the sauerkraut; whip up more if there isn't.

Cover tightly. If the pan hasn't its own lid, lay brown-bag paper completely over the top, and then cover with heavy-duty foil, crimping tightly against the outside rim.

Set pan on bottom rack of the oven for 10 minutes; reduce heat to 350° F. Bake undisturbed for 3 hours. Taste a roll on top to see if it's cooked (the top rolls sometimes need turning over toward the end of cooking). Remove pan from oven the moment rolls are tender and rice inside is cooked.

Before you refrigerate it, especially if making for the first time, taste the juices for seasoning; salt and pepper are especially important to heighten flavor here. This will keep, refrigerated, up to 4 days; frozen, up to 6 months. Thaw before reheating.

The serving: To heat for serving, set oven to 500° F. If the cabbage looks dry, pour a little water over to moisten. Set in the oven on lowest rack and at once turn heat to 300°. Bake tightly covered as before for about 1½ hours. The time depends on number of rolls and shape of the pan, more time for more rolls. You can always turn the heat to 225° to hold the rolls, so plan on more rather than less time. Taste juices for salt and pepper again before serving.

Have a big bowl of *crème fraîche* or sour cream for topping each portion. Potatoes boiled in their jackets with a sprinkling of dill are a nice and easy accompaniment, with carrot sticks and black olives on the side for contrast. Also have corn bread or French rolls, cold beer, and dill pickles. For dessert, My Grandmother's World-Famous Chocolate Cake! (see p. 275).

My Meat Loaf

8 SERVINGS

I've stood over a hot stove finishing an elegant dinner for guests while one or two of them, kibitzing in the kitchen, couldn't stop nibbling at the meat loaf on the counter, still warm from the children's supper. I keep forgetting how good it is—I should just make meat loaf for both sittings!

2 *pounds ground beef or any meat*
4 *eggs*
2 *cups loosely packed small pieces of day-old good bread*
   or cooked rice, oatmeal, any grains; see NOTE
1⅔ *cups buttermilk (or milk of any sort, and add 3*
   tablespoons more lemon juice); or less
2 *teaspoons lemon juice*
2 *tablespoons fresh chopped or 2 teaspoons dried dill*
½ *onion, finely chopped, or 1 teaspoon onion powder*
1 *large clove of garlic, minced*
1 *teaspoon salt, or to taste*
¼ *teaspoon fresh ground pepper*
⅔ *cup catsup, optional*

NOTE: If using cooked grains instead of bread, use only as much milk as will give the mixture the consistency of oatmeal.

Break eggs into meat in a bowl and mix with clean hands until thoroughly blended. Add all remaining ingredients except catsup and mix thoroughly with hands—it should have the creamy consistency of cooked oatmeal. Sauté a small bit in a pan without fat and taste for seasoning; correct if necessary. Pat into a flat 2-quart baking dish if you like your meat loaf in squares, or into a large loaf pan if you like it in slices. It's nice but not necessary to smooth catsup over the top. Cover with foil and refrigerate up to 1 day if you wish. Bring to room temperature before baking at 325° F for 1 hour; remove foil the last 10 minutes to brown. Pour off fat before serving. It will keep refrigerated 4 days.

(My mother has a clever trick: she pierced the bottom of a loaf pan with an ice pick, then she bakes her meat loaf in the pan set on a rack over a larger pan. The fat drains off as it bakes.)

When ground beef is on special, or the bulk price is cheaper, I double or triple this recipe, bake it in a large roasting pan for about 1½ hours, then divide it up and freeze it.

Put some whole unpeeled potatoes or yams on the oven rack to bake with the meat loaf, and serve with Burgundy, a big mixed raw vegetable salad and garlic toast. Hot lemon sauce over warm apple tart would make a company dinner.

And meat loaf is very good cold, you know.

Turkey Meat Loaf

8 SERVINGS

Simply use ground fresh turkey for up to *half* the ground beef in the preceding recipe. Beef and turkey combine deliciously, and the extra fat in the beef gives necessary moistness to the extra lean turkey.

Make this notion a model for other beef/turkey ideas. Time and temperature for baking are the same.

Pâté de Maison

15 TO 20 SERVINGS

This pâté is as good as any I have eaten. And it's far leaner, less rich, and less expensive than most of the great pâtés of this world. I owe it to my dear friend Rheta Resnick, who first made it for me.

> 2 pounds one-ground fresh dark turkey meat
> ½ cup Half-and-Half
> 2 eggs, lightly beaten
> ½ teaspoon salt
> ¼ teaspoon fresh ground pepper
> ⅔ cup plain fine dry bread crumbs
> 12 ounces fresh spinach, no stems
> 1 fistful parsley, no stems, chopped fine
> 1 large onion, chopped fine
> ½ teaspoon oregano
> ½ teaspoon nutmeg
> ½ pound mild uncooked Italian or Polish sausage in
>   casing, in 2 pieces (without preservatives, if possible)

In a bowl, with a light hand, mix turkey, Half-and-Half, eggs, salt, pepper, and bread crumbs. Chop spinach medium fine. Mix spinach, parsley, onion, and herbs together on the chopping board, then use a fork to blend them thoroughly into the meat. Heat oven to 350° F. Fill a wet ceramic, Teflon, or glass loaf pan with a bit less than half the pâté mixture. Lay the 2 sausages side by side down the center of the mold, then gently fill in sides and cover sausages with the rest of the mixture. The sausages should be centered in the loaf.

Cover with foil and bake in the center of the oven for 2 hours. Chill thoroughly before slicing. Refrigerated, it keeps 1 week. Frozen, it keeps 3 months.

Easy Lamb Stew

6 SERVINGS

Put it together at odd moments over the afternoon.

3 pounds shoulder, shanks, or meaty neck of lamb, cut in
*   1-inch-thick slices, or smaller cuts, if desired*
1 onion, coarsely chopped
3 cloves of garlic, minced
2 unpeeled carrots, in thin rounds
¼ cup dry red wine
1 28-ounce can of cheapest tomatoes
6 small unpeeled potatoes, quartered
1½ pounds green beans, zucchini, or frozen Italian green
*   beans*
6 ounces mushrooms, quartered, optional
2 tablespoons oil, optional
Salt and fresh ground pepper, to taste

Trim all visible fat from the lamb. Place lamb, onion, garlic, carrots, and wine in a Dutch oven. Break up the tomatoes with your fingers and add them and their juices; stir to mix ingredients, then cover and set over very low heat. Simmer about 3 hours, shaking the pot occasionally. When the lamb is very tender, turn off heat.

If there is much fat floating on the juices, ladle into a jar and remove accumulation at the top, then return juices to the pot. Or, if you wish to make this in advance, just refrigerate, covered, then lift off the congealed fat before you reheat.

When convenient, simmer the potatoes in a small covered pot in water barely to cover until tender. Lift out potatoes and set aside in a covered dish, then pour their water into a medium-sized skillet. Have the green beans trimmed and snapped in half, the zucchini cut into 1-inch chunks, or the Italian beans thawed. Simmer vegetables in the skillet, covered, over high heat until tender-crisp. (Keep an eye on them, and add water if they're in danger of burning.) At the same time, if mushrooms were reasonably priced, sauté them briefly in a small skillet over high heat in oil, stirring frequently, until they take on color. Add potatoes, green vegetables and pot liquor, mushrooms and their juices to the stew, stirring gently to mix. Taste for salt and pepper, then set over low heat until stew comes to a simmer, about 30 minutes.

For guests, have crisp hot rolls for sopping up the sauce and a light red wine. Salad can be whole leaves of romaine set beside small bowls of Silky French Dressing for dipping. And for dessert, vanilla ice cream with blackberry preserves spooned over.

Perry's Oxtail Pot

6 SERVINGS

Oxtails have a unique flavor, even though they may not be the meatiest of cuts. They're fun to eat, and this stew makes a cozy dinner for the family on an Occasion, or for guests.

Oxtails:
   3 whole oxtails (about 5 pounds) cut in 1-inch-thick rounds
   2 unpeeled carrots, coarsely chopped
   2 onions, coarsely chopped
   1 large, leafy stalk of celery, coarsely chopped
   2 cloves of garlic, minced
   Stalks of 2 green onions, coarsely chopped
   ½ cup oil
   About ¾ cup unsifted rice flour or white flour
   1 teaspoon paprika
   1¼ teaspoons fresh ground pepper
   2 generous handfuls of chopped parsley
   ½ bay leaf, crumbled
   1 tablespoon fresh or 1 teaspoon dried thyme leaves
   6 crushed juniper berries or 2 tablespoons gin
   Pinch of ground clove
   Dash or 2 of Tabasco or ½ teaspoon taco sauce

1½ cups (12 ounces) *undiluted canned beef broth
diluted equally with water, or 3 cups homemade beef
broth (see* Pot-au-Feu *broth, p. 37)*
1 *to 3 cups dry red wine, or 4 to 6 cups beef broth and
¼ cup lemon juice*
Flour paste:
2 *parts flour*
1 *part water*
Garnish vegetables:
1½ *pounds young zucchini or green beans*
16 *young unpeeled carrots*
14 *small or 8 medium peeled new or red potatoes*
1 *pound boiling onions*
12 *fresh peeled or 56 ounces of canned good-quality
drained tomatoes*
10 *ounces frozen or 2¼ pounds fresh peas*
Salt and fresh ground pepper, to taste

The oxtails: Trim oxtails of fat. In a large heavy skillet over medium-high heat, sauté the carrots, onions, celery, garlic, and onion stalks in ¼ cup of the oil until lightly browned. Lift out and set aside on waxed paper. Shake the oxtails in a paper bag with the flour, paprika, and ¼ teaspoon of the pepper. Heat the remaining oil and brown the meat on all sides over low heat.

In a large deep Dutch oven, earthenware if you have it, spread the browned vegetables on the bottom and arrange meat on top. Sprinkle over 1 handful of the parsley (wrap the rest in plastic film and refrigerate), the bay, thyme, juniper or gin, clove, Tabasco, and remaining pepper. Set oven to 500° F. Add 3 cups beef broth to browning skillet, and deglaze the pan, scraping out the good little bits, over medium heat. Pour this over the meat, then add wine or broth and lemon juice—just enough to cover.

Sealing the pot: Mix a large batch of sturdy but slightly sticky dough of flour and water. On a floured board, roll it into a broad rope long enough to fit around the rim of your casserole. Moisten the rim, then stick the rope on top of it; fit on the lid so the dough squashes out from beneath it.

Moisten the edge of the lid, then firmly press the dough up over it, thus sealing the pot. Allow no possible place for steam to break through. This is the classic means of sealing a pot which will cook a long, slow time—and sealing the flavors and juices in. However, be prepared for frustration, because steam does drive trains, after all, and it almost always bursts through. Just keep patching!

Baking the meat: Place pot in the oven on the lowest rack for about 15 minutes, or until you hear the first bubble. Listen carefully; it mustn't boil. Turn the heat down to 200° F, shake the pot a bit to mix everything up, and bake undisturbed 8 to 10 or even 12 hours. (You may bake it at 275° for about 5 hours instead, but the meat won't have the same flavor or texture.) Remove from oven, cool, and remove the seal with a knife. Now set aside the oxtails while you purée the sauce through a sieve or fine blade of a food mill.

Return the meat and sauce to the pot, and if possible, chill (up to 2 days) to let the flavors marry. Remove fat. Bring to room temperature before reheating.

The garnish vegetables: At some point before reheating the pot, cut zucchini, carrots, and potatoes into 1-inch chunks (snap the green beans, if used, in half after trimming); blanch or steam each vegetable until tender-crisp. Chop the tomatoes coarsely and thaw frozen peas, or blanch fresh peas.

One and one-quarter hours before serving, set oven to 325°. Gently mix the garnish vegetables into the pot. Taste the sauce for salt and pepper, then bake, covered, shaking the pot gently now and then. It will take about 1 hour to heat up.

Serve sprinkled with the reserved parsley. Buttered broad egg noodles are what's wanted beneath the stew, French bread, Burgundy, a light *salade de saison,* and then an apple crisp for dessert.

Breast of Lamb, Rue Dante

(Persian roasted lamb breast)
ABOUT 6 SERVINGS

As a student in Paris, I often ate at a small Left Bank restaurant that served marvelous shish kebab. Later, I recreated the taste—a pungent, golden sauce that balances the sweet meat of lamb. Of course it's superb with chunks of meat threaded on skewers and grilled. But it's even more useful for thick sheets of lamb breast, generously basted and slowly roasted to crisp and savory succulence.

> *5 pounds lamb breast or smaller riblets, in sheets*
> *½ cup oil*
> *½ cup lemon juice (about 4 lemons)*
> *1 small, whole dried hot red pepper, no seeds*
> *1 small onion, finely chopped*
> *2 teaspoons powdered ginger*
> *2 teaspoons turmeric*
> *1 teaspoon powdered or 2 teaspoons seeds of coriander*
> *½ teaspoon ground allspice*
> *2 cloves of garlic, minced*
> *Salt and fresh ground pepper, to taste*

Mix all ingredients except lamb, salt, and pepper in a flat dish large enough to accommodate the meat. Lay in and marinate the meat for several hours at room temperature, turning frequently. To roast, heat oven to 275° F. Lay the sheets of lamb on cake racks set on a rimmed baking pan with hot water beneath, but not touching them. Roast in the center of the oven 2 hours; strain the marinade and baste the meat now and then; turn meat once.

Serve on a bed of baked brown rice (use the marinade onion in the rice) surrounded by green beans and tomatoes. A light red wine would be thirst quenching, and a light tossed salad would be good afterward. For dessert, something as simple as fresh peaches or any juicy fruit in season mantled with thick plain yogurt.

Jellied Beef

ABOUT 8 MAIN-DISH SERVINGS

The Scandinavians make elegant stiff aspics of chopped simmered veal, as good on dark bread for open-faced sandwiches as on plates with lettuce and dilled potatoes. Here is my version, made with cheapest beef. It is a marvelous "cold cut" to keep on hand, a comforting resource against emergencies, and a fine dinner party hors d'oeuvre.

> 3½ pounds meaty *beef neck bones*
> 2 *pounds meatless beef shank soup bones; ask the butcher to crack them*
> 1 *large unpeeled onion, quartered*
> 2 *unpeeled carrots, in chunks*
> 1 *large leafy stalk of celery, cut up*
> ½ *bunch of parsley, stems included*
> 2 *large cloves of garlic, peeled and mashed*
> 6-inch *length of orange zest (peel with no pith, cut with a vegetable peeler)*
> 1 *bay leaf*
> 8 *peppercorns*
> 6 *beef bouillon cubes*
> 1½ *cups dry red wine*
> 2 *quarts water*
> 1 *bunch parsley*
> 1 *tablespoon unflavored gelatin, or more as needed*
> 2 *tablespoons dry sherry*

In a large soup pot over high heat, bring to a simmer all ingredients except 1 bunch parsley, gelatin, and sherry. Simmer very gently, covered, for 2½ hours, or until the meat is very tender. Pour through a strainer into a bowl. Set aside the meaty bones and discard remaining ingredients in sieve. Remove fat from broth. Measure the broth and make note of the amount. Return broth to the pot, bring to a boil over high heat and boil while you cut the meat from the neck bones. Chop meat into smallish (not too fine) pieces.

Measure the meat, packing loosely. You'll need 1 cup more broth than meat—simmer down the broth accordingly. You'll need about one-sixth as much finely chopped parsley as meat, so remove stems from the parsley and start chopping. If you found meaty bones, you'll have about 3 cups of meat; so simmer the broth to 4 cups, and chop the parsley to measure ½ cup. Soak the gelatin in the sherry in a small cup; if you will be working with less than 4 cups broth, use the same 2 tablespoons of sherry called for, but reduce gelatin proportionately.

In a bowl, lightly toss the meat and parsley together to blend, then wet a metal mold (capacity should be the total of your ingredients) and spread the mixture in the mold. When the broth has reduced to the right measure, add the sherried gelatin and stir over low heat until the gelatin has thoroughly dissolved. Place a damp cloth in a colander and slowly pour the broth through it, to clarify a little. Taste for salt. Now very slowly pour the broth over the meat in the mold, disturbing it as little as possible. Cover tightly and refrigerate until set, about 6 hours. It will keep about 1 week.

To serve, scrape off any flecks of fat on top, run a knife around the sides of the mold, dip in hot water briefly, then turn onto a serving dish. Slice in fairly thick slabs—and don't be dismayed if it doesn't always hold together. It still tastes superb.

For a light luncheon or supper, this might be served Swedish fashion, on thin brown bread over a lettuce leaf, garnished with slices of hard-cooked eggs and wedges of tomatoes, with cool potatoes in their jackets dusted with dill on the side. Have a crisp rosé wine, and for dessert, fresh or canned poached pears sprinkled with fresh chopped or dried leaves of mint, and cookies.

Pieds de Porc Sainte Ménéhould

(Crisp grilled pork trotters)
COUNT I TROTTER PER SERVING

In France, this dish is regarded as such a delicacy that, like grilled chicken at many of our markets, it is sold ready-cooked at a handsome price. If you've never tasted trotters, the first couple of bites might be baffling. But then the contrast between crisp crumbed outside and soft gelatinous inside is delicious. They are rich. The French regard these as hors d'oeuvres, but for my part, I couldn't eat anything substantial afterward (which makes them that much more economical).

Preparing this dish, there is a delicate broth for a bonus.

Pork trotters, split lengthwise
Seasonings:
    Cut-up onion
    Stalks of green onions
    Leafy celery tips
    Parsley
    Peppercorns
    Bay leaf
White vinegar
Melted margarine
Fine dry bread crumbs (unseasoned), lots
Parsley furls

Cooking the trotters: Rub trotters under cold running water until almost squeaky clean, then fit halves back together and roll tightly in a single layer of cheesecloth or scrupulously clean cloth tying tightly at ends and around the middle like a sausage. Lay in bottom of a deep pot, add seasonings (for proportions, follow Old-Fashioned Chicken Soup recipe (see p. 30), generally; you want a flavorful trotter, but you don't want to cook a cheap cut with lots of costly vegetables), add water to cover, and just a splash of vinegar to make the water tart. Cover, set over medium heat, bring to a boil slowly, then reduce heat so water just trembles. Poach trotters until a fork tests them tender, from 2 to 4 hours; remove from pot. When bundles are cool enough to handle, remove cloth and lay each half on a platter or tray; cover and chill.

Grilling the trotters: Arrange pieces on an oiled baking sheet, then brush all over with melted margarine. Sprinkle copiously on all sides with dry bread crumbs—you want as thick a coating as will stick, so pat it down firmly. You may cover and chill again, if you like. Pre-heat oven to 350° F and heat trotters in the center of the oven for from 15 to 25 minutes, depending how cold they are. Raise heat to broiling, then slip trotters about 5 inches beneath the heat and broil until a rich dark brown, about 3 or 4 minutes—the skin pops under such heat, so keep your distance. Take out sheet, turn trotters over, sprinkle with more crumbs, then sprinkle the baking sheet itself with bread crumbs, so you'll have extra toasted crumbs for the trotters. Return to broiler and brown as before; keep an eye on them and stir up extra crumbs if they brown too fast.

Transfer trotters and crumbs sprinkled over to a hot platter and garnish quickly with parsley. Serve with a brisk mustard (Dijon, if you have it), some form of potato, whipped, perhaps, mixed lettuce and spinach salad, and pickled beets. Cold beer or dry white wine is wanted, and for dessert, something made with milk, for the nutrition supplement—rice pudding, or an old-fashioned tapioca.

The leftover broth: To make a rich, delicate-yet-piquant broth you could serve as a light first course, strain the cooking stock into a smaller pot. Add about ½ bunch of parsley (stems included) and ¼ pound of ground beef for every 3 trotters you simmered. Simmer gently all day long, or at least 8 hours, then add a fair amount of salt to heighten flavor. Strain, then serve hot or cold, jellied. A Chinese friend adds a handful of raw peanuts to this soup before serving—good idea.

Boeuf à la Cuillère

(Braised beef garnished with vegetables)
10 SERVINGS

This is a model of braised beef: one of the least expensive cuts of beef splendidly garnished, superbly sauced, the meat so tender you can eat it with a spoon. The cooking isn't complicated, but it involves a number of steps—just spread them over two or three days. The composition is completely arranged ahead of time, and only needs last minute warming in the oven.

Marinade:
   3 *unpeeled carrots, chopped medium fine*
   3 *leafy stalks of celery, chopped medium fine*
   2 *onions, chopped medium fine*
   4 *large cloves of garlic, minced*
   ¼ *cup chopped parsley*
   4 *berries or a good pinch of ground allspice*
   2 *bay leaves, crumbled*
   6 *cups (48 ounces) dry red wine*
   ⅔ *cup light-tasting oil*
Beef:
   7 *pounds cheapest lean beef, bone-in chuck roast*
   ¼ *cup light-tasting oil*
   1½ *teaspoons fresh or ½ teaspoon dried thyme leaves*
   2 *split calves' feet (ordered well in advance, the butcher can get them for you)*
   2 *10½-ounce cans beef consommé; dilute equally with water*
Garnish vegetables:
   2 *pounds fresh young green beans*
   3½ *pounds small boiling potatoes*
   3 *dozen tender young unpeeled carrots*
   1½ *pounds peeled boiling onions*
   1 *cup (8 ounces) margarine*
   Coarse (kosher) or regular salt

Sauce:
   1 tablespoon cornstarch
   2 tablespoons Madeira wine
   Salt and fresh ground pepper, to taste
   1 generous bunch parsley or watercress

Marinating the beef: Trim meat of fat, then arrange into a compact shape and tie firmly with string. Mix together the carrots, celery, onions, garlic, parsley, allspice, and bay; there should be a generous 4½ cups. In a dish just large enough to hold the meat, arrange half the vegetables over the bottom. Lay on the meat, blanket with remaining vegetables, then just cover with wine and oil. Cover tightly with plastic film and refrigerate from 6 hours to 3 days.

Cooking the beef: The day before serving, lift beef out and dry well with paper towels. Pass marinade through strainer into a heavy skillet; pat the vegetables in the strainer dry and set aside. Simmer the marinade over high heat until it measures 3½ cups. At the same time, in a 7- to 8-quart Dutch oven (or casserole that will take direct heat), heat 2 tablespoons of the oil and sauté the marinade vegetables, stirring frequently until they color—about 15 minutes. Mix in the thyme, and set vegetables aside. Heat 2 more tablespoons of oil in the casserole and brown the calves' feet nicely; set them aside. In the same oil, brown the beef on all sides over medium-high heat.

Set oven to 275° F. Lift up the beef and spread half the vegetables on the bottom of the casserole. Set the calves' feet around the meat, then sprinkle with the remaining vegetables. Stir diluted consommé into the reduced marinade and pour it over the meat; it should just cover. Bring to a simmer on top of the stove. Cover tightly with 1 sheet of heavy foil crimped against the dish, and then the lid, or 2 sheets of heavy foil. Set on the lowest rack in the oven and braise undisturbed 4 or 5 hours, until very tender. (Or, like the oxtails, you could bake it at 500° F 15 minutes, then at 200° 8 to 10 hours.)

When cool enough to handle, remove the calves' feet, the

string on the roast, and the bones. Turn the meat over, cover, cool and refrigerate until the next day or until chilled.

Blanching the vegetables: The day of the dinner, blanch the vegetables whenever it's convenient. Bring a large pot of water to boil over highest heat as you nip the stem ends only off the beans and string them, if necessary. Dump in the beans, cover, and blanch. Peel the potatoes and round the edges with a vegetable peeler to plum size. Blanch potatoes in the bean water. Cut the carrots at the *top* end into equal lengths (cook the potato and carrot trimmings in some of the blanching water to make a cup or two of puréed soup); blanch them next. Peel the onions by pouring some of the boiling water over them and steeping them 2 or 3 minutes; drain, peel, then cut an X at the root end to hold their layers together. Blanch until tender-crisp. Dry all vegetables thoroughly; keep covered.

Glazing the vegetables: Next step, whenever convenient, is as follows. In your largest skillet, over medium-high heat, melt a good lump of the margarine. Sauté the green beans, stirring constantly with a rubber scraper, until they have a nice glaze but are still bright green; remove them to a plate, sprinkle with a bit of coarse salt. Add more margarine to the pan and then the carrots; sauté and shake the skillet this time until the carrots are gilded here and there, but not browned; remove them also to a plate, lightly sprinkle with salt. More margarine and now the onions, shaking the skillet until they are golden, too. Remove and lightly salt them. Add the potatoes and the rest of the margarine, and shake and turn them until they are buttery gold. Salt lightly and set aside. Cover all the vegetables.

Finishing the sauce: Remove the fat from the top of the dish, and warm up the casserole over low heat until you can lift out all the beef and place it on a board. Raise the heat under the sauce and reduce it to 4 cups. In a small bowl, mix the cornstarch and Madeira. Keep the sauce in the measuring pitcher while you turn the Madeira mixture into the casserole and use it to loosen all the deep burnished bits around the rim of the pot. Add the sauce and whisk over medium heat until it has thickened. Taste for salt and pepper.

As the sauce reduces, ease the meat into slices with a sharp knife as best you can, letting one portion rest against another. Shape into a tidy rectangle and arrange it in the center of a very large shallow baking dish (an oval gratin dish is ideal, but the casserole you cooked it in would probably be fine, too). Spoon about one-fourth of the sauce over and under each portion of meat until it is saturated. Put remainder of sauce in a small pot.

Arranging the dish: Now lay the green beans to one side of the meat, all going the same way. Set the carrots, also in a one-way bundle, on the other side. Tuck the potatoes beside the beans at one end of the dish and the onions beside the carrots at the other end. Cover tightly with foil and keep in a cool place (not the refrigerator, which is too cold and may dry things out at this point) until 50 minutes before serving.

Serving: One hour before dinner set the oven to 350° F; 10 minutes later, set the dish in, covered, on the lowest rack. Every 15 minutes, gently poke the vegetables with a rubber scraper to be sure they're warming up uniformly. Heat the sauce on top of the stove. Remove the foil, garnish the dish with flourishes of parsley or watercress, and bring to the table. Have the sauce in its own heated bowl, and ladle over the meat and potatoes as you serve.

Offer more of the red wine you made the sauce with, and some crisp dill pickles and French bread. A *salade de saison* ought to follow. Dessert could be a fine apple tart.

Cold Braised Beef

You know, braised beef is almost better the next day, cold. It's a classic dish for warm weather.

Prepare everything in the same way as in the preceding recipe, with the following exceptions. Do not glaze the vegetables in the margarine, but blanch them a few minutes longer, until tender. Arrange them as directed beside the

meat. Do not thicken the sauce with cornstarch; simply reduce it until thick, stir in the Madeira, taste for salt and
pepper, then pour all the sauce over the meat and vegetables
arranged in a deeper platter. The gelatin from the calves'
feet will thicken it handsomely when cold.

Chill, very well covered, until 15 minutes before serving
time. Then garnish with parsley or watercress and cuts of
lemon—or orange, for a Provençale touch. The same menu
accompaniments as above apply.

Good Roast Beef, Veal, Lamb, and Pork

See budget notes on individual meats at the beginning of
this section for recommendations of cuts to buy for dry-roast-
ing.

Roast the meat uncovered, fat side up, in a pan or casserole (earthenware adds a particularly pleasant flavor).
For brownest meat, use a shallow baking pan; for juiciest meat, the pan can be almost as deep as the meat is
high. One or two each of carrots, celery, onions, garlic, and
parsley sprigs, all chopped medium fine, add flavor to the
juices if scattered on the bottom of the pan. You can baste
the roast occasionally with pan juices, if you like, but a good
covering of fat on top makes basting really unnecessary.
Roast whole unpeeled potatoes or other root vegetables on
the oven rack at the same time—or set peeled root vegetables in the pan with the meat, to soak up the drippings (fattening and unhealthy, but so good!). Serve roast beef with
Burgundy, zinfandel, or claret; roast veal with zinfandel or
claret; roast lamb with claret; and roast pork with rosé or
Chablis. Add a mixed green and vegetable salad, crisp rolls
for company, and for dessert, prunes steeped in medium-
dry sherry, port, or Marsala in a crock on the counter for
3 weeks, served in their juices with crème fraîche. (Then
renew the crock, to keep a constant source.)

NOTE: Should you ever find yourself with a roast of pork
topped with a very thick white blanket of fat, there is an

English manner for it that makes a wicked but marvelous treat. Use a sharp knife or single-edge razor to score the fat diagonally, so the lines run long as possible and as close together as you can make them; cut almost down to the meat, but not quite. As the pork roasts (do not baste), fat will melt down between the wafers, resulting in a stand of luscious fine cracklings that you include as you carve the meat. To assure a good crisping start, roast at 400° F for 10 or 15 minutes and then turn the heat to a little under 325° and continue roasting according to the following key.

Key to roasting meat: Times can be no more than approximate. Calculate the maximum minutes for the oven temperature you prefer, and then you can always lower the oven heat if the meat appears to be finishing too soon. Remove roast from oven when cooked slightly less than desired; meat will finish cooking as it rests.

Good Grade meat should be roasted at 275° F; all meat profits from the slow heat.

The key is for bone-in meat; add 5 to 10 minutes per pound for boneless cuts.

Add 10 to 20 minutes to the total time so juices can settle at room temperature before serving. Then slice all meat as thin as possible for maximum tenderness.

MEAT	DESCRIPTION	DEGREES ON MEAT THERMOMETER	DEGREES OF OVEN HEAT	MINUTES PER POUND*
Beef	Very rare	125°	275°—325°	19—13
Beef	Rare	130°—135°	275°—325°	20—14
Lamb	Pink	140°—145°	325°	15—17
Beef	Medium rare	140°	275°—325°	21—15
Beef	Medium	150°—160°	275°—325°	24—18
Lamb	Medium well	155°—160°	325°	20—25
Lamb Pork Veal	Well-done	170°	325°	30—35

* Slower oven takes more time; minutes are proportionate to heat.

Just as pork and veal must *always* be roasted well-done, beef should *never* be well-done—it loses quality past 160°. Lamb, if those you're serving will accept the European standard, is infinitely juicier on the pink side. (And temperature for pork has come down 15 degrees in recent years, because research has proved that 170° is more than hot enough to kill any parasites in the meat; it's much juicier.)

Beef Steaks, Lamb Chops, and Hamburgers au Poivre

In French cuisine, this elegant treatment is reserved for finest tenderloin of beef. But why not share the wealth with more modest meats? They are far juicier cooked this way than broiled.

Buy meat or shape patties (with a light hand) about ¾-inch thick. Coarsely crush whole peppercorns with a mortar and pestle or under a heavy skillet on a chopping board. Trim solid meat of excess fat, pat dry, rub with cut clove of garlic, then brush lightly with oil. The ground meat doesn't need this. Sprinkle about ¼ teaspoon of the cracked pepper over each side of the meat (or up to ½ teaspoon), then press in gently. Cover and let flavors marry at least 1 hour at room temperature or overnight in the refrigerator.

Have accompanying dishes almost ready before you begin, because meat should not be kept waiting. Count about 10 to 12 minutes from start to finish of cooking meat.

To pan-broil: Set a dry ridged or flat cast iron skillet over high heat until just below smoking hot. Meanwhile, sprinkle the meat lightly on both sides with coarse (kosher) salt. Lay in the meat without crowding and sear (brown or score, to seal in juices) 1 to 2 minutes; turn with pancake turner or tongs and sear on other side. At once turn heat to medium-high and continue cooking, uncovered, turning frequently, until rare or medium rare. Remove to a hot serving platter, dot with parsley butter, and serve.

To sauté: Cover the bottom of a flat, heavy skillet with equal parts oil and melted margarine; heat over medium-high heat until it begins to sizzle. Lay in the meat without crowding and shake the pan over the burner to butter the meat. Sauté 3 to 4 minutes (for rare to medium rare), uncovered, then turn with pancake turner or tongs. Repeat on second side, test for doneness. Remove meat to a hot serving platter, dot with parsley butter, or keep warm while you deglaze the pan as explained below.

Parsley butter: Cream together equal measures of minced parsley and softened margarine. Any fresh herb can substitute (or any dried herb), but adjust proportions for balance. Set in knobs on cooked meats, poultry, fish, vegetables, eggs, what-you-will.

To deglaze the pan: Pour off all but a film of fat from the pan, add a handful of minced green onion, a speck of minced garlic, and a slosh of dry vermouth or red wine. Turn heat to high and scrape up the browned bits in the pan while the sauce reduces slightly. Remove from heat, swirl in a knob of margarine, then pour over the meat and serve.

See roast meat recipe for wine recommendations. For accompaniments, any grilled vegetable and any form of potato would be excellent, with French bread, and salad to follow. Dessert could be anything from chocolate cake to lemon *sherbet* to slabs of watermelon or fruit in season.

Good Braised Pork Steaks and Chops

Trim all but a thin layer of fat from the meat. Brown on both sides in a heavy skillet in a little oil over medium-high heat, then reduce heat to low. Add a little minced garlic and a knob of margarine, cover and shake the skillet and let braise 20 to 30 minutes, or until meat tests done. Turn once, and watch meat doesn't cook dry. Sprinkle with salt and pepper and remove to a hot platter. Deglaze the skillet over high heat with a slosh of dry white wine, vermouth, or apple juice (see instructions in preceding recipe); when juices have reduced to the desired consistency, pour over the meat, and serve with warm applesauce, buttered carrots, parsley-flecked simmered potatoes, dry white wine, and for dessert, saltine crackers to be spread with fresh cream cheese and strawberry jelly.

Beefsteak and Kidney Pie, Lodge Hill Cottage

8 SERVINGS

I learned to make this delectable dish while living in Medmenham ("Med'num"), in Buckinghamshire ("Bucks"), England. The recipe translates into Yankee very well.

2 pounds boneless best buy in braising beef (see p. 113)
1½ pounds beef kidneys, well rinsed
¼ cup oil
2 onions, coarsely chopped
1½ cups (12 ounces) undiluted canned beef broth
2 teaspoons Worcestershire or Chinese oyster sauce
Fresh ground pepper, to taste
2 tablespoons margarine, optional
2 tablespoons flour, optional
Salt to taste
1 package petite frozen peas
2 tablespoons minced parsley
½ recipe Best Pie Pastry (see p. 278)

The meat: Trim off all fat and gristle, then cut the beef into 2-inch chunks. Remove the membrane of the kidneys, then use kitchen scissors to "butterfly" them—cut not quite all the way through from the outside edge to the center, then pull open. Snip out the hard white centers and vascular membrane, then cut kidneys into pieces the same size as the chunks of beef.

In a medium-sized Dutch oven or heavy pot over medium heat, heat 2 tablespoons of the oil and sauté the onions until golden, stirring often. Add the beef and kidneys and stir in enough beef broth to barely cover; add the Worcestershire or oyster sauce and a grind or two of pepper. Bring to a slow simmer, cover, turn heat to lowest, and simmer gently for 1½ hours, or until all the meat is tender when tested with a kitchen fork.

The sauce: When cooked, if you like a thicker sauce, rub the margarine and flour into a paste in a small dish. This is called *beurre manié.* Drain the sauce from the meats into a small saucepan and bring it to a gentle simmer. Drop a small knob of the *beurre manié* on top of the sauce, then stir gently until the sauce thickens. Add the paste knob by knob until you reach the consistency you like; then stop simmering. Return the sauce to the meat, and stir to blend. Taste for salt and pepper. You may refrigerate this until the next day, if need be; but just a few hours is better. Roll pastry into a circle ⅛ inch thick and chill, covered, on a plate.

The pie: Bring meats to room temperature, and about 50 minutes before serving, set oven to 425° F. Arrange meat in a 2-quart deep dish, and mix gently with the frozen peas (they will thaw in the oven; if bigger peas are used, they must be thawed, however) and chopped parsley. Cover with the pastry, trim the edges to 1 inch, ruffle this border between thumb and forefinger, cut a pattern for vents on top, and bake 15 minutes. Lower heat to 375° F and bake another 20 minutes, or until the sauce bubbles through the golden crust.

Serve with a dish of buttersilk carrots served without the chopped parsley, homemade bread if possible, claret or any dry red wine, and a *salade de saison* after. Dessert may be vanilla ice cream softened and flavored with applesauce or chopped sautéed apples, then frozen in a bowl until served.

Coeur en Couronne

(Tender beef heart with gravy in a whipped potato ring)
6 SERVINGS

An "I'm glad you didn't tell me before I took my second helping" sort of dish. Buttermilk soaks out the characteristic strong flavor while tenderizing the tough muscle; the meat tastes like familiar cooked beef.

1½ pounds beef heart, trimmed of fat
Buttermilk or sour milk to cover, a generous 1 cupful
2 large onions, chopped
4 cloves of garlic, minced
3 tablespoons oil
10-ounce can of mushroom, onion, or beef gravy
¼ teaspoon powdered ginger
Salt and fresh ground pepper, to taste
Recipe for Whipped Potatoes (see p. 97) using 6 large
*   potatoes*
Generous handful of chopped parsley

Lay the meat in a flat baking dish, then cover a bit more than halfway with the milk. Soak in a cool place for at least 1 hour, turning every ½ hour or so (it will keep overnight). About 1½ hours before serving, set the onions and garlic to sauté in the oil in a large skillet over medium heat while you cut the meat into uniform ¼-inch dice. Add the meat to the skillet and toss to blend. Stir in the gravy, cover the pan and turn heat to lowest. Simmer, stirring frequently, for about 45 or 50 minutes, or until the meat is tender. Gravy will thin down after cooking awhile, then thicken again; you may want to add a splash of water if it gets too thick. Stir in ginger, then taste for salt and pepper.

While the meat cooks, simmer, purée, and whip the potatoes. Oil a 6-cup ring mold copiously, then smooth in the purée. Cover with foil and set in a 300° F oven to keep warm. If you haven't a ring mold, just keep the potatoes warm in a bowl in the oven.

To serve, either turn out the potatoes from the mold onto

a heated platter, or drop from a kitchen spoon in the shape of a ring. Heap the meat in sauce in the center of the ring, make a border of chopped parsley around the outside of the potatoes, and serve. Add a fresh butter-steamed green vegetable in season, such as green beans, zucchini, or broccoli, a lightly dressed salad and a light red wine. For dessert, fresh poached or canned pears sprinkled with nutmeg (and splashed with white port, if for guests).

Trippa alla Milanese

(Tripe in a light Italian sauce)
8 SERVINGS

Tripe is one of the best value-for-money meats there is. No waste, scant fat, rich nutrition, good flavor, interesting texture, all for comparatively little money. We were first served this at a dinner party—here is Zena Cornin's savory dish for adventurous gourmets.

> 2 *pounds honeycomb beef or veal tripe (ask the butcher*
> *how much it has been steamed)*
> 2 *ounces salt pork*
> 4 *large cloves of garlic*
> 1 *generous bunch of parsley (or 2 skinny bunches),*
> *no stems*
> 6 *tablespoons tomato paste (buy 1 small can)*
> ¾ *teaspoon fresh chopped or ¼ teaspoon dried oregano*
> *Pinch of ground allspice*
> ¾ *cup dry vermouth or white wine*
> 2 *cups light chicken broth from powder or cubes*
> *Lemon juice, to taste*
> *Fresh ground pepper, to taste*
> *Parmesan*

On your chopping board, chop the salt pork, garlic, and parsley together so finely that they blend into a paste. Turn into a Dutch oven and warm over low heat while you rinse the tripe, then use scissors to cut it into strips about ⅝ inch by 2 inches. If there is any fat on the tripe, simply scrape it off. Blend tomato paste, oregano, and allspice into the pot, then add the tripe. Stir to mix well, then let simmer about 15 minutes until meat has exuded some of its juices. Stir in the vermouth or wine, and then the broth. Cover, turn heat to lowest, and simmer 2 hours, stirring occasionally. The tripe should be *al dente*—succulent but a bit chewy. You may set the pot aside in a cool place now until needed.

To finish, warm pot gently, then taste—a little lemon juice and a generous amount of pepper will give point to the sauce. It probably won't need salt.

Serve in large soup bowls over *tagliatelle* (long noodles) boiled *al dente*—1½ recipes of pasta (see p. 215) cut ¼-inch wide, or 1 pound store-bought. Shower with Parmesan. You can add fresh or frozen peas to the tripe the last 10 minutes, if you wish. Or you can serve the tripe over boiled white beans instead of pasta. The Milanese prefer it over rice, but it's rather a regional taste.

To complete this excellent dinner, have plenty of fresh Italian or French bread, a cold, crisp dry white wine, and afterward, a simple green salad. If the budget allows, dessert could be a wedge or round of good cheese, firm apples, and melting pears—and a basket of shortbread with coffee.

Chicken and Turkey

The chickens I buy from John and Vera's poultry shop have scratched for their mash on real earth. They have breathed fresh air and have taken mild exercise, and their meat is butter-plump and sweet. I pay more for these chickens, but not that much more. Their flavor is worth double the price of supermarket chickens grown up one to a bin beneath light bulbs. Sometimes, there just isn't a way to spend less and get more. Surely somewhere in your area there are naturally raised chickens—try to find them.

Budget notes on buying poultry

How to judge tender poultry at the market? Press the breastbone; it should be pliable. The skin should be moist. And if you can bend back the wingtip, it, too, should be pliable. Also choose the breastiest chicken or turkey of the lot.

What is the best value for money in frying chicken? In my own abashedly unscientific consumer's report, I found: for 3 pounds of pure meat, buy 5 pounds of breasts, 6 pounds of thighs or 8½ pounds uncut chicken. In my part of the country, the breasts and thighs came to about the same price. The whole uncut chicken cost 20 per cent less, because it saved the butcher's labor. Every minute of his time you don't have to subsidize buys you a couple of eggs.

If you can ever buy extra-large packages of mixed pieces at a lower price per pound than even whole uncut chicken, do so. Match up the pieces and freeze them until you have enough to make a dish all of drumsticks, or thighs, or wings, or what-not. It is always best to cook just light or just dark meat when you can; light meat cooks faster and begins going dry while waiting for dark meat to finish.

Another rule broken: they cost more per pound, but breasts are a good buy for entertaining. Pound half a breast into a thin scallop, and any veal scallopine recipe will suit it. A friendly butcher will do it for you, if you give him notice and a dazzling smile.

Stewing hens. The good old girls are becoming a thing of the past; fryers are more economical to raise (they're in and out faster). When you want a chicken for the pot, use a large roasting hen, but cook it one-third the time.

For both chicken and turkey, always buy the largest bird you can use. You get more meat in proportion to bone in bigger birds because generally speaking, after a certain point, the bony frame of a bird holds its size while the meat just keeps filling out around it. To serve a lot of people, therefore, a roaster is a better buy than a fryer, if the price per pound is at all close.

Fresh or frozen? Often there are bargains in the freezer case. In turkeys, for example. For state occasions, I roast only fresh perfect birds. In between times, however, I buy the much cheaper U.S.D.A. Inspected but not Grade A frozen turkeys. They are not Grade A because the poor chaps have some part missing: A mechanism on the assembly line that cleans and plucks the birds sometimes goes awry, and skin gets torn or various parts fly off. The turkeys taste just fine.

Don't buy the self-basting frozen turkeys, the sorts with oil or fat injected into the meat by the packer. Not only is it not what you would use to baste your bird, but you are again paying for somebody else's labor. The recipe in this chapter roasts turkey to the greatest succulence imaginable, so you do the basting, and use the money you've saved to buy the wine for dinner.

How to cut a big turkey into useful small parts: If you have a freezer (or access to a shelf of one), no matter what size your family, you can take advantage of the economy of a very big Tom, especially whenever the price is very low. If it's a fresh turkey, you can divide it up and freeze it for three or four different meals, any way you wish. If it's a frozen turkey, then your options are narrowed, but still wonderfully varied.

First thing is to find yourself a darling of a butcher. Second thing is to approach him about this dividing business when he's not rushed; it will take his time and cooperation, although you *can* do most of it yourself, if you must. If it's a frozen turkey, say one of the not-Grade-A boys, ask the butcher to let it thaw slowly in his refrigerator, with your name on it. Once defrosted, and at his convenience—and this is the same if the turkey's fresh—ask him to cut it up in any combination you like:

BREAST—The herbal boned breast of turkey roast (see p. 182) is, I think, the best imaginable way to deal with this meat. Another time, you could ask the butcher for 1½-inch-thick crosswise-cut steaks from the breast for grilling. Or simply have the forequarters of the turkey cut into two small white-meat roasts, with the wings removed.

HINDQUARTERS—By all means, ask your butcher to be good enough, the last thing he does before he cleans his meat grinder, to pull out the tendons from one drumstick, and then put the leg and thigh meat of one hindquarter through his grinder. He can't argue that it will mix with other meats if you ask him to do it at the end of the day; you can pick it up the next morning, then use the same day, or freeze it at once uncooked (even if from thawed meat; because it has changed form, the raw meat may be refrozen). The other hindquarter may be roasted or grilled then eaten hot or cold, or frozen (see below).

WINGS—Have butcher remove wings from forequarters before you use the breast meat. Cook turkey wings as you would chicken, only a little longer.

To freeze poultry: Uncooked fresh meat should be wrapped well, airtight, and frozen as soon as you bring it home; it will keep up to 9 months. Uncooked fresh or thawed ground turkey wrapped airtight, will keep up to 4 months. Cooked poultry keeps best frozen in large pieces, but it may also be frozen in slices; the secret is to cover cooked poultry completely with broth, gravy, or béchamel sauce—this way, it will keep up to 6 months. Cooked poultry not covered with liquid will keep only 1 month.

How much poultry to buy? People usually regard a serving of chicken or turkey in terms of pieces rather than ounces. But it generally works out that ½ pound of meaty chicken pieces constitutes a generous serving. That would be 2 good drumsticks or thighs or ½ large chicken breast (it took me years to realize that "breast of chicken" singular is two halves). Turkey servings are a bit more complicated. For each *generous* serving, then, buy:

Bone-in very meaty chicken breasts, thighs, drumsticks,
    8 ounces
Chicken 4 pounds and over (roasters, pullets, capons,
    hens, roosters); turkeys over 12 pounds—remember
    that you lose about 16 ounces to the soup pot, 10 ounces
Meaty wings, 11 to 12 ounces
Chicken 3¾ pounds and under (broilers, fryers); turkeys
    under 12 pounds—you also lose about 16 ounces to the
    soup pot, 12 ounces
Fresh ground turkey, boned meats, giblets and livers, 3½
    to 4 ounces

If you forget these amounts at the market, as a general rule buy ¾ pound per serving of any poultry, and unless the bones are hugely disproportionate, you'll have enough.

Budget notes on cooking chicken and turkey

Thaw frozen poultry in its wrapper in the refrigerator if possible. A trick to help keep juices in while thawing is to pat the icy turkey dry and rub with oil. A realistic refrigerated defrosting time for big birds is about 24 hours for every 4 to 6 pounds.

Store uncooked poultry loosely wrapped no more than 48 hours in the coldest part of your refrigerator. Remove the giblets before chicken goes into the fridge and toss them into a pot with a handful of seasoning ingredients and water to cover (or freeze and collect giblets for One Great Broth). And don't neglect to make another saving broth of the bones and scraps from cooked chicken or turkey.

How to test chicken and turkey for doneness? Pierce the thickest part of the drumstick with a skewer or cooking fork; if the juices run clear yellow, the turkey is done. Other tests: When the thigh or drumstick meat, pinched with the fingers, is soft and tender. On roasts, when the leg, jiggled from the tip, moves easily in its socket. When the meat thermometer registers 180° F. (This moment of "Is it done?"—especially with a big turkey—can turn great cooks to jelly.)

After a roast chicken or turkey dinner, always remove any stuffing and refrigerate it separately. The carcass—and refrigerator space—can be most efficiently dealt with if you take a little time and strip the meat from the bones, wrap, and refrigerate (or freeze) it. Then crack the carcass into pieces that will fit into the soup pot; you can simmer broth with the traditional seasonings overnight, or wrap and refrigerate until the next day or two.

NOTE: *All poultry must be at room temperature before cooking to prevent shrinkage and toughness.*

Poulet à la Casserole

(Chicken browned then finished in the oven)
4 SERVINGS

This juicy chicken is simple and perfect and has endless delectable possibilities. I think you'll find it invaluable.

I call for butter because its flavor really does contribute mightily to the dish. When there are very few ingredients, and they are particularly susceptible to the sweet nuttiness of butter, one little cube is worth the small added expense. The French never flour chicken for sautéeing, and so the pure buttery juices make an exquisite light sauce.

To be perfect, braised chicken—for that's what this comes to—ought to go directly from sautéeing to baking to table without delay. But when there are other good things alongside in the pot to keep the chicken moistened, then you *can*, if you must, brown the chicken, put the casserole together, cover it and set aside in a cool place a few hours. Then you can bake it, a little longer and at higher temperature, to compensate for the lost momentum, an hour before serving. But make this basic unadorned chicken non-stop. It doesn't take that much last-minute time.

1 3-pound frying chicken, cut up
5 to 6 tablespoons (about 3 ounces) butter; buy 1 stick
3 tablespoons dry white wine, optional
½ teaspoon salt, or to taste
Fresh ground pepper, to taste
Handful of chopped parsley

Pat the chicken thoroughly dry while you heat the butter in a large heavy skillet or 2-quart earthenware casserole that will take direct heat over medium-high heat. When the butter sizzles, lay in the chicken and sauté until nicely browned on all sides; turn with tongs or nudge over with a rubber scraper. Do not cook longer than necessary.

Preheat oven to 325° F. Cover chicken and bake in the center of the oven about 45 minutes; test for doneness. It may need another 5 to 15 minutes.

You may now simply sprinkle with salt and pepper and parsley and serve in the skillet or casserole, spooning the juices over each portion. Or you can make a delectable sauce in 2 minutes:

Remove the chicken to a heated serving platter, cover with foil and keep warm in the oven with the heat off while you add the wine to the cooking vessel and set it over medium-high heat. Use a rubber scraper to stir any glazed bits off the pot into the sauce, and simmer just until the sauce is the consistency of thin cream, about 2 or 3 minutes. Add salt and pepper, and pour over the chicken. Sprinkle with parsley, and serve at once.

Accompany this with the same wine you used in the sauce, whipped potatoes and any tender-crisp green vegetable in season. A light salad after, and for dessert, thick, creamy homemade yogurt flavored with vanilla and sprinkled lightly with brown sugar.

Poulet à la Normande

(Chicken in casserole with apples)
4 SERVINGS

From the farms and orchards of Normandy, a happy marriage.

1 recipe Poulet à la Casserole (*see p. 165*); *omit the wine*
The rest of the stick of butter
3 large (1 pound) juicy green apples
½ cup apple cider
1 tablespoon Half-and-Half or crème fraîche, *optional*

Slice the apples ¼-inch thick and sauté them in the butter in a large skillet over medium-high heat while browning the chicken in the other skillet or casserole. When the apples have absorbed most of the butter, add them to the chicken. Rinse out the apples' skillet with the cider, then pour it over the chicken. Shake vessel to distribute everything evenly. Cover and continue as directed, or set aside at room temperature a couple of hours and bake at 350° F (set in a cold oven) the hour before serving. When tender, remove the chicken and apples to a heated serving dish, keeping warm, and simmer down the juices until the consistency of thin cream. A spoonful of Half-and-Half or *crème fraîche*, if you have it, is not amiss stirred in. Season to taste, then pour sauce over the chicken and sprinkle with parsley. Serve at once.

Plain brown rice baked in the oven with the chicken would be delicious with this, and peas steamed beneath a lettuce leaf in the French fashion. Have Chablis or cider to drink, perhaps a spinach salad after. And for dessert, you might have buckwheat crêpes with drizzled honey and margarine —have them made before dinner; roll or fold in four and then heat them up in a chafing dish before your guests, or quickly in the kitchen.

Sometimes, between September and November, sauté sliced quinces in place of the apples, and serve the fragrant finished dish as *Poulet aux Coings*. Or for a chicken no one will ever have tasted, use the exquisite blend of apples, quinces, and cranberries (roughly 3 small apples, ¼ cup cranberries, and 1 medium-sized quince) found in my recipe for Paradise Jelly, and call it *Poulet au Paradis!*

Poulet à la Parmentier

(Chicken in casserole with sautéed potatoes)
4 SERVINGS

A country combination—absolutely great.

1 recipe Poulet à la Casserole (*see p. 165*)
The rest of the stick of butter
5 medium (*2 pounds*) *peeled boiling potatoes*
1 more tablespoon dry white wine (*¼ cup in all*)

Cut the potatoes in ¾-inch dice. While sautéeing the chicken as directed, place the butter in another large skillet over medium-high heat. When it sizzles, add the potatoes and sauté them until they have taken on a rich color. Use a rubber scraper to stir the potatoes and turn the chicken. When the chicken is brown, turn the potatoes into the pot and shake vessel to distribute evenly. Cover and continue cooking as above, or set aside at room temperature a couple of hours and bake at 350° F the hour before serving. Do make the sauce with the white wine.

Serve the chicken on a heated platter surrounded by the potatoes and moistened with the sauce. Sprinkle with parsley, and bring to the table at once. Have the same wine you used in the sauce, Buttersilk Carrots without the decoration of parsley but with a sprinkling of dill, and a simple salad to follow. Dessert might be poached fresh or canned apricots, the syrup flavored with vanilla, and served with thick yogurt or *crème fraîche.*

Poulet à la Paprikash

(Chicken in casserole with onions and paprika)
4 SERVINGS

Paprika chicken is a classic, but so many recipes make such a fuss of it. Here is an authentic Hungarian recipe, wonderfully simple, and incomparable for taste.

> *1 3-pound frying chicken, cut up*
> *3 good-sized onions, coarsely chopped*
> *1 large fresh tomato, coarsely chopped*
> *¼ cup oil, or more*
> *1 teaspoon paprika (the best quality is not an*
> *extravagance)*
> *1 tablespoon flour*
> *½ cup Super Yogurt (see p. 77) or* Crème Fraîche
> *(see p. 73)*
> *1 teaspoon salt, or to taste*
> *Chopped fresh or dried dill*

Following the browning method as for *Poulet à la Casserole* (see p. 165), substitute 2 tablespoons of the oil for the butter. At the same time as the chicken is browning, also sauté the onions in the rest of the oil in another skillet over medium-high heat until lightly browned; use a rubber scraper to stir the onions and to turn the chicken. When the onions are lightly browned, turn off heat and stir in the tomato until blended; now mix in the paprika. Pour the onions over the chicken then shake the vessel to settle the onions. Cover tightly and bake as for *Poulet à la Casserole,* or set aside at room temperature a couple of hours and bake at 350° F the hour before serving.

Remove the chicken to a heated serving platter and keep it warm while you make a well with a spoon in the center of the cooking skillet or casserole. Sprinkle the flour there and quickly whisk it into the surrounding juices and onions; set over medium heat and whisk until thickened. Now add the yogurt or *crème fraîche* and whisk to blend. Add salt to taste, and when the yogurt is hot—after about 1 minute—pour the sauce over the chicken.

You should also be boiling broad egg noodles while the chicken is finishing up. When they are tender, lift out with a strainer, toss them in a bowl quickly with a lump of margarine, and then make a border of them around the chicken on the platter. Sprinkle the noodles with dill, and serve. A light white wine or beer is in order, and cole slaw on the side —make it with cabbage, shredded carrots, and lots of chopped parsley for color. For dessert, an apple or quince tart sprinkled with toasted chopped walnuts.

Poulet à la Basquaise

(Chicken in casserole with tomato-seasoned rice)
4 SERVINGS

Also simple and gorgeous. A lovely thing about this Basque dish—a meal in itself—is that the tomatoes on top melt down into the rice, which drifts down over the chicken as the dish bakes, resulting in a savory mix that takes comparatively little effort on the cook's part. And after the recipe, there are directions for embellishing the dish for a big party. Just multiply the recipe proportions as needed.

1 recipe Poulet à la Casserole (*see p. 165*); *omit wine, substitute light-tasting oil for butter*
1 medium onion, finely chopped
1 large clove of garlic, minced
¾ cup converted long-grain white rice
1⅔ cups boiling water
7 medium-sized (2 pounds) fresh or 3 1-pound cans of firm sliced tomatoes, drained
Peel of 1 small orange in a spiral, optional
Salt and fresh ground pepper, to taste
1½ teaspoons best quality paprika
2 to 3 tablespoons margarine

Brown the chicken in 2 tablespoons of the oil as directed. At the same time in a small skillet over medium-high heat, sauté the onion and garlic in a little oil until lightly browned. And on another burner, simmer the rice in the water in a small covered pot over low heat just 10 minutes; turn off heat and leave rice undisturbed until needed. Peel and coarsely chop the tomatoes. Use a vegetable peeler to remove the zest of the orange.

Oil a 3-quart baking dish and spread the onions on the bottom. Arrange the chicken over them, and sprinkle lightly with salt and pepper. Scrape the pan juices from the skillet over the chicken, then blanket with the rice. Sprinkle with the tomatoes, then season lightly with salt, a few rounds of the pepper mill, and the paprika. Bury the orange spiral in the casserole for an especially *Pays Basque* flavor. Dot with margarine, cover the dish and bake as for *Poulet à la Casserole*, or set aside at room temperature a couple of hours and bake at 350° F the hour before serving.

Serve with cool grilled sweet peppers if in season, or whole green beans *à la vinaigrette* if not. A light salad to follow, all drunk with cold light white wine. And for dessert, thinly sliced green apples in a baking dish, sprinkled with brown sugar and cider up to one-third their depth, then baked covered until tender, and served hot or cool.

For a full-dress Basque chicken, lay 1 pound of fresh uncooked spiced sausage (from the delicatessen) in one piece in with the chicken. Cover with 4 sweet red or green peppers cut in strips and sautéed in oil until just half-cooked. Then cover with the rice, tomatoes, poke in the orange peel, and finally sprinkle with more paprika, 2 teaspoons of the best. Bake as directed.

Serve with black olives on the table for added color, a light white wine, French bread, and salad after. The apples would still suit for dessert, but for a big party, add dollops of ice cream on top.

Chicken for Important Occasions

(Chicken in casserole with a silken sauce)
8 SERVINGS

Still simple, still perfect. The braising method raised to its highest power. At a restaurant, this dish would cost every penny of its worth. I am grateful to Julia Child and Company for its inspiration—*Poulet Poêlé à l'Estragon* (In *Mastering the Art of French Cooking*, Vol. I, Alfred A. Knopf, New York, 1966.)

> 2 *3-pound frying chickens, cut up*
> ¼ *cup light-tasting oil*
>
> *Seasoning vegetables:*
> > *1 large onion, thinly sliced*
> > *1 clove of garlic, minced*
> > *2 unpeeled carrots, in thin rounds*
> > *1 teaspoon fresh chopped or ⅓ teaspoon dried*
> > > *sweet basil*
> > *1 teaspoon fresh chopped or ⅓ teaspoon dried*
> > > *tarragon*
> > *1 teaspoon fresh chopped or ⅓ teaspoon dried*
> > > *(lemon) thyme*
> > *⅛ teaspoon fresh ground pepper*
> ¼ *cup (2 ounces) margarine*
>
> *Sauce:*
> > *3½ cups chicken broth, more or less*
> > *2 tablespoons cornstarch*
> > *1 tablespoon lemon juice*
> > *2 egg yolks*
> > *2 tablespoons Madeira*
> > *Salt and white pepper, to taste*
> *Parsley curls*

The chicken: In a small heavy skillet over low heat, heat 2 tablespoons of the oil. Sauté the onion, garlic, and carrots about 10 minutes, stirring frequently, until they turn limp. Sprinkle over the herbs and grind on a bit of pepper. Cover and set in a cool place until needed.

About 2½ or 3 hours before serving, brown the chicken as directed for *Poulet à la Casserole*, using a 4-quart earthenware casserole if possible, or 1 or 2 large skillets (and then transfer to a large baking dish); substitute 3 tablespoons of the margarine and 2 tablespoons of the oil for the butter in that recipe. Set oven to 325° F and warm up the seasoning vegetables in their skillet over low heat.

Now alternate layers of vegetables and chicken in the casserole or baking dish; cover and bake in the center of the oven about 1 hour and 10 or 15 minutes, or until it tests done. Begin to test after about 55 minutes. When the chicken is tender, hold the lid firmly over the chicken pieces, and send the pan juices through a strainer into a 1-quart measuring pitcher. Use a kitchen spoon to pick out quickly as many of the seasoning vegetables left in the casserole as you can— a few will just add to the texture of the sauce, so don't take time with this. Cover casserole tightly and return to the oven with the heat off.

The sauce: Remove fat from the juices. Add chicken broth to make 4 cups, then simmer it down to 2 cups in a wide, heavy skillet over high heat. Turn off heat, remove ½ cup of the reduced broth to a small bowl, swirl to cool, add the cornstarch to the bowl and stir with a fork to dissolve. Whisk cornstarch mixture into the broth in the skillet and turn heat to medium; add lemon juice and whisk until thickened.

Have the yolks in another small bowl; whisk constantly while you spoon a little of the hot sauce into them; return yolk mixture to the skillet, whisking constantly. At once reduce heat to very low and whisk a moment or two until the sauce coats the whisk—it must not bubble once. Take off heat, add the Madeira, a last lump of margarine, whisk again, taste for salt and white pepper.

Serving: Remove chicken from the oven. There will probably be a little juice in the bottom of the casserole by now; whisk it into the sauce, spoon a little sauce over the casserole to glaze the chicken; turn the rest of the sauce into a serving bowl. Garnish the chicken with parsley, and bring to the table at once.

NOTE: There is a bit of give in the timing. The chicken can keep up to 30 minutes in the oven, if well covered (cover lid with thick damp towels). Stop making the sauce at the point just before you add the egg yolks, and keep the sauce in a double boiler over hot water over low heat. Then, when you are just about ready to serve, finish making the sauce as directed.

A crisp and unusual *paillasson* or simply whipped potatoes and fresh butter-tossed green beans are ideal accompaniments to this superb dish. Have a light young red wine, like a zinfandel, French bread, a *salade de saison* to follow, and for dessert, a pear tart.

Sausalito Grilled Chicken

8 GENEROUS SERVINGS

This chicken is endlessly useful. Delicate and herbal, it provides a simple background to complex salads or pasta dishes. Or it can be grilled to a char and served as the center of a colorful buffet. It's good hot or at room temperature. And it's easy.

> 2 *3-pound frying chickens, cut up*
> ⅔ *cup light-tasting oil or melted margarine*
> ½ *cup lemon juice (about 4 lemons), or dry white wine*
> 3 *large cloves of garlic, minced*
> 3 *tablespoons fresh chopped or 1 tablespoon dried sweet basil, oregano, or your favorite herb*
> 1 *teaspoon salt*
> *Fresh ground pepper, to taste*

Arrange chicken skin side up on an oiled rimmed baking sheet. Mix remaining ingredients and brush over chicken—do this a few hours in advance of cooking for extra flavor, if you wish. Heat broiler to 425° F. Set chicken 5 to 7 inches below heat. Brush well every 5 minutes with the sauce; when you pull the baking sheet out to baste, turn it back to front each time if your broiler grills unevenly. After 20 minutes, turn chicken over and continue as before.

Depending on size and age, chicken should be tender after 20 minutes on each side. Test for doneness.

If using margarine, serve while hot; use oil if serving at room temperature. To keep a few hours until needed, cover with plastic wrap and set in a cool place. Baste again with the pan juices before heaping on a platter.

Serve with a light and airy dish of fresh pasta or almost any savory pastry, and a big spinach or mixed green salad. Cold white wine (the same in the baste, if you used wine), hot French bread sprinkled with Parmesan and garlic, and some sort of pickle are good accompaniments. And for dessert, slip a cottage pudding into the oven as you sit down to eat, then serve it with apricot preserves warmed with a touch of brandy, if you have some.

For a quick family dinner, I just tuck the chicken and sauce into a 325° F oven for 1 hour and baste it when I pass through the kitchen. Not so juicy, but still very good.

Chinese Chicken Wings

6 SERVINGS

Looking marvelously burnished on the platter, and tasting deliciously succulent, these humble cuts will never be disdained. I used to toss wings into the soup pot, but no more!

4 pounds (about 24) chicken wings; tips removed
½ cup honey
⅓ cup soy sauce
1 tablespoon frozen orange juice concentrate, optional
3 cloves of garlic, minced
*½ teaspoon Chinese five-spice or ¾ teaspoon
    powdered ginger*

If you're in a hurry, arrange the wings broad side down on a rimmed baking sheet; if you're not, the wings will be juicier if during the first part of their baking they snugly fit in a 3-quart flat baking dish. Mix the remaining ingredients together and pour evenly over the wings; gently shake sheet or dish to distribute sauce. The chicken can soak in the sauce at room temperature a few hours, or in the refrigerator a couple of days, if convenient.

Set the oven to 500° F. Cover the sheet or dish with foil and bake in the center of the oven. After 10 minutes, reduce heat to 300° and bake 1 hour. Lift up foil and test for doneness; give them another 10 to 20 minutes, if necessary.

Remove from oven, turn heat to 350°. Now either use tongs to place wings broad side up on a rimmed baking sheet, or turn them over if already on the sheet. Brush with the sauce, then pour the rest over, and return to oven to glaze uncovered another 15 minutes; or until the wings are a deep rich shiny brown both top and bottom.

NOTE: If your oven's source of heat is overhead, then keep wings broad side down while they glaze, so the pale upper side will darken. Ovens with the heat from below will brown the pale side if it is turned down and in the sauce. You can bake the wings early in the day, then reheat and glaze them 10 minutes longer just before serving.

Arrange wings on a heated serving platter and pour remaining sauce in a pitcher. Spoon off any fat that rises in the sauce; then serve. The sauce can be poured over rice, which is the best accompaniment; peas, a spinach salad, then lemon sherbet topped with crushed pineapple make it dinner.

Petti di Pollo alla Marsala

(Sautéed scallops of chicken breasts with Marsala)
½ BREAST MAKES I SERVING

A beautiful way with chicken that appears extravagant but isn't.

For each ½ meaty chicken breast:
Salt and fresh ground pepper, to taste
1 tablespoon margarine
1 tablespoon light-tasting oil
2 scant teaspoons flour
1 tablespoon sweet Marsala
Lemon rounds and parsley curls

Should your butcher not be free to do the boning, use a small sharp knife to detach the skin from the meat, then run the knife close to the bone, beginning at the center thick breast bone. Simply feel your way, slowly, firmly cutting the meat free in one piece.

Place the filets one by one between sheets of plastic film (or in a plastic food bag—waxed paper disintegrates) near the edge of your bread board. With the flat side of a Chinese cleaver, the bottom of a sturdy plate, or a tenderizing mallet, pound the filets ¼-inch thin. Keep giving the filet quarter-turns, so the pounding will be even.

Lightly sprinkle salt and pepper over the meat. You can wrap the scallops in plastic film at this point, and set aside until you need them.

Twenty-five minutes before dinner, put butter and oil in your largest skillet and heat over medium heat while you dust the scallops lightly with flour; shake off excess and do not rub in. When the margarine is frothy, raise heat to high and lay in as many scallops as will comfortably fit. After about 3 minutes, they should be nicely browned on the bottom. Reduce heat to medium low, turn the scallops over with pancake turner or tongs, cover and let cook gently until they test tender with a cooking fork—15 or 20 minutes.

Lift scallops from skillet to heated serving platter; cover. Keep warm in a 225° F oven while you add the Marsala to the pan juices. Raise the heat to high and stir while the juices reduce to a thin syrup—about 15 seconds. Pour over the chicken. Decorate the platter with lemon slices and curls of parsley and serve at once.

Creamed spinach (the Florentine Bed) would be excellent with the chicken, as well as roasted small red potatoes, if in season. Drink chilled fruity white wine. For a lovely finish after the salad, serve chilled Pour Custard dusted with nutmeg in wine glasses, and fresh-baked shortbread cookies. Twirl an orange peel in the coffee.

Another night for guests, prepare the scallops *alla Bolognese*. The last 10 minutes of cooking, heap a good amount of grated Parmesan cheese over each scallop. Moisten with a sprinkling of the sauce, then finish cooking; the cheese will melt. Garnish and serve as above, with the same accompaniments. (A thin slice of boiled ham beneath the cheese, covering the scallop, is a further enrichment.)

Chicken Chile

(Scallops of chicken breasts with creamy mild green chile sauce)

12 SERVINGS

Absolutely delicious—a big success at parties. This may be put together the day before it's served.

12 half chicken breasts, about 6 pounds
3 eggs, beaten lightly
1½ cups seasoned bread crumbs
⅔ cup light-tasting oil
6 tablespoons margarine
1 large green pepper, finely chopped, or 1 cup frozen
1 large onion, finely chopped
2 large cloves of garlic, minced
⅔ cup (6 ounces) chopped canned mild green
  California chilies (available from most gourmet
  grocers)
1 14-ounce can sliced baby tomatoes
8 ounces Neufchâtel cream cheese
1½ to 2 cups buttermilk

Follow directions in preceding recipe for boning and pounding. Dip the scallops in the beaten eggs, then coat lightly but thoroughly with the bread crumbs. Set scallops on a cake rack to dry 10 or 15 minutes. Sauté the scallops in oil and margarine as in preceding recipe but do not cover after turning over.

At the same time, in a medium skillet over medium heat, sauté the green pepper, onion, and garlic in 2 or 3 tablespoons of the oil until tender; add the chilies and the entire can of tomatoes. Stir over low heat, and add the cream cheese in lumps; stir and mash cheese into the vegetable mixture to make a creamy sauce. Set oven to 325° F.

In a 3-quart oval or rectangular baking dish, spoon one-third the sauce over the bottom; then lay in 5 or 6 of the scallops (depending on the shape of the dish); cover with half the remaining sauce; lay in the remaining scallops; then cover with the rest of the sauce. Pour buttermilk over, barely to cover—the amount depends on the shape of the dish. Shake the dish to distribute the buttermilk. Bake 30 minutes, uncovered, just until bubbly. You may serve at once, but the flavors will improve upon standing one day. Cover and refrigerate.

Bring to room temperature and reheat at 325° F another 30 minutes; if it looks dry, add a bit more buttermilk—just until it's bubbly again.

Serve from the casserole, with hot garlic French bread (the long, crusty loaf sliced almost to the bottom, the bread spread with margarine creamed with minced garlic), some pinto beans would be in keeping, and a big crisp green salad. If it's summer, a dessert of a watermelon shell filled with fresh fruit compote would be gorgeous—if it's a gala feast, line the shell first with lime ice. Or in winter, vanilla ice cream (laced with bourbon?) and chocolate sauce topped with slivers of fresh orange peel.

Succulent Roast Chicken

For a special family gathering or splendid dinner party, few complicated dishes can rival a perfectly roasted chicken. It does take last-minute attention, but little more than a few dippings in and out of the kitchen.

Large, breasty, golden chicken, from 3 to 6 pounds;
*   you can do 2 at once in a suitably sized dish*
Salt and fresh ground pepper
1 onion, in thick slices
Fresh sprigs or dried leaves of tarragon, or (lemon)
*   thyme and sweet basil*
Margarine
1 clove of garlic, halved
1 bunch parsley

Set oven to 425° F. This is ideally roasted in an earthenware casserole just large enough to hold the chicken, and an inch or so shallower than the chicken is high. Substitute a glass baking dish or enamelled cast iron pot, if necessary. Lightly rub the two cavities of the chicken with salt and pepper. In the body cavity, place half the onion slices, the herbs, and a lump of margarine the size of a small lemon. Use cotton string to tie the tips of the drumsticks together, then loop the string around under the tail; push the drumsticks forward to lie against the body, and this should pretty much close the cavity. Run another length of string around the front section of the bird, thus clapping the wings tight against the body; tie on top.

Rub the baking dish all over with the cut side of the garlic; discard it and add the rest of the onion. Place the chicken *breast down* in the dish, then brush all over the exposed skin lavishly with margarine. Set in the center of the oven and roast for 20 minutes; turn heat to 350° F (325° if dish is glass), and brush copiously with more margarine. Brush every 20 minutes; after awhile, you can use the drippings in the dish. Halfway through the roasting time, remove the dish from the oven and turn the chicken breast side up. Brush with drippings and return to oven, basting as before.

Timing with chicken is as uncertain as with turkey, but a 3- or 4-pound chicken will generally require roasting for 18 minutes per pound; a 5- or 6-pound chicken, 15 minutes per pound. If you begin testing the bird for doneness (see p. 165) 10 or 15 minutes before you expect it to be ready, you'll be fine.

There are sauces and gravies one can make with the rich drippings, but I prefer just the buttery juices *au naturel*. The chicken will keep, if need be, in a 225° F oven if covered with heavy foil and a damp towel. Don't make it wait more than 30 minutes.

I prefer also the French manner of not stuffing roast chicken; the cavity is so small in comparison with the number of people it will serve that any stuffing would be skimpy. But a Danish friend always tucks softened pitted prunes and coarsely chopped peeled apples into her chicken—and that makes a lovely bit of garnish.

Pull off the strings, pull out the seasonings in the cavity, and stuff a bunch of parsley stalks in the vent. Serve in the roasting dish, ladling juices over every portion after carving. If you set potatoes on the oven rack to bake as the chicken roasts, then all you need to add is a heap of butter-tossed whole green beans or whatever green vegetable is best in season, some hot rolls, and a young, light red wine. Have a *salade de saison* with a light dressing after, and for dessert, *crème brulée*.

Roast Turkey Pieces

A 3- to 5-pound forequarter of white meat or a hind-quarter of dark meat make fine small, thrifty roasts with little trouble.

Cover with cheesecloth dipped in melted margarine and set meat in a baking pan in a preheated 350° F oven. Baste faithfully every 20 minutes (especially with white meat), until meat tests done; about 26 to 28 minutes per pound. Let juices settle for about 20 minutes while you keep the meat warm, then carve and serve as usual. Freeze leftover meat.

Barbecued Turkey Pieces

Thick white meat steaks, big drumsticks, or even turkey wings taste marvelous when set over slowly burning coals, covered loosely with a tent of heavy foil, and grilled. Baste frequently with olive oil and dry vermouth, and turn every 20 minutes or so, until meat tests tender and nicely browned. Count from 1½ to 2 hours.

Herbal Boned and Rolled Breast of Turkey

AT LEAST 12 SERVINGS

This is herb-marbled cold meat, my version of Paula Peck's version of James Beard's beautiful boned buttered turkey in her *Art of Good Cooking* (Simon and Schuster, New York, 1966). It is ideal for entertaining because it's so unusual and so delicious, and really not very difficult.

See budget notes at beginning of this section about cutting a big bargain turkey into small parts. Ask your butcher to bone the breast in one piece, but he needn't bother rolling and tying it. Also ask him for its weight. Or bone it yourself, following directions for chicken breasts; it's not hard.

> *1 4- to 5-pound boned breast of turkey in one piece*
> *About 1 cup (8 ounces) softened margarine*
> *Fresh chopped or dried powdered thyme*
> *Fresh chopped or dried sweet basil*
> *Fresh chopped or dried tarragon*
> *1 large clove of garlic, minced, or garlic powder*
> *Fresh ground pepper*
> *½ lemon*
> *Salt*

The seasoning of the meat is ideally done the night before roasting, but if you're pressed for time, do it just before. Spread out the meat skin side down. Use clean fingers or a butter knife to coat the flesh completely with margarine. Then sprinkle on enough herbs to blanket the meat—a light but covering veil. Distribute the garlic as evenly as you can over the meat, then grind on a light dusting of pepper. Sprinkle with the grated zest and then the juice of the lemon; finally, dust lightly with salt.

Tightly roll up the meat lengthwise. Use cotton string to tightly tie in a roll—first tie in the center, then every 2 inches along the roll; then come back and tie again every inch, tightly as you can, trying to force the meat into as long and even a roll as possible. Coat the outside with more margarine to cover, then wrap in waxed paper or plastic film, refrigerate, and let the good seasonings sink in overnight, if possible. Bring to room temperature before roasting.

Preheat oven to 350° F. Place roll seam side down in a baking dish or earthenware casserole that just fits the meat, and that is also as deep as the meat is high. Fold cheesecloth 4 layers thick, wet, wring out, and dip in melted margarine; cover the roll completely with it (or use a discardable piece of cloth). Bake in the center of the oven, and baste faithfully with drippings in the dish every 20 minutes (otherwise, breast meat can be stick-in-the-throat dry). Count about 28 minutes per pound—but a meat thermometer inserted in the center of the roll after 1½ hours of roasting is recommended.

After 2 hours, test for doneness. When cooked to taste, remove from oven and let stand for 30 minutes. Then, remove cloth (moisten with broth so it won't stick), and slice about ⅜-inch thick; arrange pieces overlapping on a platter. Cover airtight; serve at room temperature. The pan juices, warmed up just to melt the margarine, are delicious, or good mayonnaise is a fine accompaniment, too.

Serve with any wine you please—a chilled rosé or faintly sweet dry wine, or a lightly chilled zinfandel, perhaps. And you might have *pommes chip*, some cool grilled tomatoes or halved zucchinis *à la vinaigrette*, or roasted sweet peppers. Or all four, for a party buffet. Dessert could be Persian red pears and your own homemade yogurt. Superb!

Twelve Steps to Incomparable Roast Turkey

Roasting a great big bird—economical as it may be—can be a scary process. If it isn't perfect, it's been a waste of a lot of time and money. So, I urge you to try this method. You will probably never worry again.

1. The day before roasting, get the turkey ready. If frozen, and there wasn't time to thaw it slowly in the refrigerator, then set in its wrapper in *cold* water, and change the water frequently. A large bird may take up to 8 hours. As soon as the turkey is thawed enough to be flexible, or as soon as you bring a bird home if it is fresh, remove neck and giblets from cavities and begin making broth. To continue thawing the turkey in water, wrap again in plastic bag if you can.

2. When turkey has completely thawed, or as soon as you bring home a fresh one, rinse in cold water, pat thoroughly dry, and rub skin generously with unsalted shortening. Rub cavities lightly with salt and fresh ground pepper. Wrap turkey completely in waxed paper and a damp towel; refrigerate.

3. Calculate roasting temperature and time. I realize that you probably have other cookbooks each recommending a different set of numbers—and for different tastes and circumstances, they might all be right. But do remember that turkeys grown today roast more rapidly than the turkeys of just a few years ago. And some turkeys raised in the West have been known to cook faster than turkeys in the East! Unless you know your turkey's background, the exact time it will take to cook is impossible to know until you've cooked it. (One old-fashioned book says that adding 1 hour to the time it took the gizzard to simmer to a point soft "as cold mush" is the answer. I always forget to poke it.) So always add 15 to 30 minutes, depending on the size of the turkey, to your entire roasting schedule, just in case.

Turkeys 14 pounds or under should be roasted at 325° F for 18 minutes per pound. Turkeys 15 pounds or over require a 300° F oven at 15 minutes per pound. *Add 30 minutes* at end of roasting and before carving to allow juices to settle. *Unstuffed turkeys* are calculated at ¾ the above time.

4.   The morning of the dinner, remove turkey to room temperature first thing, or no less than 2 hours before oven time. Prepare the Ohio Dressing ingredients, or your favorite, adding everything but the liquid. (No, you mustn't stuff the turkey the night before, I know there are people who have gotten away with it, but it is at best a risky business.)

5.   About 1 hour before oven time, finish making the dressing and stuff the turkey. Tuck it neck-down in a large bowl in the sink and lightly stuff the body cavity two-thirds full. Lift out onto a working surface and fill neck cavity two-thirds full. Lightly heap any extra stuffing in an oiled sheet of foil, then wrap it butcher-style, allowing room to expand; it may be baked in the roasting pan the last hour.

6.   Truss the turkey, using skewers, extra-large safety pins, or a sturdy darning or upholstery needle and cotton string. Secure neck skin over stuffing to back. Fold wings under the back; should part of the wing be missing, simply tie wing close to the body with string. Close body cavity. Tie legs at tips to the tail. (Some turkeys have a flap of skin just above the tail; if so, tuck legs under the flap.) Insert the point of a meat thermometer in the center of the thickest part of the thigh next to the body cavity, not touching the bone.

7.   Make a roux of 4 parts melted margarine and 1 part flour; use a pastry brush to paint the entire turkey with this. A trick from turkey master, Marcella Wilhelms—as the turkey roasts, the paste seals the pores, thus helping to keep in the juices, and the skin browns most beautifully. Set oven to proper temperature.

8.   Place turkey, *breast side down*, on rack in a large flat pan just big enough to accommodate the bird. (Actually, I roasted turkeys for years without a rack, just laid them on one breast and then the other.) Fold 4 layers of cheesecloth, or cut a discardable large clean soft cloth, into a rectangle large enough to cover the turkey completely. Wet, wring out, then dip in melted unsalted shortening and spread over every inch of the bird.

9. Place turkey in oven. Set timer for 20 minutes. Melt turkey fat from broth in a medium-sized pot; measure it, then add unsalted shortening (use the cheapest fat or oil —it will be discarded) to make 2 cups. Return to pot with 2 cups of the turkey broth you made, and warm up over medium heat. When timer sounds, quickly pull out the pan, stir broth and fat, use bulb baster to moisten all of the cloth with mixture, then push the pan back in and close the oven door. Baste turkey every 20 minutes faithfully the entire time—it's worth the effort. If you run out, melt more shortening and heat equal amount of broth. Toward the end, baste with pan juices.

10. Halfway through roasting, pull pan out of oven onto working surface—always close oven door as quickly as possible. Ladle basting broth liberally over the cloth, then remove cloth carefully so it doesn't pull the skin with it. Using clean, thick potholders and a strong cooking fork for leverage, turn the turkey breast side up. Replace cloth over turkey as before, baste liberally, and return to oven immediately to continue roasting. If any parts of the turkey brown too quickly, cover lightly with foil.

11. During the last hour of roasting (don't forget to put the packet of stuffing in), each time you baste, test the turkey for doneness.

12. Soak cheesecloth as before and lift off gently, then lift up turkey with potholders onto a heated serving platter. Cover with foil and several hot damp towels, and set in a corner while you finish preparing the dinner. Then after it has stood 30 minutes, unwrap and either present your gorgeous bird for carving at table, or carve in the kitchen, making separate heaps of white and dark meat. To make buffet service fast and keep the meat hot as possible, carve all the white meat first and send it to the table, calling for white meat people. Then when you bring out the dark meat, the dark meat fanciers come and get it.

Serve with your family's traditional accompaniments, and a light red *or* white wine.

Madeira Gravy

10 SERVINGS

Double or triple this recipe as needed.

Drippings from roasting pan
Turkey broth to make 5 cups, if needed; or use 3
  measures chicken broth and 1 measure beef broth
  if you run out
Chopped giblet and neck meat from broth
3 tablespoons flour
Salt and fresh ground pepper, to taste
1 to 2 tablespoons Madeira
Few drops gravy-coloring sauce, optional

While turkey rests, pour off drippings from pan into a tall container. Return a kitchen-spoonful of fat to the roasting pan. Discard rest of fat in container, and add broth to make 5 cups. Sprinkle flour over pan and set over 2 burners on low heat. Whisk constantly while you blend fat and flour, then slowly pour in the broth; if you get lumps, pull pan off heat and whisk them out before continuing. Scrape all crusty bits from pan into gravy; when smooth, add chopped meat, seasonings, and Madeira. For extra-rich color, even my grandmother always added a few drops of gravy-browning sauce. When gravy has simmered to desired thickness, turn into a keep-hot dish and serve.

What to Do with Leftover Chicken and Turkey?

I like the simple direct approach: cold sandwiches with mayonnaise and lettuce on white bread (I know, but white it must be), and hot open-faced sandwiches (also white bread) next to whipped potatoes with lots of gravy for dinner.

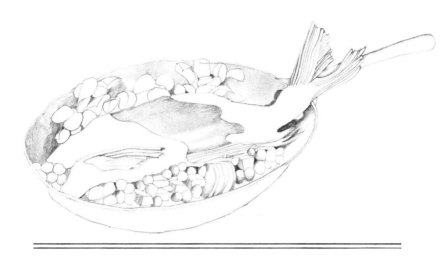

Fish

Until I stood in front of a Japanese fishmonger's case and stared at an array of glistening sea creatures I never knew existed . . . until I got up the nerve to bring home a whole large rockfish—coral-colored, bright-eyed, spiny-tailed—and gave it a glorious ending in my wok . . . until I bought fish from a man who could tell me precisely where my fish had been caught the day before, I never appreciated fish.

Nearly every bit of land in America lies close to some sort of water with some sort of fish in it. So you, too, can buy from a fishmonger with his colorful wares arranged on a bed of crushed ice rather than plastic-wrapped trays of cardboard. If far from the seas, there is still delectable variety— the strawberry bass, perch, and crappie of eastern rivers; the great northern pike, whitefish, muskies, smelts, and silver bass of midwestern lakes; the blue and channel cats, Kentucky, black, and bayou basses of southern rivers and lakes; and the graylings, rainbow, cutthroat, steelhead, Dolly Varden, and many more trouts of western lakes and streams.

But is it essential to great eating that your fish be spanking fresh? My husband thought so. A man who prides himself on his sense of taste, he has been annoyed to discover any number of times after dinner that the *sole Bercy* he raved about had been made with thawed filets from the supermarket. No, if you buy and cook such fish with care, you can dine upon some of the superb fishes of the world that don't swim anywhere nearby.

The recipes that follow are classics, and so simple and foolproof that they take the fear out of fish cookery. (They did for me.)

Budget notes on buying fish

How can you tell if it's fresh? If the fish is whole, its eyes will be full, shining, and clear as glass—there are no exceptions to this rule! That's all you need to look for, with the head on. If it's off, the gills should be bright red. If there are no gills, then ask to touch the fish; your finger should leave no impression, and the skin should be glistening as though wet.

And how can you tell if it's fresh if it's a filet? If in any doubt—if its surface is dull instead of moist, if you know it should be pearly white instead of greige—ask to smell it. Yes, even ask the supermarket butcher to open the package for you. *Fresh fish has no fishy odor.* It should smell as sweet as the waters from whence it came. Ask, too, if the fish has been frozen; most butchers don't volunteer this information, but they must tell you if you ask. If there are great pools in the package, it's probably been frozen and thawed—which is fine as long as it shows no freezer burn and the package also smells sweet and not the least bit fishy; apply the same standards as for fresh.

Buying the whole fish is always more economical, like buying a whole uncut chicken. (After fileting, or cooking whole, simmer the skin, bones, head, and tail for a beautiful broth —a saving and a bonus besides.)

When you get home, unwrap the fish and lay it on a plate, cover loosely and refrigerate. Cook thawed fish the same day. Cook fresh fish within 24 hours—or freeze it immediately, as follows: Freeze whole small fish in a block of ice—lay in a loaf pan or coffee can or any suitably sized container, cover with water, and freeze; knock out of the can, if you need it. Cut larger fish into steaks or filets and either wrap in double layers of freezer paper then vacuum-bag or ice-glaze by freezing fish on a baking sheet without wrapping. Dip in ice water, return to freezer on sheet. When glazed, repeat. When ice is ⅛-inch thick, vacuum-bag and freeze.

Always store fish in the coldest part of your freezer. It will keep 4 months.

As for crustaceans, mollusks, and so forth, the only ones affordable, it seems to me, are the ones you gather yourself —except for squid, which come frozen, and make delectable shrimp-tasting rings for garnish or mixing into a fish stew. But if you can go crabbing, or clamming, or diving for oysters, or can pull sea urchins from tidepools (legally!) and squeeze a lemon over their apricot fruit, or pluck thimble-sized limpets from the rocks for a salt velvet bite from a pin, go to it! And of course there are magnificent mussels for the taking on both coasts—*but be sure to observe seasonal quarantines.*

Shellfish may also be frozen for several months. See a standard cookbook—each species has different require-ments.

Canned fish: The cheapest form of canned fish is fully as nourishing as the costliest. So unless it's for something special such as a *Niçoise,* always buy the biggest bargain in tuna, sardines—and salmon, if the price is right. Mackerel has always been an inexpensive canned fish, but it's rather fat and strongly flavored. You might try it in your favorite creamy noodle casserole or potato puff in place of tuna. Maine sardines on toast with a squeeze of lemon make a tasty and inexpensive breakfast or lunch; or serve them over small cuts of French bread as an hors d'oeuvre.

How much fish to buy? For a 3 to 3½ ounce serving of cooked boneless fish, buy:

Whole fish (as it comes from the water): 1 pound
Whole dressed fish (eviscerated, scaled, head, tail,
    and fins removed) and steaks (dressed fish cut in
    thick crosswise slices): about 6 ounces
Filets (no waste): about 5 ounces
Canned fish: 3½ ounces

NOTE: For entertaining, remember that these are modest servings.

Budget notes on cooking fish

First, you should know that for maximum succulence and flavor, cook a whole fish with head, tail, and fins intact.

As crucial as meticulous selection of your fish is how you cook it. Cooking fish is like cooking vegetables—take care not to overcook them. You can always return the pan to the heat, but you can never recapture the succulence you've lost in too much heat.

Remember, if you're using frozen fish, to *thaw it slowly,* as you do poultry—in the refrigerator, so its loss of juices will be minimal. Thaw in its wrapping, and cook just as you would fresh fish, but do not bring to room temperature; cook while still chilled. Frozen fish has been through a bit of a trauma (more than meat, because its flesh is so fragile), and wants extra tender loving care (and not ever to be refrozen).

The great thing is to know the moment supreme—*how to test fish for doneness.* That moment is fleeting, and I'm afraid trickier to catch than with meat and poultry, so look closely at the following paragraphs.

Whole fish: Gently sink a table fork into the center of the thickest part; give the fork a little jiggle. If the meat looks opaque but still moist, feels tender, and falls into a natural pattern of flakes, it is just right. Also, the eyes will be white and quite protuberant.

Steaks: Apply the same test, using a cooking fork so it won't make a great crevice.

Filets: Use a table fork to lift up a flake of the fish near the center of the filet; if it is opaque but still moist, it is ready. If the flakes are too fine to lift, press the fish with a forefinger—flesh should be ever so slightly resilient.

Lean fish: Throughout the recipes in this section, I call for lean fish principally because such fish is usually more delicate in flavor, and is certainly less rich and fattening. For individual servings weighing 3⅓ ounces raw, fish are listed in the following paragraphs in descending order of leanness.

74 to 80 calories: Pacific, squirrel, and silver hake; Pacific whiting; cusk; Atlantic tomcod; cod; white crappie; flounder (sole, sand dabs, flatfishes); haddock; tilefish; red drum (redfish); turbot. Of these, whiting, cod, flounder, haddock, and turbot are cheaper than the rest.

82 to 90 calories: bullhead; burbot; white croaker; lingcod; chain pickerel; squid; red, black, and speckled hind grouper; Atlantic ocean perch; northern pike; yellow fin croaker; tautog, blackfish; blue pike. Squid and ocean perch are cheapest.

91 to 98 calories: yellow perch; black sea bass; walleye pike; red and gray snapper; sturgeon; butterfish from Gulf waters; Pacific ocean perch; pollock; Atlantic croaker; lake herring, cisco; black, canary, yellowtail, rasphead, and boccaccio rockfish; white bass; Pacific herring; skate; Atlantic, jack, and bay smelt. Of these, snapper, ocean perch, pollock, and smelts are cheaper.

100 to 118 calories: Atlantic and Pacific halibut; brook trout; fresh-water catfish; bass (smallmouth and large-mouth suckers; white and mullet suckers); striped bass; California halibut; southern, Gulf, and northern kingfish; carp sucker; Pacific barracuda; buffalofish; Atlantic sheeps-head; wreckfish; carp; bluefish; eulachon, smelt; swordfish. Carp is the cheapest.

The Simplest of Soles

This is an incomparable way with filets of any delicate fish—the French make it with shallots and call it *filets de sole Bercy.* Any effort more complicated seems to me just make-work.

For each ½ pound of skinned filets of lean fish:

1 bulb of a small green onion, minced
Speck of garlic, minced
Minced parsley, amount equal to onion and garlic
    combined
1 generous tablespoon Chablis, dry vermouth, or cider
A little salt and fresh ground pepper
1 scant tablespoon or so of margarine

Heat the oven to 350° F. Butter a shallow glass or ceramic baking dish that will accommodate the filets flat in a single layer (they will shrink, so you can crowd them a bit). Sprinkle the green onion, garlic, and parsley over the dish. Flick over the wine, and set the dish in the oven for 5 to 6 minutes, to warm up and melt the seasonings together.

Meanwhile, lightly salt and pepper the filets on both sides.

Lay the fish in the hot dish, dot with margarine, and lay a sheet of foil (do not let it touch the wine) or buttered brown-bag paper over the top very lightly. Bake 12 to 15 minutes if the filets are thin, or a bit longer if they have been cut thicker. Test for doneness.

Serve as is, or spoon some of the juices over the filets and slip under the broiler to glaze for a minute or two. Or drain juices into a skillet and reduce them over high heat; drop in a knob of margarine to thicken. Then pour over fish. Serve at once.

Once, for a special dinner, my mother and I laid one big fat fresh green shrimp for each guest on top of the filets (just one apiece, they weren't so costly), then encircled them with ¼-inch-wide ringlets of squid. When they were cooked, the shrimp and the squid had turned pastel pink, and couldn't have looked more decorative nor tasted more of the sea.

Little new potatoes boiled in their jackets, silky carrots or butter-steamed peas or green beans and cool Chablis are what's wanted with this. And why not poached or canned apricots sprinkled with grated orange zest for dessert?

A Simple Sauce for a Simple Fish, of Sorrel

FOR A SCANT POUND OF FISH

Have you ever been poking through pots of herbs at the nursery, and come upon a leafy plant that looked like spinach, but was marked French sorrel? Perhaps you didn't know what to do with it. Next time, bring it home, put it in a larger pot, give it lots of sun and water, and in time you can add a handful of the lemony leaves now and then to puréed potato soup (thus making it *potage santé*, or health soup), or to a bit of butter and slip it into an omelette.

Most of all, the tangy snap of sorrel complements fish. Here is a little sauce—not much, because our poor plant never seems to surrender more than a few tentative leaves at a time—but it is perfection, at a modest price.

A good 2 dozen leaves and stems of sorrel
1 tablespoon margarine
¼ cup Half-and-Half
1 egg yolk
Pinch of salt, dash of white pepper

Pluck the sorrel from the pot, rinse the leaves and tender stems; chop them fine. Melt the margarine in a small saucepan (not aluminum) and stir the mince about over medium heat until it melts. Meanwhile, in another little pot over medium heat, bring the half-and-half to the boil. At once stir the cream slowly into the sorrel with a wooden spoon—it probably will curdle, but it doesn't matter. Off heat, drop an egg yolk into the sauce and stir to blend. Return to very low heat and stir until the sauce thickens; it will uncurdle. Add a pinch of salt, then at once turn into a small hot bowl or spoon over filets of fish which have been simply cooked and drained of their juices, as in the previous recipe.

Serve with boiled potatoes, for mashing in the sauce (it's so *good*!) and sweet buttered carrots. Finish with apples and cheese, or fresh strawberries and your own cream cheese on plain crackers.

Filets Florentine

(Filets of lean fish on a bed of creamed spinach)
6 SERVINGS

This is a beautiful dish, also inexpensive. You can make the component parts a few hours in advance, then put them together and heat them up when wanted. As long as neither the fish nor the spinach is overcooked, they won't suffer from this convenience.

2 pounds (at least 6) thinly sliced skinned filets of
  lean fish
Ingredients from recipe for Simplest of Soles
  (see p. 195) for 2 pounds of fish
1 recipe Florentine Bed (see p. 98)

The sauce:
   5 *tablespoons (2½ ounces) margarine*
   1 *bulb of green onion, minced*
   Scant ¼ cup flour
   ½ cup rich milk or half-and-half
   Salt and white pepper, to taste
   ½ bay leaf
 4 *to 8 ounces mushrooms, chopped, optional*
Oil
Dash of ground mace
Dash of powdered mustard

Set oven to 350° F. Roll filets up tightly with the finest-grained side out (if there is one); fasten the roll with a toothpick through the center. Lay rolls seam side down in a baking dish that will just accommodate them all. Bake according to recipe for soles, but take them from the oven *before* they test thoroughly cooked; when they are just a trifle less than tender. Lift rolls carefully from dish with a slotted spoon; set in a single layer in a deep dish, and save the juices. Cover rolls well and set in a cool place; this may be done up to 4 hours in advance.

Prepare the Florentine bed according to directions; it's very important that the purée be taken off the heat a bit undercooked—it will finish cooking when warmed for serving. Lay plastic film directly on top of the spinach, and keep cool up to 4 hours.

To make the sauce ahead, melt 4 tablespoons of the margarine over medium heat in a heavy saucepan. Add the minced onion and sauté a minute or two. Off heat, whisk in the flour and then the milk until the paste is smooth. Return to heat and continue whisking until thickened. Now beat in fish juices from the baking dish until the sauce is just a little thicker than you would like; it will thin out in the oven. Taste for salt and pepper. Add the bay leaf and turn off heat, laying plastic film or waxed paper directly on the sauce so a skin won't form; keep it cool.

About 1 hour before dinner, sauté the chopped mushrooms in a small skillet in the remaining tablespoon of butter until they are lightly cooked, about 4 or 5 minutes over medium heat. Oil a shallow baking or gratin dish that will accommodate the fish, and spread the spinach evenly in it. Tuck the rolls of fish into the bed. Warm up the sauce, remove the bay, then season subtly with mace and mustard. Pour it evenly over the rolls, leaving the spinach a green contrast. Sprinkle over the mushrooms, if used.

Forty-five minutes before serving, set the oven to 350° F. Ten minutes later, set the dish uncovered in the middle of the oven and bake just until heated through; it will take from 20 to 30 minutes, depending on the shape of the dish. Slip beneath the broiler to glaze the sauce 1 or 2 minutes, then serve at once.

Crisp roasted red potatoes and Chablis would be fine accompaniments, and a light salad after. For dessert, cold poached or canned pears and yogurt with a dash of lemon flavoring.

A Whole Fish in the Wok

3 TO 4 SERVINGS

I have cooked any number of whole, large fish in my wok evenings when there were just three or four of us. It truly is an exciting dish—the whole, handsome fellow reclining on a bed of bright green, stir-fried vegetables, as elegant as you please.

> *3- to 4-pound whole fish; ask the fish merchant to scale and eviscerate it only*
> *2 to 3 tablespoons salt*
> *1 tablespoon oil*
> *Stir-fry vegetables:*
> > *Spinach leaves, celery crescents, shreds of Chinese cabbage, thinly sliced rounds of water chestnuts, bean sprouts, Chinese snow peas; see amounts and other possibilities under Stir-Fry (p. 91)*
> *Sauce and directions for Stir-Fry*

1.   Dry the fish thoroughly, then rub amply with salt inside and out. Have every ingredient ready. Set the wok on a ring over highest heat. Heat the empty wok until it smokes. Swirl the oil around the edge of the wok and quickly tip it so as much of the pan is oiled as possible.

2.   At once lay in the fish. Reduce heat immediately to medium low. Set timer for 4 minutes. Do not move the fish— instead, tip the wok in its stand. After 4 minutes, tip the wok so heat is directed to the shoulders of the fish. Set timer for 3 minutes; then tip wok so heat is beneath just this side of the tail. Set timer for 3 minutes; then level the wok.

3.   Very gently slide a pancake turner or a *wok chan* underneath the fish, to loosen it. If it has stuck (mine never has), moisten with a drop more oil. Now slip a wide pancake turner in one hand under the shoulders of the fish, and the other pancake turner just underneath the fish inside the tail. If someone will hold the wok steady, you can very gently nudge the fish over to cook on the other side. (You can manage alone, but four hands are better than two, here—and it's more fun to share the adventure.)

4.   Repeat the timing—4 minutes, 3 minutes, 3 minutes— with heat concentrated at different angles under the fish for the second side. Set the oven to 225° F and place a large oiled serving platter in it. After 10 minutes, test fish for doneness (see p. 194). When ready, set the hot platter in front of you, then use your two hands to gently slide the fish out of the wok onto the dish. Cover with foil and keep in the oven, door ajar.

5.   Return the wok to highest heat and wipe clean with a paper towel, and a little salt, if need be. Now make a 3-minute stir-fry with the vegetables you've prepared. Surround the fish with a frame of the brilliantly colored vegetables; the sauce of the stir-fry can be used to sauce the fish as well. Serve immediately with steamed rice.

NOTE: You can do a weightier fish in your wok as well; a 7-pound fish will take about 2 or 3 minutes more on each side. And if, when you've finished, you suspect your fish is a bit pink at the bone, set it in the oven on a heat-proof serving dish and raise oven to 350° F; cover with foil and give it 10 minutes or so while you dawdle over the first course. Then do the stir-fry when you're sure the fish is ready—the vegetables mustn't wait.

To serve, take along the pancake turner to the table; simply cut through to the skeleton and lift up a slice. When you've served the meat on the top of the fish, pick up the tail with your fingers and gingerly pull back the skeleton until the head comes too; deposit bones on a plate which you've set on the table for that purpose. Continue slicing the fish as before.

No salad—the vegetables are enough. For dessert, serve a cool slice of melon, if in season, a dish of hot peaches or plums laced with rum or pistachio ice cream. And don't forget the fortune cookies. Serve with cups of a fine black China tea.

Turbot à la Bretonne

(Turbot or any fish with white beans, as made in Brittany)
6 TO 8 SERVINGS

This is my mother's gorgeous dish, taken from a traditional recipe from Brittany. Great for a party because it's cheap, and best put together the day before. The recipe may be doubled or tripled.

2 *pounds turbot or skinned filets of any lean fish*
1 *pound dried great northern (or any white beans),*
   cooked
2 *onions, chopped medium-fine*
3 *unpeeled carrots, chopped medium fine*
1 *small stalk celery, chopped fine*
2 *large cloves of garlic, minced*
6 *to 7 tablespoons oil*
⅓ *cup flour*
¾ *cup rich milk or Half-and-Half*
¼ *cup liquor from cooking beans*
⅛ *teaspoon nutmeg*
⅛ *teaspoon white pepper*
½ *teaspoon salt*
½ *cup Parmesan, or more*
Fresh ground pepper, to taste
½ *cup seasoned bread crumbs, or more*
2 *tablespoons margarine*
Lots of chopped parsley

Pat the fish thoroughly dry. Cut into 1-inch chunks, then cut again, with the grain, in half, so the pieces are a small bite size.

At the same time, in your largest skillet over medium heat, sauté the onions, carrots, celery, and garlic in 2 or 3 tablespoons of the oil until tender, about 15 minutes. In a measuring pitcher, mix ¼ cup oil with the flour, half-and-half and bean liquor. Add nutmeg, pepper, and salt. Add to vegetables and stir until thickened. Turn beans and fish into sauce in skillet then mix gently with a rubber scraper. Turn off heat.

Butter a 3-quart baking dish. Spread a shallow layer of beans in the dish, then sprinkle with a couple of tablespoons of Parmesan and grind over a little pepper. Alternate shallow layers of fish-and-beans with light sprinklings of cheese and pepper. Mix the remaining Parmesan with the bread crumbs and spread over the top—add more if the crumbs aren't thick. Dot margarine over the top, cover with foil or lid and set in the center of the oven. Set heat at 350° F and bake the fish a good hour. Remove and chill until the next day. Bring to room temperature.

Reheat at 300° F for 1 hour or so—the heat may be turned down once everything is hot. Twenty minutes before dinner, remove the cover to let the crumbs crisp. If they have not browned, slip the dish beneath the broiler a minute or two before serving. Garnish with a thick border of chopped parsley around the edges of the dish.

Offer Chablis, beer, or cider to drink, a crisp spinach salad, hot French bread, and perhaps grilled tomatoes. For a gala spread, ask the butcher to slice a small ham as thinly as his machine can manage. Arrange on a platter, garnished with thin slices of orange. The colors and flavors all blend beautifully. For dessert, you might make little jam tarts. Shape small tartlets of tart pastry, in tins or over the backs of a muffin tin, and bake them blind. Fill some with strawberry, some with apricot, and some with blackberry preserves (or any assortment that's reasonable in price) for a shimmering variety of colors.

How to Poach a Whole Fish

6 SERVINGS

A whole fish is always a good buy for guests, because it almost certainly will be moist, and because it looks so impressive when you serve it. Poaching a whole fish—be it a big red snapper from the Mexican Gulf or a school of spotted sculpin from the Northwest coast—is a fragile matter. But simple, if you pay attention, and so rewarding. Serve it hot from the pot, or cool, as you like. Cool is easiest.

6 *pounds whole fish; ask the fish merchant to eviscerate*
and scale the fish, but leave everything else in place
Seasonings:
  4 quarts cold water
  2 onions, sliced
  2 unpeeled carrots, cut up
  2 stalks celery, cut up
  Bay leaf
  Few sprigs parsley
  Few sprigs fresh thyme or a pinch of dried leaves
  ½ cup dry white wine, vermouth, or ⅓ cup white
    vinegar
Garnish as desired

Find a pot or pan, not aluminum, sufficiently broad enough to accommodate your fish and deep enough so that the *court bouillon*—the savory broth you'll make—will cover it. If the seasonings called for won't cover the fish, add more of everything, in proportion, until they do. Then bring all ingredients except the fish to a boil over high heat—you will probably use two adjacent burners. Lower heat, cover pot and simmer *court bouillon* 1 hour. Strain and cool it, then turn it to the poaching pot.

Fold cheesecloth (or a large, clean dish towel) to a size which will enfold your fish with cloth to spare at both ends. Wet it and wring out. Spread open and arrange the fish on it. If there are several fish, then arrange them with their heads going in the same direction. And watch that no tails are bent by being crowded in the pot. Make a sling of the cheesecloth and lower the fish into the boiling broth and *at once* turn heat to very lowest. Cover the pot, pulling the corners of the cheesecloth up outside over the top of the lid. Set timer for 15 minutes. The water should not bubble nor even tremble.

When the timer rings, test the fish for tenderness. The instant the fishes are tender, lift them out by the corners of the cheesecloth—be careful of the steam. Set bundle down on an absorbent towel to drain a minute or two, then lift it onto a serving platter or tray. Very slowly pull the cloth out from underneath, using your hands to arrange the fish—one leader and the others following here and there behind, if there are several.

Now use a table fork to carefully lift off the skin on top and any fat that adheres to it, exposing the glistening meat. Remove any top fins that will interfere with serving, as well.

If you like, serve at once, garnished with lemon rounds and parsley. My grandmother made her name with hot poached salmon with egg sauce—béchamel flavored with chopped hard-cooked eggs and a flick of dry mustard. I doubt whether she'd be poaching salmon these days, but a hot whole fish of any sort whisked to the table on a platter, drizzled with melted margarine and served with small potatoes boiled in their jackets and lots of dill still will make your reputation. The trick is to have everything else prepared— the petite-sized peas, the fresh spinach salad, hot biscuits, and cold Chablis—so that when the fish reaches his *moment suprème*, everything is in readiness to receive him! For dessert, a seed cake—a package pound cake (quite pure) made with 2 tablespoons caraway seeds.

To refrigerate, up to 24 hours, very lightly paint the exposed flesh with light oil, then lay plastic film over the fish to seal airtight. To serve, remove fish from the refrigerator about 1 hour before serving; remove the plastic film at the last minute.

For a beautiful and not too expensive buffet dish for warm weather, luncheon or dinners, serve it cool on a bed of fresh spinach leaves garnished with Greek rice salad, fresh mayonnaise on the side, and hot French bread. For dessert, sautéed apples with Pour Custard flavored with grated nutmeg.

NOTE: If you are saucing the fish with something quite flavorful, such as the *aioli,* then you can forgo the fineness of a *court bouillon* for poaching, and just use plain water with a glug of white vinegar or white wine to keep the fish sleek. Even simpler, a friend butcher-wraps her fish in foil and drops the package in, counting about 18 minutes for a big fish.

Aioli Garni

(Poached fish garnished with vegetables and *aioli*, garlic
  mayonnaise as served in Provence)
  3 SERVINGS PER POUND

A traditional Friday night dinner in the south of France
is a platter of salt cod (soaked and rinsed, then simmered),
together with a fine whole poached ocean fish and an assortment of simmered vegetables arranged about them. The
platter may be a simple selection, or it may be magnificently
elaborate. On a special night it might be a platter filled with
the two fishes and framed with little potatoes in their jackets, whole green beans, whole baby carrots, little onions each
stuck with a clove, branches of fennel, small artichokes, a
whole cauliflower, chunks of zucchini, a pile of chick peas—
each vegetable simmered separately until tender—as well
as crisp raw green peppers, hearts of celery, wedges of tomatoes, black olives, and hard-cooked eggs. There might even
be snails, baby octopi, and periwinkles (steamed in half
white wine, half salted water) for a delicate border.

The dish may be served hot from the pot, or altogether
cooled. Thus for luncheon or a summer dinner party, *everything* may be cooked and readied the day before, tightly
wrapped and refrigerated. An hour or so before serving,
make your artistic arrangement upon the platter. All you
need to complete the meal is the *Aioli* (see p. 9), a chilled
jug of Chablis or apple cider, French bread, a slab of cheese
(Monterey jack or Cheddar), and a basket of fruits in season for dessert.

Le Grand Aioli

(Simmered beef and/or chicken added to *Aioli Garni*)

For a Sunday supper of gala importance in Provence,
Maman might add to her *aioli garni* (see the preceding recipe) the slow-simmered beef and chicken from her *pot-au-
feu* cooked the day before. Accompaniments are the same.

Count ⅓ pound of meat-with-a-few-bones-in per serving. For a dinner of *le grand aioli,* I would most certainly end with a fine apple tart.

You'll Love Squid

3 TO 4 SERVINGS PER POUND

Imagine shrimp in the form of ringlets, all pink and tender and sweet. That's how cooked squid looks and tastes. If you were to serve some in a sauce or as garnish for fish without a word as to its origin, your family or friends would at once join the millions of Italians, Portuguese, Spanish, French, Greeks, Chinese, and so on, who love squid. Fresh or frozen, squid is comparable to shrimp in having high protein, few calories, negligible fat (a far more desirable source of protein than sirloin steak, for example)—but it costs a fraction of the price of shrimp. So don't give time to being squeamish about preparing or eating it; squid is a delicacy you really will enjoy.

To prepare squid: Thaw if frozen. Under cold running water, pull the tentacled body from the hood. Pull out the translucent feather-shaped shell inside the hood and discard it. Express the remaining contents of the hood and discard; rinse out the hood, rubbing off the speckled membrane. This is the pure white meat that tastes like shrimp or abalone. The tentacles are useful, too, either added to stuffing for the hood or tossed into a sauce or stew (chop them up and you'll never notice them); so cut them free of the body and set aside.

Uses of squid: Cut hood crosswise into ¼-inch-wide rings. They will sauté tender in oil in a wok over high heat in about 4 minutes—so add them to a Stir-Fry. Or sauté them with the seasoning vegetables to replace meat in a sauce for pasta. Their pretty rings in a vegetable bouillon would add immensely to the esthetics and the flavor of that soup. Use them as garnish for a handsome fish cooked any way. Add the rings to a mixed fish fry, dipping first in a little flour. Or leave the hood whole and use a ½-teaspoon measuring spoon to stuff squid with a mixture of cooked rice or fresh bread crumbs seasoned with Parmesan, chopped parsley, minced garlic, the sautéed chopped tentacles, and wine or an egg to moisten. Stuff lightly (it will expand considerably) and lay in a baking dish; moisten with tomato sauce or canned tomatoes, and bake uncovered at 300° F about 30 minutes, or until tender. (Or simmer in tomato sauce over low heat about 30 minutes). Serve garnished with lemon.

You'll find many more recipes for squid in cookbooks from countries I mentioned—or invent your own. Cooking with squid is cheap, amusing, and rewarding.

What to Do with Leftover Tidbits of Fish?

Mayonnaise de poisson is a good beginning: bind the skinned, boned, and flaked cooked fish with just enough fresh or good-quality store-bought mayonnaise to make it moist; serve heaped on lettuce, garnished with olives, or rounds of cucumber, or hard-cooked egg quarters, some capers, a few cool boiled potatoes—those sorts of things, two or three each. Makes a nice, light main-dish salad.

A *gratiné* is nice, too: cream flakes of cooked fish with a medium béchamel sauce, smooth into a flat baking dish and sprinkle with Parmesan, dot with margarine. Bake in a 350° F oven until bubbly, and brown, if necessary, beneath the broiler.

The béchamel creaming—thick, this time—can turn fish into a tasty filling for crêpes; sauce with thinner béchamel, and sprinkle with chopped ripe olives before warming in a 350° F oven.

And so on.

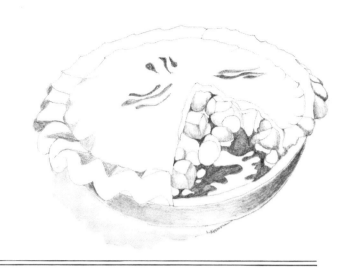

Pastas, Grains, and Savory Pastries

Grains (wheat, corn, oats, rice, millet, buckwheat, barley, and rye) and legumes (dried peas and beans, lentils, and peanuts)—"Poor man's meat," they've been called. Eaten separately, their proteins are incomplete. But a fascinating thing: eaten together, nutritional strengths bolster weaknesses with a synergistic effect, and *the protein of grains and legumes combined equals that of meat!*

Instinctively, cultures all over the world have eaten this marvelous mix. Italians love their minestrone—pasta and beans, with a boost of animal protein, Parmesan. Mexicans slather creamy refried beans over their cornmeal tortillas. And many of our children are made of pure peanut butter sandwiches.

Cheap, delicious, nourishing. So don't feel guilty if once or twice a week you serve a dinner of pasta or beans or rice. Just be certain that *both* grains and legumes are in the meal. And it's a sound idea to include cheese or milk; animal protein added to vegetable increases the nutritional value significantly.

Seeds (especially sesame, sunflower, pumpkin, and squash) and nuts (notably pignolia, cashews, and Brazil nuts) also combine with legumes to make good quality protein, particularly if milk or cheese is added. But this is trickier territory. Best use these seeds and nuts as added enrichment, rather than depend on them entirely for protein.

Poor man's meat—something super out of next-to-nothing.

Al dente: Italian for "to the teeth," means cooking pasta until it's still a bit chewy. *To test pasta for doneness,* just pull out a piece and bite down. Lift out of the water the instant it's ready—soft pasta is Very Bad Form.

Boil in ample salted water, for pasta: For every pound of pasta, the rule is 7 quarts water brought to a boil, then 2 tablespoons salt added just before the pasta; a glug of oil, to keep the pasta slithery and separate, helps.

Unbleached flour: All-purpose bleached flour may be substituted throughout the book, unless otherwise noted. Unbleached simply has been subjected to less processing than bleached flour; food value is close to the same.

Pasta Verde

(Green, or spinach, noodles)
    ABOUT 1¼ POUNDS; 5 TO 8 SERVINGS

You can buy pretty good pasta from the Italian delicatessen, although nothing really can compare to homemade. But you can't buy tender spinach-tasting noodles anywhere that I know. You have to make them yourself. And although it takes time and trouble, they are divine. If you really want to impress somebody, serve them a flat rimmed soup bowlful of your own *pasta in brodo,* fresh spinach noodles bobbing in homemade beef or chicken broth, with a whiff of freshly grated imported Parmesan cheese over the top. They will fix you with That Look, and ask when may they move in. (This is the only *pasta verde* worth making, I think, because you can actually taste the spinach.)

1¼ pounds fresh tender spinach, well-rinsed
4 cups unsifted unbleached flour, and more for the board
2 eggs
1 teaspoon salt
Good pinch of nutmeg

In a pot over medium-high heat, wilt spinach leaves and stems in just the water that clings to their leaves from rinsing. Then quickly run spinach under cold water to cool, take into your fist and squeeze the spinach absolutely dry. Chop on your chopping board very, very fine. (If you ever see a *mezzaluna*—also called *hachoir*—a two-handled, extremely sharp blade in the shape of a half-circle, grab it; it can finely mince *anything* in a trice.) Don't bother with the blender; it gets all strung up in the spinach stems.

Make a mound of 4 cups of the flour on your bread board (this is the traditional way, but if you find it easier, work in a bowl). Make a well in the center and drop in the eggs, spinach, salt, and nutmeg. Work the center ingredients together with clean fingers, then gradually work in the flour around it until all has been blended. Sprinkle the remaining flour on a board and knead for 15 minutes—knead vigorously, and add flour only as necessary. The less flour, the more tender the noodles. Do not cheat; prop up the newspaper or think Great Big Beautiful Thoughts. When the dough is blistered and smooth as silk, cut into 3 equal parts; 4, if your rolling-out area is small.

Clean up the board of any hard bits, then sprinkle again with flour. Or work on a floured table top: Roll out *paper* thin, rolling firmly, always in the same direction. Sprinkle lightly with flour and let sheets dry for about 15 minutes—they mustn't get so dry they become brittle. Roll up like a jelly roll and cut with a sharp knife into any desired width; ¼-inch is nice. Shake out each strip and either hang up to dry on a string strung across the kitchen (part of the fun, that), or lay out on a lightly floured cloth. Dry for 2 hours, or until thoroughly dried. Store in a plastic bag in a cool place until needed.

Boil in ample salted water until *al dente*, then lift out with a pasta fork, or a large strainer. Drain (do not rinse) by shaking the pasta gently, then turn into a heated bowl that has a touch of good oil on the bottom. Toss as you would salad to mix in the oil, then ladle a little of your sauce in a pool in the center of the pasta, and serve the rest on the side.

To make more pasta, multiply all ingredients evenly. You

may knead as many recipes as you can handle, but roll out no more than you can comfortably handle at a time.

A Ravishing Dish

(Green noodles with fresh tomatoes and mussels or clams)

From Apulia, the hot, fecund spur and heel of the Italian boot, a treasure. If made with canned clams (sometimes cheaper than tuna, incidentally), the flavors are gorgeous. But if made with mussels, not only are the flavors a poem, but the colors are, too. Make this for someone special.

Per person:

1 pint mussels
Or: 2 ounces canned minced clams, drained
Green onion bulb, minced
Garlic, minced
Parsley, minced
Margarine
Splash of dry white wine
Peeled fresh tomato, coarsely chopped
Lemon juice, to taste
Drizzle of light-tasting olive oil
3 to 4 ounces Pasta Verde (*see p. 212*)
Fresh ground pepper
Coarse (Kosher) salt

Scrub mussels well under cold running water and cut off beard (the byssus). Lay mussels in a large skillet on a bed of onion, garlic, parsley, a bit of margarine, and wine. Cover pan and shake over highest heat (like popcorn) for just a few minutes, until shells have opened up. Pull the fruit from the shells (any that remain closed, toss out) and keep hot in a covered dish. Strain their liquor for the cook's reward, a hot, buttery sea-draught. If canned clams are used instead of mussels, simply warm them gently.

Also have the tomatoes, lemon juice, and olive oil ready. And the spinach pasta on the boil. When pasta is *al dente,* lift it out with fork or strainer, shake gently, then turn into a heated bowl with a bit of oil on the bottom. Toss to blend, then add the hot mussels or minced clams, chopped tomatoes, and a light dressing of the oil and lemon juice. Grind on the pepper—not too much—and give a quick shower of coarse salt. Toss gently at table before your hungry family or friends, then serve with hot Italian bread, cold white wine, and a little salad after. A dish of chocolate ice cream garnished with a sprinkling of chopped candied orange peel (save a cupful from holiday baking in the freezer; it will last until the peels appear at the grocer's again) might be dessert.

Pasta Fresca all'Uovo

(Fresh pasta made with eggs)
12 OUNCES; 3 TO 5 SERVINGS

If you're not close to a source of really fine fresh pasta, then for special occasions—a *trenette col pesto* occasion, for example (see following recipe)—here is a delicate noodle, as good as you'll ever eat. The recipe is Tina's, a gifted Triestina cook.

> 2 *cups unsifted unbleached flour, and more for the board*
> 2 *eggs*
> 4 *eggshell halves of water*
> ¼ *cup olive oil*
> ¼ *teaspoon salt*

Make the pasta as directed for *pasta verde,* adding water and oil with the eggs in the center of the mound of flour instead of spinach. If dough is too sticky and you really can't work with it, add a bit more flour. Knead this dough 20 minutes, then cut in half to roll out as directed. It may be rolled paper thin or penny thin, as you choose, and cut as narrow or broad as the sauce warrants—every shape of pasta, although cut from the same dough, has its own nuance of flavor.

You may increase the recipe as needed, but only roll out as much as you can handle easily on your working surface.

Trenette col Pesto

(Thin noodles with fresh sweet basil sauce)
    3 TO 5 SERVINGS

Trenette are a specialty of Genoa, where they are sauced with what many cognoscente regard as the noblest dressing of all for pasta. (And worth a winter's wait for the first crop of sweet basil in late spring. You can surely buy a pot or two of the herb cheaply from a nursery—keep it in a sunny window, and, although it is an annual, some kitchen gardeners have managed to make it last until spring.)

> *1 recipe* Pasta Fresca all'Uovo (*see preceding recipe*), *or*
>   *12 ounces good-quality thin store-bought pasta*
> *Oil*
> *Pesto:*
>   *1 full cup of fresh sweet basil leaves (dried won't do)*
>   *½ cup grated (2 ounces) Parmesan*
>   *2 large cloves of garlic, peeled*
>   *¼ cup (2 ounces) pine nuts (pignoli, available from*
>   *most delicatessens or European grocers), or*
>   *substitute walnuts*
>   *2 tablespoons light-tasting olive oil*
>   *¼ cup melted margarine*

The trenette: Roll the paste in 2 separate sheets as thinly as possible—that won't be thin enough. Dust lightly with flour, then roll up lengthwise and cut to the fineness of 3 broom straws, between $\frac{1}{16}$-inch and ⅛-inch wide. Gently shake each length out and hang up on a line to dry, or lay on a floured cloth. Just before dinner, boil pasta in ample salted water until *al dente*. Lift out with fork or strainer, shake gently, turn into a heated bowl with good oil in the bottom, toss to coat the strands. Serve individually in flat soup bowls or on plates, with *pesto* in the center; let everyone mix up his own.

The pesto: Crush the basil leaves in a mortar with a pestle or in wooden bowl with the back of a wooden spoon. Add the Parmesan and stir and pound until the mixture becomes a paste. Gradually pound in the garlic, and then the pine nuts. When smooth, blend in just enough oil to moisten, and then the melted margarine. This much may be done 1 or 2 hours in advance; cover and set in a cool place. Then ladle in only as much of the water from cooking the *trenette* as it takes to make a thick and creamy sauce. Remember, the pasta will have some water clinging to it, and will thin the sauce further when mixed.

Serve with a lightly seasoned salad garnished with garbanzo beans, some good French bread, chilled Chablis, and a compote of fresh fruit for dessert. Should you ever come across a bottle of imported Italian maraschino liqueur, try to invest in it; to my taste, it is the single best flavoring for fresh fruit, and you can use it judiciously, so it will last. For dinner, you might make the *trenette* a first course, in the Italian manner (after the antipasto), then follow it with grilled chicken, served cool and without the herb.

Tagliatelli alla Spinaci

(Baked creamy spinach and noodles)
2 10-INCH ROUND DISHES OF 8 SERVINGS EACH

This is a delicate dish, wonderfully versatile. It can be the party accompaniment for something simple like grilled chicken or fish steaks or meat loaf for lots of people. Or it can be a luncheon dish served with a vegetable soup and green salad. It's also a natural for turning into a complete casserole: Chunks of tuna, cooked turkey or chicken, beef, lamb, or pork, or a pound of ground beef or lamb sautéed until still a bit pink and drained of fat, can be folded in after the spinach.

There are few meats, fowl, or fishes that creamy spinach doesn't complement, and noodles taste good with everything. The recipe makes plenty; you can serve it all at once or freeze one portion, or just cut the ingredients in half.

> *1 pound tagliatelle or any long noodles; or 3 recipes of*
>   *fresh pasta (see p. 215) cut ¼-inch wide*
> *3½ pounds fresh spinach, well-rinsed*
> *½ cup (4 ounces) margarine, plus more for the top*
> *2 eggs, beaten to blend*
> *2 tablespoons oil*
> *1 large onion, finely chopped*
> *3 tablespoons flour*
> *1½ cups extra rich milk*
> *1½ teaspoons salt*
> *1 teaspoon lemon juice*
> *⅛ teaspoon nutmeg, plus more for the top*
> *1½ teaspoons fresh chopped or ½ teaspoon dried sweet*
>   *basil, plus more for the top*
> *Lots of ground pepper*
> *1½ cups Parmesan*

Stem spinach, then set leaves in a very large heavy pot over low heat to wilt with just the water from rinsing. Place in a strainer and press out any extra water. Chop very fine. Boil noodles in ample salted water for about 8 minutes—less if homemade, until they are just a shade chewier than *al dente*. Lift out with a pasta fork or strainer and turn into a heated deep bowl. Add the margarine in bits and toss to blend into the pasta with wooden spoons. Blend in eggs as well. Cover noodles and set aside.

In a large skillet over medium heat, sauté the onion in the oil; when golden and tender, stir in the flour with a wooden spoon, then the chopped spinach. Still over the heat, stir in 1 cup of the milk, ½ teaspoon of the salt, the lemon juice, nutmeg, basil, pepper, and ½ cup of the Parmesan. Cook, stirring continually, just until spinach is creamy and thick.

Turn spinach into the noodles and toss with wooden spoons to blend, adding another ½ cup of milk, ½ cup of Parmesan, and 1 teaspoon salt. Oil 2 10-inch glass pie dishes, or 1 shallow dish with a 1½-quart capacity. Spread the mixture in the dishes, and sprinkle each with Parmesan, more nutmeg, basil, and pepper. Dot with margarine and set aside in a cool place, covered, until ready to heat.

Forty-five minutes before serving, set oven to 375° F. Bake in the center of the oven about 25 minutes for the 2 dishes, or 35 minutes for 1 dish—until the top is nicely browned. Serve with a platter of sliced tomatoes and white beans vinaigrette on crisp lettuce. Offer cold Chablis, and for dessert, orange sherbet garnished with a handful of the cheapest fresh or frozen berries.

Lasagne al Forno, Verde

(Baked lasagne with delicate spinach and meat filling)
6 SERVINGS

This is also from Triestina Tina. It would get three stars from Michelin.

1 recipe Pasta Fresca all'Uovo (*see p. 215*); *or 12 ounces store-bought lasagne*
1½ tablespoons salt
1 large pair of chicken breasts
8 ounces lean, boneless pork (ask for "trimmings")
3 tablespoons oil
Few leaves of rosemary, fresh or dried
8 ounces lean ground beef
Handful of mushrooms, chopped
2 pounds fresh spinach or beet greens, well rinsed
1 tablespoon Parmesan
Pinch each of nutmeg and cinnamon
2 eggs
2 tablespoons margarine
2 tablespoons flour
1¼ to 2 cups milk
2 egg yolks
Salt and freshly ground pepper, to taste
3 cups tomato sauce
½ pound mozzarella or Monterey jack cheese, sliced thin

The lasagne: Prepare the *pasta* as directed; roll into 4 large penny-thin sheets. Cut into strips 2 inches wide, and a smidge shorter than the 2½-quart flat baking pan or dish you'll be layering them in. You'll need 12 strips of lasagne. Boil in about 5 quarts of salted water until *al dente;* then lift out and turn into cold water. Store-bought lasagne should be boiled 12 to 15 minutes, or until *al dente*, and also turned into cold water until used.

The filling: Skin and bone the chicken; cut chicken and pork in small pieces. In a large heavy skillet over medium-low heat, warm 2 tablespoons of the oil. Then sauté the chicken and pork with the rosemary until nearly tender. Add the beef toward the end, as it will cook faster. Drain off any fat, and add the mushrooms—you may want to add a bit more oil. When meats are tender, pass everything through the coarse blade of a meat grinder, or chop fine.

Cook the greens until wilted in a pot over low heat in just the water that clings to their leaves. Turn into a sieve and press out the water so greens will be fairly dry; pass through the meat grinder into the meats or chop fine. Add the Parmesan, spices, and eggs. Mix all together lightly but thoroughly with a wooden spoon.

In a small pot over medium heat, make a béchamel sauce with the margarine, flour, and milk according to directions in Step 2 on p. 64.

NOTE: If you'll serve the lasagne the same day you make it, use 1¼ cups milk; if made the day before serving (and it's best this way), use 2 cups milk. When sauce is thick, off heat, drop in the yolks and whisk to blend, then return to a low heat and whisk 1 minute, or just until the sauce coats the whisk; do not simmer. Stir into the filling; taste for salt and pepper.

The layering: Now lift the lasagne from the water and pat dry on towels—be careful not to tear the noodles. In baking dish, layer ingredients in this order:

Tomato sauce to cover the bottom; lasagne to cover; sauce to moisten; layer of meat filling; lasagne; sauce; filling; and

Pumpkin Bread

2 cups unsifted flour
1/2 tsp. salt
1/2 tsp. baking powder
1 tsp. baking soda
1 tsp. cinnamon
1 Tsp. nutmeg
2 cups sugar
1/3 cup butter or margarine
2 eggs
1 cup (1 lb. can) pumpkin
1/3 cup chopped walnuts

Grease 9 x 5 x 3 pan. Preheat
oven - 325°.

Sift flour, salt, baking
powder + soda + spices

In large bowl beat sugar + butter
at med speed until blended.
Add eggs, one at a time, beating

well after feel addition.
Continue beating until light
& fluffy.

(Roast in pumpkin -

At low speed beat in flour
mixture until combined. Pour
into greased pan.

Bake 1 hr. 45 min, or until
cake comes out clean -

Stuffed Mushrooms

12 large whole mushrooms (stems only to be chopped fine)
3 onions, diced (1 lb.)
2 Tbls. butter
½ cup fine bread crumbs
½ ts. salt
¼ ts. pepper
¼ ts. paprika
1 Tbls. chopped parsley

Saute diced onions in a dry, heated skillet. When onions start turning brown, add 1 tbl. of butter. Add chopped stems. Cover for 2 min. Uncover & add bread crumbs & lump of butter. Season with salt, pepper, paprika chopped parsley. Stir well & stuff mushroom caps.

$$\begin{array}{r} 3.4 \\ 4\overline{)13.5} \\ 12 \\ \hline 1.6 \\ 12 \\ \hline \end{array}$$

$$2.5\overline{)2}$$
$$62$$
$$2.5\overline{)1.66}$$
$$5$$
$$16$$

$10/15$

$\frac{1}{3}\quad\frac{1}{2}$

$\frac{2}{3}\quad 5/6$

$$\begin{array}{r} 3.4 \\ 4.0 \\ 4.00 \\ 160 \\ 1200 \\ \hline 40 \end{array}$$

$5/3\quad ^2/5\,^8/2$

$2/3\,^5/2 = ^{10}/6$

$6\cdot 2\frac12$

$$\begin{array}{r} 11.8 \\ 3.4\overline{)40.1} \\ 34 \\ \hline 61 \\ 34 \\ \hline 27 \\ 272 \end{array}$$

$\begin{array}{l}
11.8 \\
4.7 \\
2.36 \\
3.53 \\
-.06 \\
-.12 \\
3.53
\end{array}$ a2.

$$\begin{array}{r} 2.36 \\ 3.4\overline{)8} \\ 6\cdot8 \\ \hline 1\,2 \\ 1.02 \\ \hline \phi\,2 \end{array}$$

$$\begin{array}{r} 47 \\ 34\overline{)16} \\ 136 \\ \hline 24 \\ 238 \\ \hline 2 \end{array}$$

$$\begin{array}{r} .12 \\ 3.4\overline{).9} \\ 34 \\ \hline 6 \end{array}$$

$$\begin{array}{r} 3.53 \\ 3.4\overline{)12} \\ 102 \\ \hline 18 \\ 17 \\ 1 \end{array}$$

$^2/5 = .02$

$$\begin{array}{r} .6 \\ 3.4\overline{)2} \\ 1 \end{array}$$

$$\begin{array}{r} 27 \\ 36 \end{array}$$

$$\begin{array}{r} 18 \\ 24 \end{array}$$

Escarole Pie

1 head escarole
½ cup olive oil
1 onion, diced
1 clove garlic, minced
½ cup ricotta cheese
½ cup parmesan cheese
⅛ lb. minced prociutto (ham)
2 eggs, beaten
S + P

Partially baked pie shell

Boil 2 or 3 qts. salted water.
Immerse escarole a few minutes
in boiling water until it wilts.
Remove + douse in cold water.
Chop or dice + set aside.
Heat olive oil in skillet. Sauté
onion + garlic until golden.

Stir onion & garlic into escarole.
Mix with remaining ingredients.
Fill pie shell. Bake 20 minute
375°

Niçoise Dressing (salad for 8-16)

2 tsp Dijon mustard
2 tbl. wine vinegar
1½ tsp. salt
1 or 2 cloves garlic - finely minced
8 tbls. olive oil
8 tbls. peanut oil
½ tsp. thyme
Black pepper

Combine cooked string beans,
boiled & sliced potatoes,
hard-boiled egg, tuna, anchovies,
cherry tomatoes, green pepper,
celery, red onion, scallions,
parsley, basil.

so on to the top, finishing with lasagne and sauce, then the slices of cheese over all.

Cover and refrigerate until the next day, or bake in a preheated 375° F oven the same day for almost 1 hour, or until everything is bubbling and the cheese is nicely melted. If chilled, add about 20 minutes.

A salad of mixed lettuces can go with this, and some crisp carrots and radishes if you wish. Chianti and French bread, then cheese afterwards if you want to linger at the table, and for dessert, ice cream with coffee beans folded in.

Manicotti al Forno

(Pasta tubes stuffed and baked)
6 SERVINGS

Manicotti and *tufoli* are "little muffs" meant for stuffing and then baking. If you fill the pasta *uncooked*, then cover with sauce and bake, it's much easier than fussing with fragile cooked tubes that tear and slip through your fingers. Just bake the dish in the morning and chill it so the sauce can soften the pasta through the day.

These are good for parties, as they are easy, cheap, and have a festive air about them. Consider manicotti instead of the inevitable spaghetti for teenagers—a big hit.

12 manicotti or tufoli shells, uncooked
1 recipe filling for Lasagne al Forno, Verde (see p. 219)
Oil
3 tablespoons margarine
3 tablespoons flour
1 quart milk
Pinch of nutmeg
Or: 4 cups (32 ounces) tomato sauce instead of the
*   margarine, flour, milk, and nutmeg*
Salt and white pepper, to taste
½ cup grated Romano cheese if you have some
1 cup Parmesan
Or: 1½ cups Parmesan if you have no Romano

Prepare the filling. Divide it among the shells, stuffing from both ends with a teaspoon, or better still, clean fingers. Oil a 3-quart flat baking dish, and lay the shells in; they must be one layer deep.

Make a *besciamella* (béchamel) sauce in a medium-sized pot over medium heat with margarine, flour, milk, nutmeg, salt, and pepper according to directions in Step 2 on p. 64. Stir, then cover manicotti evenly with the sauce. Or use tomato sauce another time. Shake dish to even out sauce. Cover tightly with foil and bake manicotti covered in the center of a preheated 350° F oven for 40 minutes. Refrigerate up to 24 hours. Reheat by baking as before. Remove foil, sprinkle on cheeses, then return to the oven uncovered and bake another 10 or 20 minutes.

Serve with a mixed green salad and French bread garlicked and toasted. For dessert, sherbet (raspberry after the *besciamella* manicotti, or lemon if tomato sauce was used) with fresh crushed strawberries, and fresh shortbread cookies.

Cheese Filling for Manicotti

For the family, or to serve manicotti as a side dish, this filling is easy.

> *2 cups (16 ounces) ricotta cheese, or 2¾ cups (22*
> *ounces) low-fat, small-curd cottage cheese*
> *5 tablespoons Parmesan*
> *2 eggs, beaten to blend*
> *⅛ teaspoon nutmeg*
> *Fresh ground pepper, to taste*

If you use cottage cheese, dry the curds by twisting in a damp cloth until most of the milk has been expressed. In a bowl, whisk cheeses, eggs, and spices until blended. Fill manicotti and sauce as above, either *besciamella* or tomato. Continue as directed.

Macaroni and (Cottage) Cheese

4 TO 6 SERVINGS

Don't worry about measurements—this is a last minute what's-in-the-icebox dinner. A good dish for hungry kids because you can easily double it should everybody suddenly show up with a friend.

½ pound large-size macaroni sort of pasta, any shape
3 or 4 whole large green onions
2 cloves of garlic
2 tablespoons oil
3½ teaspoons salt
½ cup parsley, no stems
1 pint low-fat cottage cheese
¾ cup Super Yogurt (see p. 77)
⅓ cup grated Parmesan
*¾ teaspoon fresh chopped or ¼ teaspoon dried sweet
    basil*
Fresh ground pepper, to taste
Paprika

Set oven to 325° F. Put a large, covered pot of water on to boil over high heat while you chop the onions and mince the garlic. Sprinkle onions, garlic, and 2 tablespoons of the oil over the bottom of a 2-quart casserole and set in the middle of the oven.

When the water boils, add 1 tablespoon of the salt and the *pasta;* stir well and let boil just until *al dente.* Chop the parsley and set aside. Remove casserole from oven and lift out the pasta with a large sieve, shake free of water, and turn it into the casserole. Add the cottage cheese, yogurt, 3 tablespoons or so of the Parmesan, the remaining ½ teaspoon salt, the parsley, sweet basil, and pepper; use two rubber scrapers or wooden spoons to mix gently but thoroughly. Taste for seasoning, then sprinkle on the rest of the Parmesan and paprika, and set uncovered in the oven to warm through, about 30 minutes. If you refrigerate it (well covered), add another 20 minutes to the warming time.

While it's baking, you might make a spinach and chopped tomato salad and toss it with French dressing. For dessert, sliced fresh or canned peaches sprinkled with grated orange zest.

Dinah's Easy Pasta Sauce

4 TO 5 SERVINGS

Here is another opportunity for using up the lone tomato, a sad bunch of celery, or that mere handful of the roast meat you had two night ago. Our eldest daughter's specialty.

1 onion
1 unpeeled carrot
1 leafy stalk of celery
½ green pepper, optional
5 tablespoons oil
3 cloves of garlic, minced
1 pound uncooked ground beef or 2 cups chopped leftover
    meat; or rings of 1 to 1½ pounds squid
1 16-ounce jar of tomato sauce
1½ teaspoons fresh chopped or ½ teaspoon dried sweet
    basil
1 teaspoon fresh chopped or generous pinch dried oregano
Glug of red wine, optional
Salt and fresh ground pepper, to taste
12 to 16 ounces of pasta
Parmesan

Chop the onion, carrot, celery, and green pepper medium fine. Heat 3 tablespoons of the oil in a large, heavy skillet over medium heat, and sauté them with the garlic, stirring often. In another skillet, cook the ground beef without add- ing fat until still a bit pink; press in a strainer to drain off fat. Add cooked ground beef or leftover meat to the vege- tables when they are tender, together with the tomato sauce, herbs, and wine. Bring to a simmer, taste for salt and pep- per, and let mellow, covered, over lowest heat until you are ready. Or make it a day or two before you'll need it, cover, and refrigerate. It also freezes well.

Cook pasta in ample boiling, salted water until *al dente*, then lift out, shake gently, and turn into a bowl with a touch of oil on the bottom. Toss to blend. Ladle some of the sauce into the center of the pasta, and serve the rest separately in a bowl, so diners may take as much as they wish. Serve pasta in flat soup bowls or on plates; offer Parmesan for sprinkling on top.

Serve with a green salad and French bread, if you like, and why not ice cream cones covered with chocolate jimmies for dessert?

There are lots of other good things you can add to the sauce—a handful of chopped mushrooms (lightly tossed in a bit of oil first, to brown), or some chopped fresh tomatoes, or zucchini, or eggplant—whatever is plentiful and cheap. And you can do very well indeed without any meat in the sauce—just add more vegetables to make it thick, and be liberal with the Parmesan.

Gnocchi Madame Iribe

4 SERVINGS

This special way with Italian *gnocchi* comes from California ranchland via Paris—from a special woman whose roots were in both.

> *10 tablespoons farina (old-fashioned Cream of Wheat)*
> *3 cups water*
> *1 tablespoon oil, and more*
> *1 very large onion, very finely chopped*
> *2 cups grated Swiss cheese or Monterey jack*
> *Salt to taste*
> *Margarine, softened*

Bring 3 cups of water to boil in the top of a double boiler over high heat, put hot water to boil in the bottom pot on another burner. When top is boiling, slowly whisk in the farina. Simmer over medium heat, stirring a minute or two, then cover and set over simmering water in the bottom pot. Stir occasionally to prevent lumps. Cook 15 minutes.

Meanwhile, sauté the onion in oil in a medium-sized skillet over medium heat until tender and golden. With a wooden spoon, stir 1 cup of the cheese into the thickened farina, then all but 2 tablespoons of the sautéed onions. Taste for salt.

Oil a 1½-quart flat baking dish and smooth the *gnocchi* —for that is what it is, now—into it. Brush with margarine and lay plastic film on top. Wrap well and refrigerate until firm, about 2 hours.

Cut into squares of desired size and arrange gnocchi, overlapping, in a shallow oiled baking dish. Heat in a 375° F oven for 12 minutes, then sprinkle with the remaining onion and cheese and bake until cheese has melted and browned.

Use *gnocchi* as you would pasta—as the basis upon which to build. It may be simply served, with a homemade meat sauce or bottled store-bought tomato sauce, as a luncheon or supper dish, after soup, before or with salad. Or as one of the layers in a casserole, with sautéed onions, a bit of diced green pepper, tomatoes, black olives, and so on, and shredded cooked chicken, turkey, or ground beef (anything left over, really).

Old Country Kasha

(Buckwheat groats with noodles)
4 TO 5 SERVINGS

A traditional Eastern European side dish, quickly made, nourishing, cheap, and comforting.

1 cup kasha (buckwheat groats)
1 egg, beaten to blend
2 to 3 tablespoons margarine (chicken fat is better)
2 cups boiling water or homemade chicken broth
2 cups (4 to 6 ounces) broad egg noodles
1 medium onion, chopped
Salt and fresh ground pepper

Put a big covered potful of water on to boil over highest heat. Stir the kasha and egg together in a bowl with a fork; heat 1 tablespoon of the margarine in a medium-sized pot over medium-high heat. Sauté the kasha mixture in it, stirring constantly with the fork, until grains are dry and separate. Add the 2 cups boiling water or broth, turn heat to low, cover, shake the pot, and simmer undisturbed 15 minutes.

Meanwhile, add a bit of salt to the big potful of water, then boil the noodles in it until just tender; drain and keep hot. While the noodles cook, heat the second spoonful of margarine in another larger skillet and sauté the onion over medium-high heat until browned. Add noodles and kasha to the onions, season to taste, and stir gently over low heat until thoroughly blended. Add more margarine, if needed. Serve at once.

Should you see plump fresh chicken giblets for a good price at the market, simmer them in chicken broth until tender, then chop them coarsely while they're hot and toss them in at the end. With green salad, some crunchy carrot sticks, and a crisp apple with cheese for dessert, that's a good dinner.

Crêpes

(Paper-thin French pancakes)
45 TO 50 VERY THIN CRÊPES

With a stack of crêpes in the freezer, there is practically no meal you can't serve on the spur of the moment. They are wonderfully versatile, and nothing to make. It just takes a flexible wrist. Whip up a batch one solitary afternoon, and wrap them for the freezer. They keep forever—they're not supposed to, but they do.

4 eggs
2 cups milk
2 tablespoons oil, and more for baking
1 cup unsifted unbleached flour

Blend the eggs, milk, and oil together in bowl or blender until mixed; dump in the flour and continue whisking or blending until smooth. If batter is not the consistency of heavy cream, add a little water if too thick, or more flour if too thin.

With this recipe you may bake the crêpes at once, or cover and let the batter rest in a cool place up to 2 days; refrigerate if the weather is warm. Have the batter not too cold, and whisk to blend.

To make the crêpes, set a fairly heavy skillet of about a 7-inch diameter over next-to-highest heat. When skillet is hot, brush all over with oil (on brush or scrap of paper towel); at once ladle in a generous tablespoonful of batter, and swirl the batter around the skillet in order to completely cover the bottom before it sets—you want an even, paper-thin cake. The crêpe should bake the instant it hits the pan. If the batter pools up somewhere, or there is too much, simply turn the skillet upside down over the bowl and pour the runny batter back.

In about 20 seconds, the crêpe should be golden about the edges. Run a long, thin spatula around the edges to lift up the crêpe and flip it over. Bake about 10 seconds more on the other side until it browns in dots and patches, then dump out onto a board. (The first one or 2 might stick; keep going until the pan heats up.) Continue thus until batter is used up; use only a swipe of oil for each cake. Perhaps you can pick up some second-hand already seasoned skillets (enamel are best because they are heavy enough for baking but don't exhaust your arm as you swirl and so on). With 4 pans on 4 burners, you can make and bake this whole batch of up to 50 *crêpes* in one-half hour.

Cool crêpes and use within a few hours, or freeze them by interleaving with squares of foil (you can re-use them) or freezer paper.Vacuum-bag. You can fill the crêpes straight from the freezer, as they practically defrost on crossing the kitchen.

To fill crêpes: Place the brownest side down. Spread a heaping tablespoon of filling in a roll across the bottom edge of the crêpe, leaving a 1-inch margin above the filling at either side. Fold these margins over, to seal in the filling, then roll the crêpe up, fairly snugly, but if there is something which will expand with the heat, roll more loosely. Lay seam side down (the thin crepe will stick to itself, and there is little danger of the filling coming out) in an oiled baking dish, touching one another. A single layer is best, but for reasons of space, if you must bake double, then without sauce, lay a piece of foil between the layers; with sauce, lay the second filled crêpe directly on top of the first, so that when you reach down with your spatula to serve them, you won't involuntarily slice into a filled crêpe beneath.

Most fillings may be frozen; simply lay filled crêpes in a freezing box or dish, cover tightly and freeze up to 1 month for maximum quality. Bring to room temperature before baking.

Blintzes

(Filled crêpes from classic Jewish cuisine)
COUNT 3 FOR DESSERT, 6 FOR MAIN COURSE SERVING, AT LEAST

There is no finer example of how great cooks can make something delicious out of bits and pieces. Jewish cooking, for the most part, is very direct—few herbs, few flourishes. The art comes in deft use of comparatively cheap seasonings such as melting browned onions, lemon peel, and lots of margarine (it should be chicken fat, but that's loaded with cholesterol and saturated fat). The following three recipes are for three sorts of blintzes which may be served for almost any meal—or make them all and have a blintz party.

To bake blintzes: Place blintzes in a single layer touching one another (but not crowded) in a flat oiled baking dish. They may be covered and refrigerated a day in advance, if helpful, but the sooner they are baked, the better. Just before baking, melt ½ cup margarine for every 14 to 16 blintzes, then use a bulb baster to moisten every blintz well with the margarine. Cover and bake in a preheated 400° F oven until bubbling, about 20 minutes. Serve at once, with accompaniments—applesauce is a favorite. Have raw vegetables instead of salad, and you really don't even need dessert—the applesauce will have done for that.

Cheese Blintzes

(The classic, from Julia Samuels)
ABOUT 18

Crêpes (see p. 227)
2 cups (16 ounces) dry cottage cheese (hoop, farmer, pot)
1 egg, beaten to blend
2 tablespoons melted margarine
2 tablespoons sugar
Grated zest of 1 large lemon
⅓ cup raisins, optional
Crème Fraîche (see p. 73), sour cream, or Super Yogurt (see p. 77)
Apricot, red cherry, blueberry, or your favorite preserves
Applesauce

In a bowl, whisk cheese, egg, melted margarine, sugar, and zest until blended. Spread on crêpes, strewing a few raisins over if for dessert. Continue as for crêpes, then bake as directed for Blintzes (see p. 229). Serve garnished with something creamy on top, a spoonful of preserves on top of that, and applesauce on the side.

Potato Blintzes

(From Frieda Schor, a fabled cook.)
ABOUT 16

The delicate wrapping of crêpe around the savory light potato, sour creamed and applesauced—my favorite.

Crêpes (see p. 227)
3 peeled medium-large (1 pound) baking potatoes
1 large onion, finely chopped
¼ cup (2 ounces) margarine (it should be chicken fat)
1 egg yolk
½ teaspoon salt, or to taste
Fresh ground pepper, to taste
Dash of nutmeg
Crème Fraîche *(see p. 73), sour cream, or Super Yogurt*
    (see p. 77)
Applesauce

Slice potatoes thinly into a small pot, cover with water, set lid ajar, and set over medium-high heat. Simmer until tender. Drain off water (save for soup) and pass potatoes through the medium blade of a food mill or a ricer—do not pack down, but let them dry out. Meanwhile, sauté the onion in the margarine over medium-high heat until golden brown (it will take about the same time as the potatoes). Turn off heat. Turn the fluffy potatoes into the onions, stir to blend, stir in the yolk, salt, pepper, and nutmeg, scraping the bottom of the skillet clean. Fill as directed for crêpes, bake as directed for blintzes. Serve with something creamy, and applesauce on the side.

Meat Blintzes

(From Claire Calof)
ABOUT 12

From chicken to liver to a handful of pot roast—a thrifty delicious dinner.

Crêpes (see p. 227)
1 cup cooked leftover meat or chicken, finely chopped
1 large onion, diced
1 or 2 tablespoons margarine
1 egg, beaten to blend
Pinch of nutmeg
Salt and pepper to taste
Crème Fraîche (see p. 73), sour cream, or Super Yogurt
    (see p. 77)
Applesauce

Sauté the onion in the margarine over medium-high heat
until golden brown. Remove from heat and stir in the meat;
when cooled slightly, stir in the egg, nutmeg, then salt and
pepper. Fill crêpes as directed, bake, and serve for supper
with the creamy topping and applesauce on the side.

The Best Cannelloni of All

(Crêpes filled with creamy meat and spinach)
4 SERVINGS

Another of Tina's legacies.

1 cup ricotta cheese
2 pounds fresh spinach, well rinsed
¼ cup (2 ounces) margarine, plus a bit more
3 tablespoons flour
½ cup milk
½ pound lean ground beef (finely chopped cooked
    chicken, veal, or ham, or sweetbreads, may replace
    some of this, if you have it)
3 ounces mushrooms
¼ cup Parmesan
⅛ teaspoon nutmeg
Salt and freshly ground pepper, to taste
1 recipe Crêpes (see p. 227)
16-ounce jar of tomato sauce
6 ounces mozzarella, coarsely grated

Place ricotta in a mixing bowl. Stem spinach and put the leaves in a pot over low heat and let them wilt with just the water that clings to their leaves. Press spinach in a sieve to work out all the moisture, then pass through the fine blade of a meat grinder into the cheese; or chop very fine.

Melt 2 ounces of the margarine over medium heat in a large skillet, whisk in the flour and then the milk, stirring until thick. Remove from heat and place the pan under a meat grinder. Through the grinder send the beef, then the mushrooms; if you haven't a grinder, chop them as fine as possible. Mix thoroughly with a fork, then stir over medium heat until the mixture begins to bubble and the beef has almost lost its pinkness. Stir and cook another 2 or 3 minutes, then add the Parmesan and nutmeg.

Remove from heat, and when cooled a bit, stir in the spinach mixture until blended. Taste for salt and pepper, then cover and refrigerate while you bake the crêpes. Refrigerate anyway, if crêpes are already made.

Oil 1 large shallow baking dish or 2 smaller, with about 2½-quart total capacity. Fill and roll as directed in crêpe recipe. Moisten the bottom of the dish or dishes with sauce, and arrange the rolls side by side, seam side down. It is better to bake them in a single layer because in serving, you're apt to slice down and through the fragile *cannelloni* beneath.

If you must do it in 2 layers in 1 dish, cover the first with tomato sauce and sprinkle with mozzarella. Place each of the second layer of *cannelloni* directly on top of the first, this way you know where the bottom rolls lie, and you can cut right down and bring up 2, for each serving.

Finish with a light cover of more tomato sauce and cheese. Wrap airtight and refrigerate overnight if for lunch, or up to 24 hours if for dinner. Let come to room temperature 1½ hours before serving, then bake in the center of a 375° F oven for about 25 minutes, or until bubbly. Be *very* careful not to overcook.

For lunch, just a vegetable *à la vinaigrette*—broccoli, for example—with the *cannelloni,* and something like cold pears poached in red wine for dessert. For a superb dinner party, add grilled chicken after the *cannelloni.*

NOTE: *Béchamel* instead of tomato saucing is lovely, too.

Crêpes de Sarrasin

(Large buckwheat crêpes from Brittany)
10 10-INCH CRÊPES

Sarrasin is from the old French word for "Easterners," the
Saracens who, twelve centuries ago, brought to the lands
they conquered distilled spirits, flaky pastry, ice cream, rice,
spinach, tarragon—and buckwheat, the Breton *sarrasin*.

These crêpes are rare and delicious. Make them for breakfast and drizzle with honey. Make them for luncheon and
heap with your own fresh cheese, lots of chopped green
onions and *crème fraîche*. Serve them for supper with broiled
kippered herrings slathered with melted margarine and
crème fraîche. Or for dessert after a light dinner, filled with
vanilla-scented applesauce, folded in quarters, and dolloped
with yogurt or *crème fraîche*.

> 1¾ *cups unsifted buckwheat flour (available at health*
>   *food stores)*
> ¾ *cup yellow corn meal*
> ¾ *teaspoon salt*
> 2¼ *cups milk*
> 2¼ *cups water*
> 3 *eggs*
> *Oil*
> *Margarine*

Heat a 10-inch heavy griddle or skillet over medium-high
heat (400° F, if electric) as you measure the buckwheat,
corn meal, and salt into a mixing bowl. Stir to mix the flours.
Whisk the milk, water, and eggs in a second mixing bowl
until blended, then beat into flours just until smooth. Oil the
griddle lightly, then stir up batter well—you'll have to stir
each time before you ladle it out— and pour ⅝ cup of batter
in a spiral to cover the pan, tipping it to spread as thinly as
possible.

Bake 2 minutes on each side, or until browned; shake the
skillet to loosen the cake, then use a long spatula to flip over.

Turn out, first side down onto the plate. Cool and store as for crêpes, then spread with soft margarine, and either fold in quarters or roll up with something good inside, heat and serve.

Tortitas de Legumbres

(Mexican vegetable pancakes)
    6 SERVINGS

A delicate use for those stray vegetables in the crisper that can't make anything important on their own. Make these little cakes of whatever vegetables you like, but the colors do shimmer through the batter, so make a bright mix. And no one vegetable flavor should predominate. For example, the following.

> *3½ cups (about 1 pound) finely chopped or shredded*
> *raw unpeeled vegetables:*
> *2 zucchini*
> *2 small carrots*
> *½ green pepper*
> *1 tomato*
> *3 whole green onions*
> *6 fresh spinach leaves with stems*
> *Generous fistful of chopped parsley*
> *1 clove of garlic, minced*
> *3 eggs*
> *½ cup unbleached flour*
> *1½ teaspoons single action or 1 teaspoon double-action*
> *baking powder*
> *¾ teaspoon salt*
> *Oil*
> *Crème Fraîche (see p. 73) or Super Yogurt (see p. 77)*

Prepare the vegetables—shred on the number 3 blade (⅛-inch) of a vegetable shredder—while you heat a griddle or large heavy skillet over medium heat. Mix vegetables together gently on a sheet of waxed paper or in a bowl. In another bowl, whisk the eggs, flour, baking powder, and salt together just until smooth; fold the vegetables in thoroughly.

Add oil to the griddle to a depth of ⅛ inch, raising heat to medium-high. When oil is hot, ladle out batter in kitchen spoonfuls, then flatten each cake with a pancake turner so it will be about 4 inches in diameter, and very thin. Bake until browned, then turn and brown on the other side. Lift out onto brown paper to blot excess oil, and keep warm in a 225° F oven while you add more oil and bake the rest.

Serve 3 or 4 *tortitas* per person, topped with *crème fraîche* or yogurt. To make it lunch or a light supper, add a salad of whole romaine lettuce leaves dipped individually in French dressing, cottage cheese, black olives, and cold beer. For dessert, chunks of pineapple canned in their own juice heaped over pineapple sherbet.

More Fillings for Crêpes

Almost anything shredded or chopped—and cooked, or ready to eat—with an egg, thickening, or sauce to bind it together, can fill a crêpe. Then arrange in an oiled baking dish, moisten well with sauce (never bake dry), and probably a shower of grated cheese wouldn't hurt. Bake uncovered at 375° or 400° F about 20 minutes.

Cornish Pasties

6 ENORMOUS PASTIES

These are a tradition for the night before Thanksgiving in our house. Not hard to make, and so good to eat. And they're almost as tasty cold the next day. (I like my leftover pasty for breakfast.) The recipe is from Cornishwoman Marion Lauren.

1 recipe Best Pie Pastry (see p. 276) with these changes:
  1 cup shortening, no margarine
  1 cup water in all
4 peeled medium-sized white turnips
4 peeled medium-sized baking potatoes
1 pound ground beef (or chopped, if you wish to be
  authentic)
6 thin-cut end cuts of pork loin chops
3 onions, sliced very thin
Salt and fresh ground pepper, to taste
Margarine

Mix pastry as directed; handle as little as possible. This does seem like a great deal of water, but it's the original recipe and it's always been excellent, both for working with and for eating. If this much water makes you nervous, use less. Divide dough into 6 equal parts, make a flat ball of each, wrap in plastic film or waxed paper and refrigerate up to 2 days in advance. Or fill at once, a little less than 2 hours before serving.

Roll out each ball between sheets of plastic film, or on a pastry cloth. Find a 9-inch plate or a pot lid to use as a cutting guide for your circle. Range the 9-inch circles before you in a line. Slice the turnips and potatoes very thin. Cut pork into ¼-inch-wide strips.

On one-half of each circle, leaving a small margin, divide ingredients evenly among the 6: layer turnips, then potatoes over them, then dot around the ground beef, add strips of pork, and finally the onions—sprinkle well with salt and pepper as you go. Dot well with margarine.

Set oven to 375° F. Dampen the margins with a bit of water, fold the empty half of the circle over the filling, and press with a fork along the margin to seal edges together. Turn up the edges as well, to be sure the juices won't seep out. On the top, cut the initials of each person at table—a Cornish miners' custom. Arrange on an ungreased baking sheet and bake on the lowest rack of the oven 1 hour.

Let pasties cool a few minutes before you call everyone to dinner—they are very hot! Serve with a watercress or spinach salad garnished with chopped hard-cooked egg, then perhaps chilled pears and apples for dessert.

Torta Rustica

(Sandwich loaf with filling baked right in)
2 LOAVES OF 8 DINNER SERVINGS EACH

Here is an idea so obvious it has escaped everyone but the Milanese. A *torta rustica* is a natural for a picnic, since it is as good cold as hot. It makes a marvelous hors d'oeuvre for lots of people. Depending upon the filling, of course, it freezes beautifully after baking, and can be popped into the oven on demand. Here is our favorite tuna filling for 2 9-inch round loaves.

> *24 ounces tuna, well-drained*
> *2 onions, thinly sliced*
> *1 clove of garlic, minced*
> *½ green or red sweet pepper, finely chopped*
> *3 to 4 tablespoons oil*
> *8 ounces Neufchâtel cream cheese, at*
> *   room temperature*
> *½ teaspoon lemon juice*
> *¼ teaspoon salt, or to taste*
> *Pinch of freshly ground pepper*
> *1½ teaspoons fresh chopped or ½ teaspoon dried oregano*
> *1 small can sliced black olives, drained*
> *1 small jar sliced pimientos, drained*

Sauté the onions, garlic, and sweet pepper in the oil in a medium skillet over medium heat until tender; add the cream cheese to the pan and stir until melted. Crumble in the tuna with the lemon juice, salt, pepper, and oregano. Mix lightly but thoroughly with a fork. Spread over dough as directed, then sprinkle over the olives and pimientos before covering with the lid.

Other fillings: Experiment with your own. Some we like in this house are sautéed onions and tomatoes with chopped black olives and shredded natural cheese. Cubes of ham, sautéed onion and green peppers, with leaves of mozzarella. Sliced sautéed onions; sliced mushrooms; lumps of cream cheese seasoned with dill, lemon juice, and paprika. And such.

The dough for torta rustica: The easiest thing to do is to use frozen bread dough. Or if you're making your own White Bread, set aside a little less than one-third the batch for 2 loaves of the *torta*. You'll need a little less than 1½ loaves of raw bread dough for 2 loaves of torta rustica.

Begin with 2 9-inch cake pans or pie dishes, well oiled. After your homemade dough has risen once and been punched down, or after the frozen dough has thawed sufficiently to work, roll out ¼-inch thick. Cut 2 rounds to fit the pans and lay a round in each. Spread on the filling ½-inch thick or thicker. Then cover with another layer ¼-inch thick: it may be a plain lid, or thin strips woven into a lattice, or anything else that suits your fancy.

Cover pan lightly with plastic film and set in a warm place. Let rise until the dough is puffy and, when you poke it at the edge of the pan with the tip of your little finger, the dimple doesn't undimple—about 30 or 40 minutes. About halfway through the rising, turn the oven to 350° F. When the dough is ready, brush with beaten egg, and set on the lowest rack of the oven. Bake 35 to 40 minutes—longer, until nicely browned, if you don't plan to freeze and reheat it.

Cool in pan for 5 minutes, run a knife around the rim and carefully turn the *torta* out into your hand, then lay it bottom side down on a wire rack to cool. Serve warm, cool, or cold, depending on the filling and what you want it for. Or cool thoroughly and wrap airtight and freeze. Bake frozen tortas 1 hour on the bottom rack. Cut in wedges to serve.

Another time, spread thin dough in rectangular baking dishes; a 15½-inch by 11-inch dish holds a dinner for 8 or 10 people, or 15 or 16 servings as an hors d'oeuvre. You can decorate the top with sesame or poppy seeds, or Parmesan and herbs. The rules for shaping these loaves are quite flexible—as long as the dough layers are at least half as thick as the filling before rising. Feel free to create new shapes and fillings of your own.

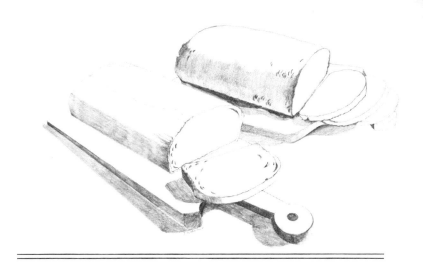

Homemade Breads and a Featherlight Baking Mix

I bake bread because it is so satisfying. The sensuous feel of sleek dough in my hands. The scent of it baking in the oven. The shrieks of children as they come crashing through the door, smelling new bread in the air. The way it's gobbled up. Time given to baking bread is worth it for such pleasure.

But baking bread is worth it for more pressing reasons as well. Scientists are increasingly concerned that we don't get enough indigestible fiber in our diet, particularly unprocessed wheat, oats, rice, corn, and barley ("the roughest of roughage"). Bread is a primary source of this crucial fiber. True, in many areas of the country, one can buy rough whole grain bread at the supermarket—home-style bread that is indeed gourmet stuff. But the prices are mind-boggling!

You can bake healthful bread that tastes even better for half the price. The trick is to bake regularly. The more bread you bake, the finer it seems; also you can buy ingredients in bulk—that's where costs really come down. Twenty-five pounds of stone-ground, finely milled whole wheat flour at the health food store recently cost twice what unbleached all-purpose white flour was at the supermarket. (And this whole wheat was from Deaf Smith County, where soil and climate combine to produce exceedingly good grain.) But in addition to the inestimable value of its fiber, whole wheat has essentially *twice* the nutrient value of white flour—so the price is *the same!*

In addition, if you go to the health food store and buy dry granular yeast, honey, steel cut (or Scotch) oats, and nonfat milk powder (see that the label says it is spray-dried) in

the largest containers you can afford—and store and *use*—
you will make superbly healthy bread at a healthy saving. I
figured my whole wheat batch out, ounce for ounce, and it
really does come to half the cost of comparable store-bought
bread. Store the grains in as cool as place as possible (the
freezer, for what fits), or at least a high and dry, well-venti-
lated area; yeast in the refrigerator; honey and milk powder
in a cool cupboard. That way, they will stay spanking fresh,
and what seems like a staggering sum all at once can be comfortably amortized in the budget over a period of months.

If, however, your family is small and even a 5-pound sack
of something seems ridiculous, buy the unrefined ingredients as inexpensively as you can, and bake these breads anyway. The worst you can do is break even. And your bread will
still be purer, better-tasting, and give you greater pleasure
than store-bought off the shelf.

NOTE: Flours in the following recipes are unsifted, and
ingredients must be at room temperature. Many ingredients
are available at the supermarket, all at health food stores.

Great Bread

5 TO 7 LARGE LOAVES

Please don't be put off by the length of these directions.
This is all that I know about baking bread, it has taken me
years to learn it, and I wish I'd had such a recipe when I
began. If you follow the recipe patiently, you'll have magnificent loaves with a minimum of problems. (The only better
advice I can give is to watch an expert baker in action.) It
takes a mere four hours to bake what might be a week's
supply of bread. You can begin in the early afternoon, and
have fresh bread and soup for dinner!

3 tablespoons (1 ounce) dry granular yeast
4½ cups very warm (110° F) water or potato water
(water potatoes were cooked in)
2 tablespoons salt
¼ cup oil
¼ cup honey
7 to 8 cups unbleached hard wheat white bread or all-
purpose flour (bread flour gives a bit more yield and
lighter texture)
1 cup steel-cut (Scotch) or old-fashioned rolled oats
1 cup low-fat soya flour
1½ cups nonfat milk powder
Oil

Whole wheat bread: A dense, hearty bread you can slice exceedingly thin.

Substitute 10½ to 11½ cups whole wheat for white flour;
buy a finely ground, stone-ground flour, if possible
Substitute oats for soya flour (makes 2 cups in all)
Add ½ cup (3 ounces) sesame seeds

Pumpernickel bread: Lighter than whole wheat bread, and wonderfully flavorful.

Substitute 7 to 9 cups whole wheat for white flour
Substitute molasses for honey
Substitute 1½ cups 100 per cent whole bran cereal for
soya flour
Add 3 cups rye flour
Add 2 tablespoons caraway seeds

Oatmeal bread:

Add 3½ cups oat flour (whirl rolled oats in the blender
until fine)

High protein white bread:

Add 3½ cups more white flour
Use rolled instead of cut oats for smoother texture

Egg bread (*challah*):

> *Add 3 eggs*
> *Add 4½ to 5 cups more white flour*
> *Use rolled instead of cut oats for smoother texture*

Raisin bread:

> *Add 3 or 4 handfuls of raisins to any of these doughs in step 4.*

1. If grains are cold, warm them on a cookie sheet in a 300° F oven. Rinse a large bowl (if your mixer will handle stiff dough, use its bowl) with hot water. Place ¾ cup of the water called for in it and sprinkle the yeast on top; stir to blend and let dissolve 5 minutes.

2. Add remaining water, salt, oil, and honey. For egg bread, add the eggs now. Use a whisk to blend everything together.

3. Add 6 cups of the whole wheat flour for whole wheat and pumpernickel breads, or the white flour for all other breads. Beat hard with a wooden spoon or at low speed on the mixer for 2 minutes, until there are no lumps. Scrape bowl often with a rubber scraper.

4. Beat in the oats, soya flour or its substitute, milk powder, and seeds or raisins (if you're using them). Now take 1 cup from the amount of the main flour you're using and dump it on your bread board or counter. Continue to beat the dough while you slowly add the other flours called for. Scrape bowl often and beat until the dough is no longer damp, gives resistance, and leaves the sides of the bowl in a great mass. The dough will be sticky and it should be firm enough to knead, but bear in mind that, at this point, the less flour you add, the lighter your finished bread will be. Add more only when kneading is impossible.

5. Stop and have a sip of wine or orange juice for strength. Dust your board or counter with a little of the reserved flour, then turn dough onto it—do not scrape out all the tiddly bits in the bowl; leave them. Take off your rings, roll up your sleeves, set the timer for 10 minutes, turn on some Bach or Handel (one wants perpendicular, joyous music for kneading), and wash your hands. Knead thus:

6.   Rub your hands with flour, then, with both hands, bring the opposite side of the round of dough toward you and fold it firmly over onto itself. Push the two layers down to seal them with the heels of your hands, then give the dough a quarter turn. Repeat the folding, sealing, and turning process called kneading—work rhythmically and firmly but gently; do not slap or whack at the dough. Unlike noodle dough, which needs whacking, a yeast dough is a living growing thing.

The dough will stick maddeningly to your hands and working surface at first—a *bit* more of the flour on both is the answer, but see how little you can use. Because of the soya flour, it will still be a bit sticky, but stop kneading at the point that the dough, when your hands are freshly floured. feels silky and resilient—when you poke it smartly with the flat of a forefinger, it bounces back. (Dough with rye flour in it will be particularly sticky.) It will be covered with a hundred small blisters beneath the surface. Do not under-knead—5 minutes will do it for some doughs, but the full 10 minutes is essential for most, so give it that much, if in doubt.

7.   Warm a 2-gallon pot or bowl and oil it lightly. Place the dough in it, then turn the ball over so the top is oiled. Cover with a lid or plastic film; if it's a very dry day, add a warm damp towel. Wrap in a cozy blanket (on cold days, I simply tuck it in bed beneath the blanket and pillows!) and set out of harm's way. Let rise undisturbed anywhere from 45 minutes for light doughs to 90 minutes for whole wheat dough. Light doughs will have risen to more than twice their original size; the whole wheat dough will just have doubled. Thrust 2 fingers knuckle-deep into the dough in the center; if the impressions stay, the dough is ready for the next step, but if the dough springs back even a little, try again in 10 or 15 minutes. Keep an eye on it and do not let dough rise more than to fill the 2-gallon pot.

8.   Punch down with a floured fist to the bottom of the pot or bowl; push the rest of the dough down as well. Turn onto the lightly floured work surface and knead a few strokes to force out all the air. Oil the pot again, turn the ball oiled side up again, cover and return to its blanket. Let rise undis-

turbed from 35 to 65 minutes, or until it has risen just a shade below the line in the pot where it rose the first time; less than doubled in bulk.

9.   Punch down and knead out any air as before. Cover the dough on the working surface with a towel while you prepare the pans. For white wheat doughs, oil 7 4½- by 8½-inch pans or 1-pound coffee cans, or 2 large baking sheets. For wheat doughs, oil 5 pans or coffee cans or 2 baking sheets. (You need 2 ovens for the bread pans; coffee cans are ideal for baking in one oven.) No matter what shape or size of baking pans—or material: you can use baking dishes as well—dough should fill them about two-thirds full. They needn't even all be the same.

10.   Cut white flour dough into 7 portions, wheat flour dough into 5 portions, and egg bread to be braided into challah into 4 portions. Shape traditional loaves by flattening out each portion—into a rectangle for pans, into a round for cans. Fold the rectangle in thirds, bringing the ends toward the center and overlapping them so that the loaf, right side up, is mounded in the middle. Roll it tightly lengthwise to make a firm submarine-sort of roll. Pinch it together underneath lengthwise to seal. Fit it into the pans; the ends should fit into all four corners, and the top should be two-thirds the height of the pan.

For the coffee cans, fold edges of the rounds toward the center and pinch together; place seam side down in the can. Push down the center a bit so the top piece of the loaf won't be too rounded to fit in the toaster or make a sandwich.

For braided egg bread, divide each portion into 3. Braid the bread, beginning in the middle of the plait, then turn the braid around and finish the other side; pinch the 3 pieces together at each end and tuck underneath so they won't pull apart in baking. Arrange on baking sheets so they don't touch.

NOTE: If you have more loaves than oven space or you wish to bake some of the loaves another day, you may freeze the dough at this point *up to 2 weeks*. Use the pans just as a gauge for size, but form loaves about ¼ smaller on the bottom, because the dough will continue to rise in the freezer. Brush dough with oil, then wrap in plastic film or foil, drugstore style, set on a flat surface and freeze. To bake, unwrap and set loaf in oiled pan, cover and let thaw and rise at room temperature until not quite doubled in bulk; it will take from 4 to 6 hours. Bake as directed.

11.   Brush all exposed dough lightly with oil, cover with plastic film and then a towel. Set to one side in your kitchen where bread will be sheltered from a draft, *at a temperature no more than 80° F.* This dough has a super-amount of yeast in it, so if it's a cold day, no matter—the bread will just rise more slowly. But too much heat will kill the yeast, so don't be helpful and put it over the pilot light on the stove or over the oven!

If the dough has risen at about 80° F, in 20 minutes for light doughs and 35 minutes for whole wheat, set the oven to 400° F. Ten minutes later, the dough should have risen well up out of the tin, not quite doubled in bulk. You can tell when it's ready by touching the tip of your little finger to a corner of the bread; if the dough half-heartedly springs back, it's ready—it should raise the last one-fourth of its volume in the oven.

If you want a crisp glazed crust, as for challah, beat an egg with a little milk and very gently brush all exposed dough with it just before baking. A sprinkling of sesame or poppy seeds isn't amiss over this glaze.

12.   Place pans or cans on the bottom rack of the oven, spaced as evenly as possible. Place baking sheets on the lowest and next-highest racks. Bake 10 minutes, then, without opening the door, reduce heat to 350° F and bake another 40 to 50 minutes, or until bread starts to come away from the sides of the pan and it sounds hollow when you rap on the bottom of the pan with your knuckles (it's hot—rap sharply!). Turn out loaves at once onto cooling racks. If you like a soft crust, brush with oil and cover with a cloth. Keep out of a draft until cold; vacuum-bag, and refrigerate or freeze.

A good serrated knife for cutting your bread is essential. And a saving hint: with children in the house, slice the loaf yourself before they get to it, or a lot can be lost in the enthusiasm.

Clouds

AT LEAST 2 DOZEN ROLLS

These are miraculous never-fail dinner rolls.

1½ *tablespoons* (½ *ounce*) *dry granular*
   yeast
¼ *cup very warm water* (*about 110° F*)
1 *cup milk*
¾ *cup shortening*
¾ *cup sugar*
2 *teaspoons salt*
1 *cup cold water*
3 *eggs*
6 to 6½ *cups unbleached flour*
Melted margarine

Please follow bread-making directions above; this recipe will skip the finer details. Soften the dry yeast in the warm water. Heat the milk, shortening, sugar, and salt and stir until dissolved; add water to bring temperature to 110° F (slightly warm on the inside of the wrist). Beat in the yeast solution and whisk until blended; beat in the eggs and whisk to blend all thoroughly.

Add 3 cups of the flour and beat 2 minutes with a wooden spoon or on the low speed of the mixer until there are no lumps. Add 3 to 3½ cups more flour to make a very soft dough. Beat well to make smooth and springy—the dough should give a bit of resistance as you beat and it should be blistered. Cover with plastic wrap and set in a warm place until fully doubled in bulk. Use a spoon to knock it down and work all the air out of it.

At this point, you may cover the dough with plastic film and a plate and refrigerate it up to 3 days. Keep an eye on it, because it will need punching down when it doubles in bulk. When ready to bake, punch it down thoroughly and continue with the recipe:

Let dough rise until fully doubled in bulk a second time before shaping—uless it has risen fully in the refrigerator— then punch down thoroughly. Now flour a board well and spoon out one-third of the dough. Roll it out into a circle ¼-inch thick—you're going to make crescent-shaped rolls. Use flour to keep the soft dough from sticking, but try not to let the dough absorb too much of it as you work.

Brush with melted margarine and cut the circle into pie slices, as wide or narrow as you like—the rolls will bake up more than twice the size you cut. Roll tightly from wide to narrow end. Place seam down on a greased baking sheet, giving room for rolls to more than double their size. Brush completely with melted margarine and cover lightly with plastic film. Roll out, shape and raise the remaining dough the same way. Set baking sheets in a warm place to rise not quite fully this time. When you touch a corner of a roll with the tip of a little finger, the impression should spring back only a little (when the dough is fully doubled, the impression remains).

About ½ hour after you finish shaping the first sheet of rolls, set the oven to 375° F. When rolls are ready, bake in the center of the oven 10 to 12 minutes, until golden. Serve at once, if possible, or cool on racks and then vacuum-bag. Refrigerate up to 3 days or freeze up to 6 months. Reheat on baking sheets the same temperature and time as for baking.

Bolillos

(Crisp and tender shuttle-shaped rolls)
3 DOZEN

These you can only buy in Mexico, I'll wager. They are a superb stand-in for French or Italian bread, if you can't buy that. *Bolillos* are easy to make, and may be reheated; but if you can put them together about 4 hours before serving, they are out of this world warm from the oven.

3 tablespoons sugar
5 teaspoons salt
¼ cup margarine
5 cups water
2¼ tablespoons (¾ ounce) dry yeast
11 cups unbleached flour
Oil
2 teaspoons cornstarch
1 cup water

Please read bread-making directions (see p. 246).

In a medium-sized pot over low heat, bring the sugar, salt, margarine, and 4 cups of the water to 110° F—stir often. Mix in the yeast and let set until frothy.

Turn into a large, warmed mixing bowl and add 5 cups of the flour. Beat with a wooden spoon or on low speed of the mixer for 2 minutes, until there are no lumps. Add another 5 cups of flour and continue beating until you have a dough that can be kneaded and that comes away from the sides of the bowl as you beat.

Dust a board with flour and knead dough for 10 minutes, until it is blistered beneath the surface, and feels silky and elastic. You may have to add flour as you knead. Place in an oiled bowl twice the size of the dough. Turn dough oiled side up, cover with plastic film and set in a warm place to rise until not quite doubled in size. This will take about 1 hour. Punch down and knead out all the air with a few strokes.

Divide the dough in half. Shape into 2 rolls 18-inches long. Using a ruler, cut each roll into 18 1-inch pieces. Oil the baking sheets: ideally, you would have 4 14- by 7-inch rimless baking sheets. If you haven't that size, then try to extend the pans you do have to that size with heavy foil.

Form each piece of dough into a ball, then pinch at opposite sides to get the shuttle shape. Lay 9 to a sheet, brush with oil, and cover lightly with plastic film. If you have 2 ovens, set all 4 sheets to rise in a warm place. If you have 1 oven, cover 2 pans of *bolillos* more tightly and set in the refrigerator for 30 minutes (set the timer), to slow down their rising.

After 15 minutes of rising, set the oven(s) to 375° F. Mix

the cornstarch in 1 cup of water in a small pot, then stir over medium-high heat until it boils and thickens. Cool slightly. When the rolls have risen to nearly twice their original size (25 or 30 minutes), brush with the cornstarch solution. Set 1 sheet on the top rack of the oven, and the other sheet on the next-to-bottom rack. After about 17 minutes, rotate the pans, to bake both sheets evenly. Bake until rolls are golden and hollow when rapped—about 35 minutes. Turn out onto racks to cool.

If you have chilled 2 pans, remove rolls after 30 minutes and let rise (it will take longer with these). Brush with cornstarch and bake. The first batch will be finished baking by the time the second is ready to bake.

If the *bolillos* are to be kept a few hours before serving, cool and wrap them airtight. Refrigerate or freeze and keep up to 3 months. To reheat, lay them directly on the middle oven rack in a 350° F oven for 15 or 20 minutes.

Featherlight Baking Mix

13½ CUPS

I'll really catch it from the General, but am I proud of this! Take 10 minutes, and toss together a saving, versatile, *super* baking mix of your own. You save about one-third the cost of packaged mixes, but you get considerably more nourishment. And it doesn't even taste healthy!

> 5 cups unsifted unbleached white flour
> 2 cups unsifted whole wheat flour
> 1 cup untoasted wheat germ
> 1½ cups nonfat milk powder
> 6 tablespoons single action or ¼ cup double action baking
>   powder
> 1 tablespoon salt
> 1½ cups shortening

In a bowl, with clean fingers, lightly but thoroughly toss all ingredients but shortening together until blended. Add shortening and rub together with your fingers or a pastry blender until the texture of corn meal. Vacuum-bag (see p. 4) or pack in a 3-pound coffee can and store in the freezer, up to 3 months. (When mixing up, use warm water if mix is very cold.) You can double the recipe, if helpful.

When measuring mix, do not pack in cup.

Biscuits

22 2-INCH BISCUITS

You can halve this recipe, if you like.

3 cups Featherlight Baking Mix (see preceding recipe)
1 cup less 1½ tablespoons water
Flour

Heat oven to 450° F. Dust working surface with flour. Add water to mix in bowl and blend with a fork; it should be a light, fairly soft dough. Beat 20 strokes with the fork, then turn out with rubber scraper onto floured surface and knead gently 10 strokes. Roll out ⅜-inch thick—or thick or thin as you like, remembering the biscuits will double in height. Cut with a 2-inch cutter, or any size (a glass works, if you've no cutter). Fit into 2 9-inch cake pans, not oiled, and bake on the bottom rack of the oven about 15 minutes, or until golden. Serve at once, with lots of margarine and Paradise Jelly.

Drop Biscuits, Dumplings or Shortcake

ABOUT 1 DOZEN MEDIUM, OR 6 LARGE

Omit the sugar, should you want to play around with the possibilities of adding a little Parmesan to the dough, or sesame seeds, herbs, or what-not.

2 cups Featherlight Baking Mix (see p. 253)
2 tablespoons sugar, for sweet recipes
5 ounces (10 tablespoons) water

Mix into a soft dough with a fork as above, but do not knead. For biscuits or individual shortcakes, drop onto an unoiled baking sheet a few inches apart and bake at 450° F until golden—about 15 minutes. Or simmer as dumplings dropped from a teaspoon in soup or stew or over sweetened fruit, over low heat, 20 minutes without lifting the lid.

Pancakes

ABOUT 20 3- TO 4-INCH PANCAKES

2½ cups Featherlight Baking Mix (see p. 253)
2 tablespoons sugar
1⅔ cups water
1 egg

Have griddle hot—a drop of water should bounce (about 400° or 425° F, if electric). Have mix and sugar in a bowl, beat water and egg together in measuring pitcher, then whisk wets into the bowl with just enough strokes to blend —do not overblend. Bake as usual. If made with double action baking powder, the batter can be put together up to 8 hours before baking; the single action baking powder mix can't.

Buttermilk Pancakes

20 3- TO 4-INCH PANCAKES

To the mix and sugar in the recipe above, add 1 teaspoon baking soda; substitute 2 cups buttermilk for the water; add egg. Blend and bake.

Waffles

---

4 DOUBLE WAFFLES

To pancake batter, add ¼ cup oil. Mix and bake as usual, being certain the waffle iron is brushed with oil before you bake the first waffle.

Buttermilk Waffles

---

4 DOUBLE WAFFLES

To buttermilk pancake batter, add ¼ cup oil, mix and bake.

Coffee Cake

---

8 GENEROUS SERVINGS

This can be pulled from the oven not much more than half an hour after you decide to make it. It is best warm—a simple treat.

1⅔ cups Featherlight Baking Mix (see p. 253)
½ cup sugar (brown or white)
1 teaspoon cinnamon
3 tablespoons margarine
1 egg
½ cup less 1 tablespoon water
2 teaspoons vanilla or ½ teaspoon almond extract and
*   1 teaspoon vanilla*
1 tablespoon cinnamon sugar
Oil and flour

Set oven to 400° F. Oil and flour an 8- by 8-inch square or 9-inch cake pan. Blend mix, sugar, and cinnamon in a bowl, then drop in margarine in small bits. Add egg, water, and flavoring. Beat with a whisk or mixer at medium-low speed until very smooth, about 2 minutes. Smooth into pan and bake (the oven should be ready by now) in the center of the oven for 25 minutes, or until it tests dry with a broom straw. Run a knife around the edge of the pan and turn out onto a serving dish. Dust with cinnamon sugar and serve.

Streusel Coffee Cake

8 GENEROUS SERVINGS

Make Coffee Cake dough as in the preceding recipe, then cover with this streusel before baking:

Scant ⅔ cup brown sugar
½ cup unsifted unbleached flour
2 tablespoons (about ½ ounce) toasted and chopped
    cheapest nuts (except peanuts), optional
1 tablespoon wheat germ
½ teaspoon cinnamon
¼ teaspoon salt
2⅔ tablespoons (1⅓ ounces) cold, firm margarine

In a medium-sized bowl, crumble the sugar, flour, nuts, wheat germ, cinnamon, and salt together; flake in the margarine, then crumble mixture until the consistency of corn meal. Makes 2 cups. May be vacuum-bagged and frozen until needed.

Bake as above, and serve from the pan.

Ohio Dressing

FOR A 12- TO 15-POUND TURKEY

This dressing, from Marcella Wilhelms, is incredibly light, and the crisp little nubbins of celery and onion are a delightful contrast in the soft, fluffy bread. Use it to stuff anything from turkey to breast of veal to a hollowed-out oversized zucchini. Like many great old-fashioned cooks, Marcella isn't quite sure how she does things, so all measurements are approximate. Which is to say, don't worry about precise amounts—just bear the general proportions in mind.

> 1½ loaves (*about 32 medium slices*) *of* bone-dry *bread*
> 3 cups finely chopped raw celery
> 1 cup finely chopped raw onion
> ½ cup chopped parsley
> 1 to 1½ teaspoons salt
> ½ teaspoon fresh ground pepper
> 4 eggs
> ⅓ cup (2⅔ ounces) melted margarine

Save bits, pieces, and ends of bread (not toast) a week or two before you plan to make stuffing. Any kind except rye or sourdough will do. Store in a brown paper bag, not airtight, in a warm dry place, and it won't mold.

Now, this is tricky, but you'll get it. Fold each slice of bread in half and hold together. Run quickly under cold running water on both sides. Break the 2 pieces into a stack of 4 and shake off the water—it will still feel dry and hard inside. Now crumble into a bowl. It should crumble without lumping, and have just enough moisture in the crumbs. Add the chopped vegetables, 1 teaspoon of the salt, and the pepper. Work the dressing lightly with your hands until thoroughly blended. Add the eggs and toss thoroughly with a fork, then the melted margarine. Mix well, then taste for salt. Pack loosely when stuffing.

What to Do with Leftover Bread?

1½ CUPS

Turn it into seasoned bread crumbs! Amounts are proportionate, so make up whatever you have in terms of the following (cheaper than store-bought and very useful for topping baked dishes):

Dry bread to make 1 cup crumbs
½ cup Parmesan
½ teaspoon dried oregano
¾ teaspoon dried sweet basil
½ teaspoon garlic powder
¼ teaspoon onion powder
¼ teaspoon fresh ground pepper

Lay bits and pieces of bread on a baking sheet, and dry *thoroughly* in a 275° F oven. Whirl in blender or crush with rolling pin into crumbs, then toss to blend with remaining ingredients with a fork. Store airtight in a cool, dry place.

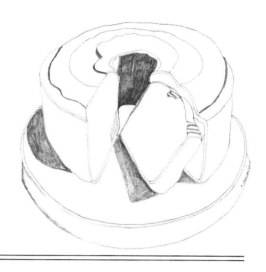

Desserts

Dessert should be simple but dramatic. These desserts are. Classical jewels which comprise a treasury of the only desserts you should ever need, no matter what your menu. They are marvelously versatile. Easy to make. Inexpensive. Foolproof. And all may be prepared in advance. So that when you stagger in with dessert for your guests, you will hear little gasps of pleasure.

(Be careful they don't turn to gasps of dismay—the temptation, out of worry or enthusiasm, toward too-rich-too-much dessert absolutely must be stifled. One perfect jewel in simple taste will serve.)

For the family, nobody needs a sweet. Fresh fruit eaten out of hand while you linger at table, or some stewed fruit stirred into yogurt are foods we do need—and really, nothing tastes much better.

Flan ring: A simple metal hoop which permits a tart to be baked on a baking sheet then slipped onto a rack to cool; the pastry stays crisp, and then the tart can go directly onto a plate to be served. Rings are inexpensive, but you can fashion your own that will last if you hang it up out of harm's way.

Using 18-inch-wide heavy duty foil, cut a length which measures the diameter of the ring you'll want multiplied by 3.1416, then 2-inches added (for example, 9 inches × 3.1416 = 28.27 inches + 2 = 30¼ inches). Then fold the foil double the long way bottom to top 3 times, so you end up with a long strip 1⅛-inch wide. To strengthen, staple in a line along the top and bottom of the strip every 1½ inches, staggering the staples, and keeping the smooth sides of the staples all on the same side. Now overlap the strip to make the desired size ring, and staple together, keeping smooth sides of staples on the inside. Stretch over anything the size and shape you want it to be, to mold it evenly.

You can also shape flan rings in rectangles—long narrow shapes are traditionally used for serving thin slices to many people. To find length for your foil, just add up the 4 sides you'd like plus 2 inches for overlapping.

Ice milk: In place of ice cream, this is lighter as a topping. It's also cheaper and less full of fat. A good idea.

Quinces: I understand that quinces, which already have a short season, are rarely seen in some parts of the country. But if you ask your produce man to get some for you, chances are good he can find them. A magnificent fruit for cooking.

Unbleached flour: As mentioned elsewhere in this book, all-purpose flour may be substituted in baking, unless otherwise specified.

NOTE: *One last time, anything that goes into the oven should be at room temperature, unless otherwise noted.*

Persian Red Apples, Quinces, or Pears

(Fruit baked in wine and served cold)
   6 SERVINGS

These three fruits are of a family—the rose family—and very ancient. Men cultivated them thousands of years before they built pyramids. Of all desserts, I think this is my favorite. Poached in wine, apples, quinces, and pears turn Persian red, and they are the crowning touch to almost every sort of menu.

6 *medium-sized* (2 *pounds*) very *hard, flavorful cooking*
   apples, quinces, or pears (*choose them with stems*
   attached, if possible)
Handful of raisins, if using pears
3 *inches of orange zest*
3 *inches of lemon zest*
⅜ *cup sugar*
⅜ *cup honey*
About 2⅔ cups dry white (*for quinces*) *or red wine*
About 2⅔ cups water
1 *cinnamon stick*
A few allspice berries, optional
Crème Fraîche (*see p. 73*), *Super Yogurt* (*p. 77*),
   Pour Custard (*p. 273*), *or sour cream*

To prepare: Apples and pears are best peeled and cored
from the bottom, then left whole with the stems on. Quinces
are best peeled, cut in eighths, then cored.

Place the fruit in a deep earthenware or glass baking dish;
stuff the pears with raisins, so they won't float. Arrange the
zest around them, sprinkle on the sugar, drizzle over the
honey; cover the fruit halfway up with the wine, add water
to cover. Add the spices, then set in the oven in the center,
turn to 225° F, and bake uncovered overnight, or until a
broom straw, when gently poked in, tests the fruit tender,
and the color is Persian red.

Carefully lift out the fruit with a slotted spoon onto a
serving dish. Turn the syrup into a wide, heavy skillet (not
aluminum) and boil hard to reduce it until very thick; you
may want to add more sugar or honey if too tart. Pour syrup
over the fruit, cover with film and chill; baste the fruit occasionally with the syrup. This may be made 1 or 2 days in
advance.

Remove from refrigerator 1 hour in advance of serving;
serve on plates, moistening fruit with its syrup. Pass something thick and creamy on the side.

Country Fruit Crisp

==

(Almost any fruit, baked with streusel)
6 SERVINGS

This simple dish is ideal after a peasant sort of dinner. To serve, you might knot two ends of two gaily-colored napkins together, pull napkins around the dish (it may even take three), then tie the loose ends snugly together to fasten.

> *4 cups fruit—buy whatever's cheapest that suits your menu: 4 large cooking apples, pears, or quinces; 5 large peaches or nectarines; about 14 medium plums or large apricots; 2 pounds cherries; 1¼ pounds rhubarb (good mixed with a handful of strawberries); 1 pound cranberries; or 2 generous pints fresh or 20 ounces thawed frozen berries*
> *6 tablespoons (3 ounces) margarine*
> *¼ cup honey, or more as needed*
> *2 to 4 teaspoons lemon juice, as needed*
> *Scant ½ teaspoon cinnamon*
> *½ cup (about 2 ounces) toasted and chopped cheapest nuts except peanuts*
> *1½ recipes Streusel Coffee Cake (see p. 257)*
> *Oil*
> *Hot Lemon Sauce (see p. 274), Pour Custard (see p. 273), vanila-flavored yogurt, Crème Fraîche (see p. 73), vanilla ice milk, or Half-and-Half*

Prepare the fruit you've chosen: Peel, core, and thinly slice apples, pears, or quinces. Blanch, slip off skins, pit, and thinly slice peaches or nectarines. Pit and slice plums or apricots. Stem cherries; pit if you have a cherry stoner, otherwise, just warn people. Slice rhubarb in ½-inch cuts. Stem berries. Oil a 1-quart-sized baking dish. Set oven to 375° F.

Arrange one-fourth of the fruit evenly over the bottom of the dish, sprinkle lightly with cinnamon, drizzle with sweetening, dot with margarine, squeeze on a little lemon, and flick over a few nuts. Continue in this manner for 3 more layers. Cover evenly with streusel—it should barely fit. Bake in the center of the oven. Test fruit for tenderness with a broom straw after about 35 minutes if soft fruit; after 1 hour if firm. Serve warm (cool about 20 minutes) from the dish with any topping you like. If you make it a few hours ahead, warm up before serving.

Cottage Pudding

(Warm light cake topped with fruit or sauce)
8 SERVINGS

Once a popular dessert, this modest but delightful dessert may be served probably a hundred different ways. (Not the least of which is as a shortcake, blanketed with fruit and—in springtime, when cows are full of cream and it's likely to be reasonable—billowing with whipped cream.)

> *1 recipe Coffee Cake (see p. 256)*
> *1½ cups or more crushed sweetened fresh peaches,*
>   *apricots, plums, berries; or warm cooked apples,*
>   *quinces, rhubarb, prunes; or Hot Lemon Sauce*
>   *(see p. 274), cold Pour Custard (see p. 273), or vanila-*
>   *or-other-flavored yogurt; or preserves warmed and*
>   *dashed with a little liqueur*

Bake and turn out cake onto dish as directed. Sprinkle with cinnamon sugar, then serve warm in bowls topped with one of the above—or something else delicious.

Winter's Tart

(Tart of sautéed apples, pears, or quinces)
8 SERVINGS

Whether made of Pippins, Jonathans, Northern Spys, Granny Smiths, or windfall apples from the country . . . whether made of Comices, Anjous, Boscs, Winter Nellies, or pears from your very own tree . . . whether made of Smyrna, Pineapple, Gors de Provence, or quinces from a neglected tree someone's grandfather grew . . . this is, to me, the best tart on winter's table.

1 recipe Best Tart Pastry (see p. 278) in a 9-inch ring
8 cups peeled and sliced (about 6 medium, or 2¼
    pounds) hard, juicy, flavorful apples, pears, or quinces
½ cup (4 ounces) margarine
3 or 4 tablespoons honey
1 or 2 teaspoons lemon juice
Few drops of vanilla or almond extract
½ cup (4 ounces) quince jelly (hard to find, but worth
    looking for) or apple jelly; or ⅔ cup apricot preserves

NOTE: You shouldn't bake this much more than 4 or 5 hours before serving. But you can sauté the fruit and refrigerate it and line a flan ring, cover and refrigerate or freeze it up to 2 days in advance.

Melt the margarine in a large skillet over medium heat, then add the fruit, and toss to blend with the margarine, using a rubber scraper. Cook over medium-low heat until the fruit is tender and fragrant. Shake skillet frequently so slices don't stick; turn them infrequently to cook evenly. When they are tender, golden (quinces will be rosy), and fragrant, remove from heat and drizzle over them 3 tablespoons of honey and probably 1 teaspoon of lemon juice, unless the fruit is just the right balance of sweet and tart. Scent the apples and quinces delicately with vanilla, the pears with almond, then stir to blend gently with a rubber scraper. Taste—add more honey or lemon if necessary, but do not oversweeten; the glaze will add its sweetness.

Set oven to 400° F. Melt the jelly in a small pan or warm the preserves, then strain them. Paint the bottom and sides of the shell with jelly or preserves, then turn the fruit into the shell; if there is much juice in the skillet, lift slices out with a slotted spoon. The simplest way to decorate the tart is to smooth fruit out; some will be distinct slices, some will have turned to thick sauce. Pull slices out as you go, and arrange them in a swirl over the top. Curl one last slice like a rosebud in the center. Bake on the lowest rack in the oven for 35 minutes, or until the crust has pulled away from the ring.

Remove tart to cooling rack as directed, melt jelly or preserves again, and pour evenly over the fruit, using the pastry brush to coat every slice and fill in every space. Serve warm; slip into a 250° F oven when you sit down to dinner, if tart has cooled completely (most serving plates will take that low heat).

The Trick to Chilling and Freezing Fresh Fruit So It Keeps Its Color and Flavor

5½ CUPS; FOR 8 TO 10 PINTS FRUIT

I used to pass up bargains of marked-down fruits at the height of their season—slightly bruised, blemished, or under-ripe goodies—because I just couldn't go through the canning routine to save them. And when I did buy such fruit, I used to wish I could make lots of fruit compote to keep on hand, but I couldn't, because it would all go dark, and then no one would eat it.

Then I discovered the magic of ascorbic acid—good old vitamin C. A pure, safe, and healthy color protector, a little bit added to a simple syrup keeps sliced fresh fruit sparkling for days (even bananas). More exciting, you can freeze fresh fruit without any processing, for the most part, and pull out an astonishingly fresh fruit cup in the dead of winter.

Buy ascorbic acid from the druggist; and when he hands you the jar, don't drop it from the shock of the price. Although you can buy commercial combinations of ascorbic acid, citric acid, and aluminum salts for color protection for less than half the money, in practical terms, pure ascorbic acid is three times cheaper because you use so little of it—and it keeps indefinitely in a cool, dry place. So considering the money you'll save putting up windfalls of bargain fruit, it's worth every penny. (You should also use it in canning; add ¼ teaspoon ascorbic acid powder to each quart of fruit that discolors in air or with light.)

Here are the basic syrups which you can quickly make up:

1.   *Simple syrup for chilling* all fresh fruit:

> 2¼ *cups sugar*
> ¾ *cup honey* (*or use 3 cups sugar, if you prefer*)
> 4 *cups cold water*
> ½ *teaspoon powdered ascorbic acid*

2.   *Simple syrup for freezing* apples, berries, citrus fruits, grapes, nectarines, peaches, pineapple (use juice as part of the water), plums, quinces:

> 2¾ *cups white corn syrup*
> 1½ *cups sugar*
> 2 *cups cold water*
> ½ *teaspoon powdered ascorbic acid*

3.   *Simple syrup for freezing* apricots and pears: Add ½ teaspoon powdered ascorbic acid to syrup number 2.

4.   *Simple syrup for freezing* sweet cherries, musk-type melons:

> 2½ *cups white corn syrup*
> 1 *cup sugar*
> 2 *cups cold water*
> ½ *teaspoon powdered ascorbic acid*

5.   *Simple syrup for freezing* figs:

> 2⅔ *cups white corn syrup*
> 1¼ *cups sugar*
> 2 *cups water*
> 1 *teaspoon powdered ascorbic acid*

To prepare the syrup: If making up in advance, stir everything but the ascorbic acid together until thoroughly dissolved and blended (do not heat). Add ascorbic acid just before the fruit goes in; stir to blend.

To prepare the fruit for freezing: Add the ascorbic acid to the syrup, then drop fruit in as you prepare it. Cut out any flaws, then peel, core or pit, and slice apples, apricots, citrus fruits, figs, melons (also in balls or cubes), nectarines, peaches, pineapples (also in cubes). Apricots, figs, nectarines, peaches, or unpeeled plums may also be halved or quartered. Berries (strawberries may be sliced in thirds), pitted cherries, figs, grapes, or plums may be packed whole. *To prepare pears for freezing* (the only fruit that takes a brief cooking), cut out flaws, then peel firm fruit, quarter, and core. Lay in *boiling* syrup number 2 without ascorbic acid; cook for 1 to 2 minutes (depending on size). Lift out, cool, pack in cold syrup number 3.

To freeze fruit in syrup, fill canning jars one-third full of cold syrup (just hold fruit back and pour in syrup). Place fruit in jar with slotted spoon up to jar's shoulders; cover fruit with cold syrup. Crumple a large piece of waxed or freezer paper and press on top, to keep fruit beneath the syrup. Cap and freeze at once.

Fruit keeps 9 to 12 months in the freezer. Thaw unopened jars rapidly by setting in cool water. Serve fruit while still glistening with crystals (although fruit will keep its color and flavor for days in the refrigerator after thawing). Or use in cooking as you would fresh fruit.

Danish Caramelized Custard

8 SERVINGS

A sublime dessert from Ellen Kristensen—much more silky and creamy than the usual custard.

1¼ cups sugar
1 quart half-and-half or rich milk
Split vanilla bean or 2 teaspoons vanilla
2 eggs
4 egg yolks (for a less rich custard, use 4 whole eggs and no extra yolks)

The caramel: Melt 1 cup of the sugar in a small heavy pot over medium-low heat until it turns completely liquid and a clear tawny gold; you may want to stir with a wooden spoon now and then, to help it along. Do not let it burn. Pour it into a smooth-sided 6-cup mold, and swirl over the bottom and sides to cover.

The custard: Meanwhile, in a medium pot over medium heat, stir the half-and-half with ¼ cup of sugar and the vanilla until sugar is dissolved. Slowly whisk some of the hot cream into the eggs and extra yolks in a mixing bowl. Turn eggs into the pot off-heat, and pour through a sieve into the mold. Cover tightly with foil.

Set the mold very carefully on a trivet or several layers of dishtowels in a very deep pot. Pour very hot water 1-inch deep around the mold. Cover the pot and steam the custard over *low* heat from 45 to 60 minutes. The water must never boil. The custard is finished when you lift the foil (watch for steam) and the custard feels semi-firm to the touch; it will tremble in the center but firm more as it cools. Lift it out and refrigerate at least 4 hours before serving. It may be made the day before.

NOTE: The texture won't be the same, but if you are more comfortable baking the custard, then set mold in hot water in a 325° F oven and bake 45 minutes, or only until a knife emerges from the center clean—be careful not to overcook.

To serve: Run the tip of a knife around the rim of the mold, place a deep serving dish on top of it, and quickly invert. Caramel will sheet down over the custard.

Crème Brulée

(Praline-covered custard)
   8 SERVINGS

Delicious and intriguing. For fancy dinner parties.

  1 recipe Danish Custard (see preceding recipe); omit the caramelizing
  1 pound light brown sugar, sifted or rolled free of lumps

Make the custard with 4 whole eggs and no extra yolks. Pour through a sieve into a glass baking dish in which the custard will be 1½ inches deep. Steam or bake as directed; chill, covered, at least 3 hours.

When cold, sprinkle on the brown sugar to a depth of a generous ¼ inch. Heat the broiler, and slip custard about 6 inches beneath it. Let the sugar glaze—it will melt together and become quite brittle and shiny. Watch carefully, because it can burn in an instant. Once nearly all the sugar has melted, pull from broiler. Cover with waxed paper and chill for another 3 or 4 hours.

Crack the praline top with the bowl of a spoon before serving. This is even handsomer if made individually in little *pot de crème* custard dishes; in which case, set them all in an oven-proof pan of ice water for the glazing.

Pour Custard

I GENEROUS PINT

Wonderfully useful sauce—pour it cool from a pretty pitcher over simple warm stewed fruit, or over fresh sliced fruit or berries. Over chocolate cake. Over fruit pies. Or dash it with Marsala and serve it in wine glasses rather as an English *zabaione*. (The English adore it; if you ever come across a checkered box of "Dessert Powder" imported from England, it is an inexpensive and recommended shortcut for this custard.)

These are particularly delicate proportions.

2 cups rich milk
1 teaspoon cornstarch
3 tablespoons sugar
3 egg yolks
1 teaspoon vanilla

Reserve 1 tablespoon of the milk and mix with the cornstarch and sugar in a small bowl. Bring the rest of the milk in a pot to a simmer over medium heat. Stir a little hot milk into the cornstarch solution, then, when blended, whisk it back into the pot. Whisk sauce over medium heat until lightly thickened.

Beat yolks to blend in another small bowl; whisk in a little of the sauce. When blended, whisk yolks into the pot over very low heat. Keep whisking a moment or two, just until the sauce coats the whisk. Remove at once—do not let simmer—and pass through a nylon sieve into a serving pitcher or bowl. Cool; then stir in the vanilla.

Place plastic film directly on the sauce so a skin won't form; refrigerate at once. Give it overnight to thicken. Stir lightly before serving. Keeps at least 3 days.

San Joaquin Valley Hot Lemon Sauce

6 SERVINGS

Absolutely gorgeous stuff for ladling over hot apple anything, tarts, puddings, or almost any light dessert.

¾ cup sugar
½ cup margarine
1 egg
1 large lemon; grated zest and juice (or more, to taste)
1 teaspoon nutmeg
½ cup boiling water

Cream sugar with margarine in small saucepan until fluffy. Beat in egg, lemon zest, juice, and nutmeg. Whisk well, then whisk in water. Whisk over low heat until thickened—do not let simmer. May be held over hot water (not boiling), or chilled then reheated the next day over hot water.

...

My Grandmother's World-Famous Chocolate Cake

12 SERVINGS

Throwing caution to the winds every once in a while can be super. Here's the way to blow it with style. (The only thing it isn't bad for is the budget . . .) From the same very old cookbook as the lemon sauce.

Chocolate:
> *2 ounces unsweetened chocolate (although you can use up to 4)*
> *1 cup light brown sugar*
> *½ cup buttermilk*

Batter:
> *2 medium-sized peeled baking potatoes*
> *½ cup shortening*
> *1 cup light brown sugar, rolled free of lumps*
> *2 teaspoons vanilla*
> *1¾ cups sifted cake flour*
> *1 teaspoon baking soda*
> *½ teaspoon salt*
> *3 egg yolks*
> *1 cup warm buttermilk*
> *Oil and flour*
> *Confectioner's sugar*

Oil and flour a tube or any baking pan or pans with a total of 12 cups capacity. Place chocolate ingredients in a small pot over low heat, bring to a simmer, and stir often while chocolate cooks until thick, about 10 minutes. Remove from heat and cool.

Meanwhile, cut up potatoes into a saucepan, cover with water, cover and set over medium-high heat to simmer until tender. Now cream shortening with wooden spoon or at medium speed on the mixer 3 minutes; add brown sugar slowly as you continue to beat. Keep beating as you add vanilla. Set oven to 350° F. If using a mixer, stop and scrape bowl and beaters, then set to medium-low speed and keep beating while you sift the flour, soda, and salt together 3 times. Rice the potatoes through a sieve or medium blade of a food mill and keep warm (important). If beating by hand, go back to beating after doing this, and beat until mixture is ever so creamy and light; about 10 minutes after adding vanilla.

Scrape bowl and beaters again. Add egg yolks one at a time, beating 1 minute after each. Then measure the potatoes; you'll need ½ cup; beat them in hot. The mixture will thin out, but beat 2 or 3 minutes more and it will thicken again. Add the cooled chocolate now and beat to blend. Turn into a larger bowl.

Working quickly, spoon one-third of the flour over the batter, then whisk it in in 15 strokes (do not beat). Add half the buttermilk, half the remaining flour, remaining buttermilk, and remaining flour—15 strokes, or less, after each. Turn into pan or divide among pans, smoothing away from the center. Rap on the counter once or twice, then bake in the center of the oven until sides of the cake begin to pull away from the pans; 45 minutes for the tube, about 30 minutes for a large flat layer, 25 minutes for 3 8-inch pans. Cool 5 minutes in the pan, then turn out onto racks.

These days, I wouldn't dream of icing this cake—a drift of sifted powdered sugar before serving is dramatic enough.

Best Pie Pastry

10-INCH DOUBLE CRUST

For old-fashioned melt-in-the-mouth pies, this is our family formula.

3⅓ cups unsifted unbleached flour
¼ teaspoon salt
10 tablespoons cool shortening
10 tablespoons (5 ounces) chilled stick margarine
4 tablespoons ice water, or a bit more

In a bowl, rub flour, salt, and shortening together with your fingers until the texture of corn meal. Flake in the cold margarine and rub together until the texture of tiny peas. Sprinkle 4 tablespoons of the ice water over the mixture, never hitting the same place twice, tossing all together with a fork. As you sprinkle, begin to press the moistened flour together with the fork; whatever sticks in the fork lift out and turn onto waxed paper. Keep picking up dough with the fork and setting it on the paper, adding more water only when the dough will no longer hold together.

Pat dough on waxed paper together into 1 or 2 flat rounds, depending on size of crust you'll want. For a 2-crust pie, make 1 round slightly larger than the other. Wrap in waxed paper or plastic film and chill at least 1 hour; overnight is best. Then roll out on a pastry cloth or between sheets of plastic film with a very little flour. Usually, ⅛ inch is the thickness wanted (mark ⅛ inch on a toothpick with a ruler, then stick it into the dough here and there to measure). Roll out 2 inches wider than the dish you're lining. Roll always away from you, from the center of the dough outward; turn dough occasionally so you'll get even coverage.

Dust the pastry lightly with flour and fold the bottom round in half, then in half again. Set in pie dish with the point of the triangle right in the center, then unfold and gently press pastry against the dish—never stretch dough as you work with it. Leave the edges ragged; you'll trim later.

Roll out the lid of the pie ⅛-inch thick and 2 inches wider than the diameter of the dish. Place between waxed paper on a large plate; mend any tears with a drop of ice water. Chill both rounds another hour if possible. Or freeze, well-covered.

Just before baking, fill pie, run a wet finger around the top of the rim, then lay on the lid. When softened a bit, press edges together to seal, then trim with a sharp knife. Flute the edge by pressing a fingertip slantwise along the rim, making a swirled effect. Or pinch together between thumb and forefinger, also on the slant, making little ripples. Prick holes in the top with a fork, or slash with a knife making a pattern.

To bake the bottom crust blind (before filling):   Follow same directions as for tart pastry in flan ring, baking with foil and beans for 10 minutes (20, if you put the pastry in frozen, which you may, and it only makes it crisper), then empty for 10 minutes more, or until it is crisp and golden. Cool in the pan on a rack.

For a shiny crust, before baking, brush the top or the rim of the pastry with milk. Egg mixed into the milk makes the crust sleek and brown. Sugar or cinnamon sugar on top makes it sparkle. You can use this pastry for turnovers, too, either savory little ones, filled with chopped cooked meats and cheeses, or sweet ones, filled with fruit and jam. Use up any trimmings this way.

Best Tart Pastry

I 9-INCH FLAN AND A JAM TART, OR I 9½-INCH FLAN, OR 12 TO 24 TARTLETS

Here is a no-worry crisp pastry for sweet and savory tarts with many advantages: Easy to mix, no need to chill (although it may be chilled, for the sake of convenience), and no need to roll out. That means it can be ready for the oven in two shakes of a lamb's tail. It is also tender as can be.

1¾ cups unsifted unbleached flour
1 tablespoon sugar; omit for savory fillings
¼ teaspoon salt
½ cup (4 ounces) chilled stick margarine
2 tablespoons ice water or a bit more
Soft margarine

Set flan ring on a foil sheet on a rimless baking pan (or the back of a rimmed one). Use the soft margarine to butter the inside of the ring and the foil making a bottom.

Making the pastry: In a bowl, use a fork to toss flour, sugar, and salt together, then flake in the cold margarine.

Rub together with your fingers until mixture is like corn meal. Sprinkle the water over the flour, never hitting the same place twice, mixing lightly with the fork as you go. Gently work the dough together with your fingers into a ball that holds together and is malleable. Set it in the center of the flan ring. If 9-inch, remove and set aside 2 tablespoons of the dough. Set oven to 400° F.

Shaping the flan: Now, working gently, use your fingers and flat of your knuckles to coax the dough over the bottom and up the sides of the ring ⅛-inch thick. There will be just enough dough to cover; watch that it doesn't get too thick where it makes a right angle from ring to bottom. Pinch distinctly between thumb and forefinger at an angle all around the rim of the ring to make a fluting, then run a sharp knife along the top to cut away excess. (Add bits of trimmings to the reserved dough, and pat into a thin round at one edge of the baking sheet; place 1 tablespoon of preserves to one side of the round, lift foil to fold dough over, press with fork to seal, prick top, then bake as a little jam tart for the pastry cook.)

Baking the tart: Bake filled on the bottom rack of the oven as directed in recipe. Pastry is done when it has pulled away slightly from the ring, and is golden. At once remove from oven; slip foil off baking sheet, pulling the tart along, easing it onto a cooling rack. Run a spatula completely underneath the tart to free it from the foil, then slip the tip of a knife between shell and ring to hold the ring in place while you ease the foil from beneath the tart. Now run the knife around the ring to free any stuck places, and lift the ring up. Cool; most fruit tarts are best warm, so allow about 30 minutes before serving. You can slip the ring back over the tart when you slide it off the rack onto a serving plate—it gives the fragile edges support.

To bake pastry blind (before filling):   Set oven to 400° F. Line the unbaked shell (prepared as above) with a piece of foil, molding it right against the dough. Press with the fluting, as well, if you want the fluting distinct. Fill bottom with 2 cups of dry beans, pushing some up against the sides of the tart. Bake in the center of the oven 20 minutes, then pull out, carefully lift out foil and beans (later, pack beans away, and label them "For Tarts"). Your jam tart is ready, so remove to cooling rack. This is *a partially-baked shell*, and may now be used for baking a custard filling, such as a quiche. *To bake completely*, return to the oven for 7 or 8 minutes, or until golden, and pulled away from the ring. Slip onto cooling rack as directed above. Keep out of harm's way in a cool place, and fill and serve within 24 hours.

To bake tartlets: Line small molds with ⅛-inch-thick pastry, arranging them on a baking sheet. Or turn muffin tins upside down and form a shell over the back of each muffin mold. Bake blind; the upside down pastries should be well-pricked with a fork, but gravity ought to keep them from losing their shapes.

Amanda's Shortbread

4 DOZEN SMALL COOKIES

The feeling among many cookie connoisseurs is that shortbread is the quintessential cookie—buttery, rich, not too sweet. After baking a mountain of shortbread—Scotch, Danish, English, Irish, and heaven knows what—my daughter Amanda, the Cookie Queen, devised this marvelously no-nonsense shortbread, the best any of us has tasted. Excellent cookies to accompany light desserts; being rich, they go a long way.

> *1 cup (8 ounces) soft margarine (if good-tasting,*
>   *it needn't be butter)*
> *¾ cup sugar*
> *2½ cups unsifted unbleached flour*
> *Pinch of salt*
> *Quick glug of vanilla (about ½ teaspoon)*
> *Margarine*

In a mixing bowl, beat at medium speed (use a dough hook,

if you're lucky enough to have one for your machine) until dough holds together and pulls away from the sides of the bowl. If it won't do this, cover and chill about 1 hour, and then it will. Heat oven to 350° F. Divide in half. Butter a large baking sheet with margarine, then lay the 2 lumps of pastry on the sheet. Use your fist (Amanda's is tiny— perhaps you ought to use your knuckles) to pat into 2 ¼-inch-thick squares. Prick with a fork all over. Bake in the center of the oven just until the color of sand, about 25 minutes, maybe 30. Cut before it cools into pieces of desired size, and lift onto rack to cool. Stored in airtight tins, these will keep indefinitely (ha!).

Amanda is thinking of rolling out this dough to make Christmas cookies this year. Good idea.

Smart Cookies

DOZENS AND DOZENS (AT LEAST 8 DOZEN)

These are healthful enough that the children could eat them for breakfast. (The trick here is to keep grownups out of the cookie jar!) Also very useful for saving cereal in the cupboard everyone ignores.

1 cup margarine
1 cup oil
2 cups raw or light brown sugar
2 teaspoons vanilla
4 eggs
¼ cup brewed coffee
2½ cups unsifted unbleached flour
1 cup whole wheat flour
2 teaspoons baking soda
1 teaspoon salt
6 cups any "granola" cereal (except one with more sugar than grains); oatmeal may be substituted
2 cups raisins (or 1 cup raisins, 1 cup chopped nuts)
6 ounces chocolate chips (optional, but I force myself to use them)
Oil

Set oven to 350° F. Oil some baking sheets. Beat the margarine until soft, cream in the oil, then the sugar and vanilla. When fluffy, beat in the eggs, then the coffee. Now mix the flours, soda, and salt in a bowl until blended, and stir them in. Add the remaining ingredients and mix well.

Drop onto sheets in any size you like and bake about 15 minutes. Cool on racks, and hide what you can.

Paradise: The Best of All Possible Jellies

ABOUT 20 GLASSES

One of the lasting pleasures of my life is making jelly. No, not so much making it as giving it. Here is a favorite— my gift to you—an exquisite rose-colored jelly you can't buy, easy and inexpensive enough to make, and very satisfying to have on hand.

> 20 *medium-sized* (6⅔ *pounds*) *juicy tart apples*
> *1 pound cranberries (fresh or frozen)*
> *10 medium-sized 3⅓ pounds juicy quinces*
> *Sugar*
> *1 vanilla bean, split (expensive, and optional)*
> *20 scented geranium leaves, should you have them*
> *Paraffin for sealing*
> *19 or 20 8-ounce jars for jelly (or 4 or 12-ounce—*
>   *it doesn't matter)*

Rinse and quarter the apples, cut out the blossom, and turn them into a deep pot with the cranberries; *barely* cover with water. Bring to a boil, lower heat, and simmer, covered, until apples are soft. At the same time, rinse, quarter, and core the quinces, and turn into a second pot; barely cover them with water, bring to a boil, lower heat, and simmer, covered, until they are also soft.

Set a large colander over a very deep pot and line it with a rinsed and wrung out clean cloth. Gently pour *both* juices into the colander and let them strain from the fruit into the pot. Toward the end, you can gather the corners of the cloth, tie them in a knot, and hang the cloth on a hook over the pot so the weight of gravity will drain out more juice.

NOTE: At no time should you press the fruit—that would make the jelly cloudy instead of crystal clear. Give it time, and wait until the last drop has fallen.

Save the fruit in the bag. Set the juice over medium-high heat, bring to a boil and simmer 12 minutes uncovered. Prepare pulp for Paradise Jam (see next recipe) and reserve as much juice as you'll need. Now measure 4 cups of juice into a deep kettle. Bring to a boil and boil hard over high heat for 5 minutes, skimming off foam if necessary. Stir in 4 cups of granulated sugar with a long-handled wooden spoon just until dissolved. Scrape the tiny seeds from a 1-inch section of split vanilla bean into the pot. Continue to boil rapidly. Five minutes after adding the sugar, test for the jelly stage —it will be 222° F on the candy thermometer, or 2 large drops of jelly will sheet together from the side of the wooden spoon. Remove from heat and skim off any foam.

Have hot, dry jelly glasses ready. They must be sterilized by simmering, ¾ full of water for 20 minutes on a folded towel in a roasting pan (if you have a sterilizing cycle in your dishwasher, great). Place a scented leaf, if you have some, in the bottom of each glass. Pour in the jelly to within ¼-inch of the top. Wipe the inside lip of the glass clean with a damp towel, then cover with a ⅛-inch film of melted paraffin (don't let paraffin get smoking hot—just melt over medium heat). Place the glasses in a cool place out of a draft to set. Repeat until all juice has been used up. Then cover with lids or plastic film and store in a cool, dark place.

This is worth a good day's work in autumn, when quinces are ripe and cranberries have been culled from their bogs. But you could do it in stages, juices made one day, jellying the next. And in a pinch, just freeze the juices against making jelly at a more convenient time.

Yes, you can use the short method with powdered commercial pectin (follow any good recipe for apple jelly). But this old-fashioned simmering gives a far finer, fruitier flavor.

Paradise Jam

ABOUT 12 GLASSES

Pass the fruit in the cloth through the fine blade of a food mill or a sieve. To 3 cups of purée, blend in 1 cup of the juices and 4 cups of sugar. Cook 4 cupfuls at a time in a deep pot over high heat until thick and fragrant, about 20 minutes—stir often, or it will burn. Pack and seal as for jelly.

Moneysaving Budget Notes

The wines and spirits in this book

While nearly everything in the world is more costly than it once was, there is a shining exception: good jug wines. With them, we no longer need deny ourselves the depth a splash of wine will add to a dish, nor the warmth a glass of wine will give to a dinner.

A couple of hints. Decant red wine into a carafe two hours or so before you pour it. The wine will then have time to breathe, its bouquet will blossom, and it will taste smoother. Chill the decanter as well as the white wine, and it will keep cool longer. And here's an Italian peasant trick: slice fresh peaches in season, or apples or pears into glasses of really cheap wine. We've had wine served this way in fruit glasses, and the sharp edges were delightfully softened.

California fortified wines—Madeira, port, and sherry— for a modest investment, reap delicious rewards in your cooking. Keep them on a cool shelf. As for brandy, a good California bottle will last and last. After all, you only use it by the spoonful. Same is true of fruit-flavored brandies and liqueurs. Buy 40 proof—much cheaper than more potent ones, and all you use is a dash for flavor anyway. A light slosh of orange or cherry or mint liqueur adds glamor for pennies; a bottle in the cupboard can be a lifesaver when all you've got is a tub of ice cream or a can of peaches on hand.

A help at the market

The Canadian Department of Agriculture makes a plastic-coated pocket-sized card with a price-per-unit wheel that is invaluable for shopping. To find which of several items is the best buy (is the large economy size truly an economy?), you just dial the answer. The Department assures me there is ample supply, so do send for one. Ask for the *Consumer's Cost Calculator* when you write to Information Canada, Ottawa, Ontario, K1A 0S9, Canada. The price outside Canada, to be included with the order, is 30¢. Remittances are payable to: The Receiver General of Canada.

How to change proportions in a recipe

You would like to make Cherry Crisp for 10. The recipe is for 6 and calls for 2 pounds of cherries. How many pounds of cherries should you buy for 10? Say it to yourself this way:

2 pounds are to 6 people as x pounds are to 10 people
Or: 2   :   6 $= x$:   10

1. Multiply the end factors: $2 \times 10 = 20$.
2. Multiply the inside factors: $6 \times x = 6x$
3. Divide the x product *into* the other: $20 \div 6x = 3\frac{1}{3}$

That's your answer—buy 3⅓ pounds (or 3 pounds 6 ounces) of cherries for your crisp. Figure the other ingredients the same way. *Except for salt,* which does not increase or decrease proportionately. You have to taste it as you go. Herbs, too.

You can alter any recipe up or down by the same formula.

NOTE: Most baked goods won't work more than 4 times their amount—twice is safest.

Index

About the Author

SYLVIA VAUGHN THOMPSON writes frequently for magazines such as *Woman's Day, Gourmet, Family Circle, Sphere, Travel & Leisure,* and others. She is the author of *Economy Gastronomy,* a book which is the favorite cookbook of some of the best cooks in America. Mrs. Thompson grew up in Hollywood and is the daughter of a film writer and an actress. She lives in Malibu in California with her husband and four children.